Other Books and Series by Jeff Bowen

Applications for Enrollment of Chickasaw Newborn Act of 1905
Volumes I thru VII

Cherokee Intermarried White 1906 Volume I thru X

Applications for Enrollment of Creek Newborn Act of 1905
Volumes I thru XIV

Applications for Enrollment of Choctaw Newborn Act of 1905
Volume I, II, III, IV & V

Visit our website at **www.nativestudy.com** to learn more about these and other books and series by Jeff Bowen

APPLICATIONS FOR ENROLLMENT OF CHOCTAW NEWBORN ACT OF 1905

VOLUME VI

TRANSCRIBED BY
JEFF BOWEN

NATIVE STUDY
Gallipolis, Ohio
USA

Other Books and Series by Jeff Bowen

1901-1907 Native American Census Seneca, Eastern Shawnee, Miami, Modoc, Ottawa, Peoria, Quapaw, and Wyandotte Indians (Under Seneca School, Indian Territory)

1932 Census of The Standing Rock Sioux Reservation with Births And Deaths 1924-1932

Census of The Blackfeet, Montana, 1897- 1901 Expanded Edition

Eastern Cherokee by Blood, 1906-1910, Volumes I thru XIII

Choctaw of Mississippi Indian Census 1929-1932 with Births and Deaths 1924-1931   Volume I
Choctaw of Mississippi Indian Census 1933, 1934 & 1937, Supplemental Rolls to 1934 & 1935 with Births and Deaths 1932-1938, and Marriages 1936-1938 Volume II

Eastern Cherokee Census Cherokee, North Carolina 1930-1939
Census 1930-1931 with Births And Deaths 1924-1931 Taken By Agent L. W. Page Volume I
Eastern Cherokee Census Cherokee, North Carolina 1930-1939
Census 1932-1933 with Births And Deaths 1930-1932 Taken By Agent R. L. Spalsbury   Volume II
Eastern Cherokee Census Cherokee, North Carolina 1930-1939
Census 1934-1937 with Births and Deaths 1925-1938 and Marriages 1936 & 1938 Taken by Agents R. L. Spalsbury And Harold W. Foght Volume III

Seminole of Florida Indian Census, 1930-1940 with Birth and Death Records, 1930-1938

Texas Cherokees 1820-1839 A Document For Litigation 1921

Choctaw By Blood Enrollment Cards 1898-1914 Volumes I thru XVII

Starr Roll 1894 (Cherokee Payment Rolls) Districts: Canadian, Cooweescoowee, and Delaware Volume One
Starr Roll 1894 (Cherokee Payment Rolls) Districts: Flint, Going Snake, and Illinois   Volume Two
Starr Roll 1894 (Cherokee Payment Rolls) Districts: Saline, Sequoyah, and Tahlequah; Including Orphan Roll Volume Three

Cherokee Intruder Cases Dockets of Hearings 1901-1909 Volumes I & II

Indian Wills, 1911-1921 Records of the Bureau of Indian Affairs Books One thru Seven;
Native American Wills & Probate Records 1911-1921

Other Books and Series by Jeff Bowen

Turtle Mountain Reservation Chippewa Indians 1932 Census with Births & Deaths, 1924-1932

Chickasaw By Blood Enrollment Cards 1898-1914 Volume I thru V

Cherokee Descendants East An Index to the Guion Miller Applications Volume I
Cherokee Descendants West An Index to the Guion Miller Applications Volume II (A-M)
Cherokee Descendants West An Index to the Guion Miller Applications Volume III (N-Z)

Applications for Enrollment of Seminole Newborn Freedmen, Act of 1905

Eastern Cherokee Census, Cherokee, North Carolina, 1915-1922, Taken by Agent James E. Henderson   Volume I (1915-1916)
Volume II (1917-1918)
Volume III (1919-1920)
Volume IV (1921-1922)

Complete Delaware Roll of 1898

Eastern Cherokee Census, Cherokee, North Carolina, 1923-1929, Taken by Agent James E. Henderson   Volume I (1923-1924)
Volume II (1925-1926)
Volume III (1927-1929)

Applications for Enrollment of Seminole Newborn Act of 1905 Volumes I & II

North Carolina Eastern Cherokee Indian Census 1898-1899, 1904, 1906, 1909-1912, 1914 Revised and Expanded Edition

1932 Hopi and Navajo Native American Census with Birth & Death Rolls (1925-1931) Volume 1 - Hopi
1932 Hopi and Navajo Native American Census with Birth & Death Rolls (1930-1932) Volume 2 - Navajo

Western Navajo Reservation Navajo, Hopi and Paiute 1933 Census with Birth & Death Rolls 1925-1933

Cherokee Citizenship Commission Dockets 1880-1884 and 1887-1889 Volumes I thru V

Copyright © 2013
by Jeff Bowen

ALL RIGHTS RESERVED
No part of this publication may be reproduced
or used in any form or manner whatsoever
without previous written permission from the
copyright holder or publisher.

Originally published:
Baltimore, Maryland
2012

Reprinted by:

Native Study LLC
Gallipolis, OH
www.nativestudy.com
2020

Library of Congress Control Number: 2020918113

ISBN: 978-1-64968-099-0

Made in the United States of America.

This series is dedicated to the descendants of the Choctaw newborn listed in these applications.

This map of Indian Territory shows how large the Choctaw and Chickasaw Nations' land base was that contained huge deposits of asphalt and coal. Just the size and territory involved was flooded with the "Grafters".

DEPARTMENT OF THE INTERIOR.
Commissioner to the Five Civilized Tribes.

NOTICE.

Opening of Land Office at Wewoka,
IN THE SEMINOLE NATION, INDIAN TERRITORY.

Notice is hereby given that on Monday, September 4, 1905, the Commissioner to the Five Civilized Tribes will establish a land office at Wewoka, in the Seminole Nation, Indian Territory, for the purpose of allowing citizens and freedmen of the Seminole Nation to select allotments of land for their minor children enrolled under the Act of Congress approved March 3, 1905 (33 Stat. L 1060), and for the further purpose of allowing citizens and freedmen of the Seminole Nation, whose allotments are incomplete, to select additional land in order to bring the value of their allotments up to the standard of $309.09, as nearly as may be practicable.

Each child whose enrollment in accordance with the Act of March 3, 1905, has been duly approved by the Secretary of the Interior, is entitled to receive an alllotment of forty acres without regard to the character or value of the land selected.

Selection of allotments for minor children must be made by their citizen or freedmen parents or by a duly appointed guardian, or curator, or by a duly appointed administrator.

TAMS BIXBY,
Commissioner.

Muskogee, Indian Territory,
July 29, 1905.

This particular notice for the Seminole and Creek Newborn makes mention of the Act of 1905. It is likely that a similar notice was posted in the Choctaw and Chickasaw Nations for the registration of newborn children.

DEPARTMENT OF THE INTERIOR,
Commission to the Five Civilized Tribes.

Rules and Regulations Governing the Selection of Allotments and the Designation of Homesteads in the Choctaw and Chickasaw Nations.

1. Selections of allotments and designations of homesteads for adult citizens and selections of allotments for adult freedmen must be made in person except as herein otherwise provided.

2. Applications to have land set apart and homesteads designated for duly identified Mississippi Choctaws must be made personally before the Commission to the Five Civilized Tribes. Fathers may apply for their minor children and if the father be dead the mother may apply. Husbands may apply for wives. Applications for orphans, insane persons and persons of unsound mind may be made by duly appointed guardian or curator, and for aged and infirm persons and prisoners by agents duly authorized thereunto by power of attorney, in the discretion of said Commission.

3. At the time of the selection of allotment each citizen and duly identified Mississippi Choctaw shall designate as a homestead out of said selection land equal in value to one hundred and sixty acres of the average allottable land of the Choctaw and Chickasaw Nations, as nearly as may be.

4. Each Choctaw and Chickasaw freedman, at the time of selection shall designate as his or her allotment of the lands of the Choctaw and Chickasaw Nations, land equal in value to forty acres of the average allottable land of the Choctaw and Chickasaw Nations.

5. Citizens, freedmen and identified Mississippi Choctaws who are married, whether they have attained their majority or not, will be regarded as of age for the purpose of making selections.

6. Selections may be made by citizen and freedman parents for unmarried male children under twenty-one years of age and for unmarried female children under eighteen years of age, and a male citizen or freedman may make selection for his wife, if she is entitled to make selection, unless she shall, at the time or previously thereto, protest in writing.

7. Where the father of an unmarried minor citizen, freedman or identified Mississippi Choctaw is a non-citizen, the citizen, freedman or identified Mississippi Choctaw mother of such children must make selection in person in behalf of said children.

8. Selections of allotments and designations of homesteads for minor citizens and selections of allotments for minor freedmen may be made by the citizen father or mother or freedman father or mother, as the case may be, or by a guardian, curator, or an administrator having charge of their estate, in the order named.

9. Selections of allotments and designations of homesteads for citizen, and selections of allotment for freedmen, prisoners, convicts, aged and infirm persons and soldiers and sailors of the United States on duty outside of Indian Territory, may be made by duly appointed agents under power of attorney, and for incompetents by guardians, curators, or other suitable person akin to them.

10. Selections may be made and homesteads designated by duly identified Mississippi Choctaws, who have, within one year after the date of their identification as such, made satisfactory proof of bona fide settlement within the Choctaw-Chickasaw country, at any time within six months after the date of their said identification.

11. Persons authorized to make selections by power of attorney, as provided in rules 2 and 9 hereof, must be the husband or wife, or a relative not further removed than a cousin of the first degree of the person for whom such selection is made.

12. It shall be the duty of the Commission to the Five Civilized Tribes to see that selections of allotments and designations of homesteads for the classes of persons mentioned in rules 2, 6, 7, 8 and 9 hereof, are made for the best interests of such persons.

13. Selections of allotments for citizens, freedmen and identified Mississippi Choctaws who have died subsequent to September 25, 1902, and before making a selection of allotment, shall be made by a duly appointed administrator or executor. If, however, such administrator or executor be not duly and expeditiously appointed, or fails to act promptly when appointed, or for any other cause such selections be not so made within a reasonable and practicable time, the Commission to the Five Civilized Tribes shall designate the lands thus to be allotted.

14. In determining the value of a selection the appraised value of the land selected shall be increased by the appraised value of such pine timber on such land as has heretofore been estimated by the Commission to the Five Civilized Tribes.

15. Selections of allotments may be made only by citizens and freedmen whose enrollment has been approved by the Secretary of the Interior, and by persons duly identified by the Commission to the Five Civilized Tribes as Mississippi Choctaws, and by none others.

16. When a selection of land has been made by a citizen, freedman or identified Mississippi Choctaw, and the land so selected is claimed by a person whose rights as a citizen or freedman have not been finally determined, contest for the land so selected may be instituted by the person claiming the land, formal application for the land being first made as is required by the Rules of Practice in Choctaw and Chickasaw allotment contest cases.

THE COMMISSION TO THE FIVE CIVILIZED TRIBES.
TAMS BIXBY, Chairman.

Muskogee, Indian Territory, March 24, 1903.

The above statement published prior to 1905, was established for what was supposed to be a set of guidelines when it came to allotments. But with supplemental agreements and Congressional legislation, time frames as well as rules and regulations often changed and were not the same for every tribe.

INTRODUCTION

The *Applications for Enrollment of Choctaw Newborn Act of 1905*, National Archive film M-1301, Rolls 50-57, are found under the heading of Applications for Enrollment of the Commission to the Five Civilized Tribes. For this series, I have transcribed the application forms filled out by individuals applying for enrollment in the Five Civilized Tribes under the Dawes Commission. These applications contain considerably more information than stated on the census cards found in series M-1186. M-1301 possesses its own numerical sequence, separate from M-1186. To find each party's roll number you would have to reference M-1186.

The Choctaw as well as the Chickasaw allotments were likely some of the most sought after properties in Indian Territory. There was supposed to be a 25-year restriction on the sale or lease of any Indian lands so as to insure that the owners wouldn't be swindled, but that isn't what happened. This fact is borne out in the Dawes Commission General Allotment Act, of February 8, 1887, Section 5, which "Provides that after an Indian person is allotted land, the United States will hold the land 'in trust [1] for the sole use and benefit of the Indian' (or his heirs if the Indian landowner dies) for a period of 25 years. (Land held in trust by the United States government cannot be sold or in anyway alienated by the Indian landowner, since the United States government considers the underlying ownership of the land held by itself and not the tribe. After the period of trust ends, the Indian landowner is free to sell the land and is free from any encumbrance from the United States.)"[1] Instead, Native Americans were exploited by the devious. The Choctaw and Chickasaw Districts both had huge asphalt and coal deposits, so there was pressure from outsiders to acquire them from the minute they were discovered. After repeated attacks throughout the years and many legislative changes, President "Roosevelt finally signed the Five Tribes Bill at noon on April 26, 1906, the forces seeking to end all restrictions were disappointed. Section 19 removed restrictions from the sale of all inherited land but directed that no full-bloods could sell their land for twenty-five years. The Act also prohibited leases for more than one year without the approval of the Secretary of the Interior."[2]

Angie Debo described the opportunists that wanted these Native American allotments as, "Grafters". The parents of the newborns enumerated within this series would no sooner receive the approval for their child's allotment than there would be someone there with cash in hand holding a new deed or lease for the parents to sign their child's birthright away. Angie Debo said it best, "As the business incapacity of the allottees became apparent, a horde of despoilers fastened themselves upon their property." According to Debo, "The term 'grafter' was applied as a matter of course to dealers in Indian land, and was frankly accepted by them. The speculative fever also affected Government employees so that it was almost impossible to prevent them from making personal investments."[3]

---

[1] General Allotment Act, Act of Feb. 8, 1887 (24 Stat. 388, ch. 119, 25 USCA 331)
[2] The Dawes Commission and the Allotment of the Five Civilized Tribes, 1893-1914 by Kent Carter, pg. 173
[3] And Still the Waters Run, Angie Debo, p. 92.

INTRODUCTION

According to the Department of Interior in 1905, "It is estimated that there will be added to the final rolls of the citizens and freedmen of the Choctaw and Chickasaw nations the names of 2,000 persons, including 1,500 new-born children to be enrolled under the provisions of the act of Congress approved March 3, 1905."[4]

The quote below explains, in detail, the requirements for qualifying as a newborn Choctaw, "By the act of Congress approved March 3, 1905 (H.R. 17474), entitled 'An act making appropriations for the current and contingent expenses of the Indian Department and for fulfilling treaty stipulations with various Indian tribes for the fiscal year ending June 30, 1906, and for other purposes,' it was provided as follows:

'That the Commission to the Five Civilized Tribes is hereby authorized for sixty days after the date of the approval of this act to receive and consider applications for enrollment of infant children born prior to September twenty-fifth, nineteen hundred and two, and who were living on said date, to citizens by blood of the Choctaw and Chickasaw tribes of Indians whose enrollment has been approved by the Secretary of the Interior prior to the date of the approval of this act; and to enroll and make allotments to such children.'

'That the Commission to the Five Civilized Tribes is authorized for sixty days after the date of the approval of this act to receive and consider applications for enrollment of children born subsequent to September twenty-fifth, nineteen hundred and two, and prior to March fourth, nineteen hundred and five, and who were living on said latter date, to citizens by blood of the Choctaw and Chickasaw tribes of Indians whose enrollment has been approved by the Secretary of the Interior prior to the date of the approval of this act; and to enroll and make allotments to such children.'

"Notice is hereby given that the Commission to the Five Civilized Tribes will, up to and inclusive of midnight, May 2, 1905, receive applications for the enrollment of infant children born prior to September 25, 1902, and who were living on said date, to citizens by blood of the Choctaw and Chickasaw tribes of Indians whose enrollment has been approved by the Secretary of the Interior prior to March 3, 1905."[5]

Following is the scope of these transcriptions: Besides the applications themselves, researchers will find the identities of other individuals within these applications -- doctors, lawyers, mid-wives, and other relatives -- that may help with you genealogical research.

Jeff Bowen
Gallipolis, Ohio
NativeStudy.com

---

[4] Annual Reports of the Department of the Interior For the Fiscal Year Ended June 30, 1905, p. 609.
[5] Annual Reports of the Department of the Interior For the Fiscal Year Ended June 30, 1905, p. 593.

Applications for Enrollment of Choctaw Newborn
Act of 1905   Volume VI

Choc New Born 308
   William R. Slinker
   (Born Nov. 4, 1902)

BIRTH AFFIDAVIT.

DEPARTMENT OF THE INTERIOR,
COMMISSION TO THE FIVE CIVILIZED TRIBES.

IN RE *Application for Enrollment,* as a citizen of the   Choctaw   Nation, of   William R Slinker , born on the   4   day of   November , 1902

Name of Father: James Slinker   a citizen of the United States Nation.
Name of Mother: Lizzie Slinker   a citizen of the   Choctaw   Nation.

Post-Office: Durant, Ind. Ter.

AFFIDAVIT OF ~~MOTHER~~. Aunt

UNITED STATES OF AMERICA, ⎫
   INDIAN TERRITORY.   ⎬
   Central   District. ⎭

   I,   Rebecca Maytubby , on oath state that I am   26   years of age and a citizen by   blood , of the Choctaw Nation; that I am ~~the lawful wife~~ a sister of Lizzy Slinker , who is a citizen, by   blood   of the Choctaw Nation; that a   male child was born to ~~me~~ her on   4th   day of November , 1902, that said child has been named   William R Slinker , and is now living.

                                       Rebecca Maytubby

WITNESSES TO MARK:

   Subscribed and sworn to before me this   24   *day of*   December , 1902

                                       L.C. Humphrey
                                          NOTARY PUBLIC.

Applications for Enrollment of Choctaw Newborn
Act of 1905   Volume VI

AFFIDAVIT OF ATTENDING PHYSICIAN OR MID-WIFE.

UNITED STATES OF AMERICA,
   INDIAN TERRITORY.
Central   District.

I, Harriet Tomlinson, a Midwife, on oath state that I attended on Mrs. Lizzie Slinker, wife of James Slinker on the 4th day of November, 1902 ; that there was born to her on said date a male child; that said child is now living and is said to have been named William R Slinker

                    her
          Harriet x Tomlinson
WITNESSES TO MARK: mark
 { Wm C Brown
   (Name Illegible)

Subscribed and sworn to before me this 24th *day of* December, 1902

                L.C. Humphrey
                    NOTARY PUBLIC.

NEW-BORN AFFIDAVIT.

Number

Choctaw Enrolling Commission.

IN THE MATTER OF THE APPLICATION FOR ENROLLMENT, as a citizen of the Choctaw Nation, of William Raymon Slinker

born on the 4th day of November 1902

Name of father   J.I. Slinker   a citizen of   white
Nation final enrollment No ——
Name of mother Lizzie Slinker   a citizen of   Choctaw
Nation final enrollment No 12162

                Postoffice   Durant I.T.

AFFIDAVIT OF MOTHER.

UNITED STATES OF AMERICA,
   INDIAN TERRITORY,
Central   DISTRICT

I Lizzie Slinker on oath state that I am 26 years of age and a citizen by blood of the Choctaw Nation, and as such have been

Applications for Enrollment of Choctaw Newborn
Act of 1905   Volume VI

placed upon the final roll of the   Choctaw   Nation, by the Honorable Secretary of the Interior my final enrollment number being   12162 ; that I am the lawful wife of   J. I. Slinker, who is a citizen of the   white   Nation, and as such has been placed upon the final roll of said Nation by the Honorable Secretary of the Interior, his final enrollment number being ———— and that a   male   child was born to me on the   4th   day of   November   190 2 ; that said child has been named   William Raymon Slinker   , and is now living.

WITNESSETH: Lizzie Slinker

Must be two Witnesses who are Citizens.   J. J. Gardner

   Rebecca Jackson

Subscribed and sworn to before me this   14   day of   Jan   190 5

W. A. Shoney
Notary Public.

My commission expires   Jan 10 1909

AFFIDAVIT OF ATTENDING PHYSICIAN OR MIDWIFE

UNITED STATES OF AMERICA
INDIAN TERRITORY
   Central   DISTRICT

I,   Dr R A Lively   a   physician   on oath state that I attended on Mrs.   Lizzie Slinker   wife of   J I Slinker   on the   4th   day of   November   , 190 2, that there was born to her on said date a   Male   child, that said child is now living, and is said to have been named   William Raymon Slinker

Robt A Lively   M.D.

Subscribed and sworn to before me this, the   14th   day of   Jan   190 5

W. A. Shoney
Notary Public.

WITNESSETH:

Must be two witnesses who are citizens and know the child.   J.J. Gardner

   Rebecca Jackson

We hereby certify that we are well acquainted with   Dr R A Lively   a   Physician   and know   him   to be reputable and of good standing in the community.

J.J. Gardner

Rebecca Jackson

Applications for Enrollment of Choctaw Newborn
Act of 1905 Volume VI

BIRTH AFFIDAVIT.

DEPARTMENT OF THE INTERIOR.
COMMISSION TO THE FIVE CIVILIZED TRIBES.

IN RE APPLICATION FOR ENROLLMENT, as a citizen of the Choctaw Nation, of William R Slinker, born on the 4" day of November, 1902

Name of Father: James Slinker a citizen of the U.S. Nation.
Name of Mother: Lizzie Slinker a citizen of the Choctaw Nation.

Postoffice Durant, Ind. Ter.

AFFIDAVIT OF MOTHER.

UNITED STATES OF AMERICA, Indian Territory,
Central   DISTRICT.

I, Lizzie Slinker, on oath state that I am 26 years of age and a citizen by blood, of the Choctaw Nation; that I am the lawful wife of James Slinker, who is a citizen, ~~by~~ of U. States of the ——— Nation; that a male child was born to me on 4th day of November, 1902; that said child has been named William R Slinker, and was living March 4, 1905.

Lizzie Slinker

Witnesses To Mark:
{

Subscribed and sworn to before me this 15th day of April, 1905

L. B. Wilkins
Notary Public.

AFFIDAVIT OF ATTENDING PHYSICIAN OR MID-WIFE.

UNITED STATES OF AMERICA, Indian Territory,
.... DISTRICT.

I, R A Lively, M.D., a Physician, on oath state that I attended on Mrs. Lizzie Slinker, wife of James Slinker on the 4" day of November, 1902; that there was born to her on said date a Male child; that said child was living March 4, 1905, and is said to have been named William R Slinker

Robt A. Lively, M.D.

Witnesses To Mark:
{

Applications for Enrollment of Choctaw Newborn
Act of 1905 Volume VI

Subscribed and sworn to before me this 15th day of April, 1905

        L. B. Wilkins
        Notary Public.

               N. B. 308
         COPY
      Muskogee, Indian Territory, April 7, 1905.

James Slinker,
  Durant, Indian Territory.

Dear Sir:

  There is inclosed you herewith for execution application for the enrollment of your infant child, William R. Slinker, born November 4, 1902.

  The affidavits heretofore filed with the Commission were of the physician and a sister of the mother. You will notice from the inclosed application that the affidavit of the mother is required.

  In the event that the mother is dead, it will be necessary for you to procure the affidavits of two persons who have a actual knowledge of the fact, that the child was born, was living on March 4, 1905, and that Lizzie Slinker was his mother.

  In having these affidavits executed care should be exercised to see that all names are written in full, as they appear in the body of the affidavit, and in the event that either of the persons signing the affidavit are unable to write, signatures by mark must be attested by two witnesses. Each affidavit must be executed before a Notary Public and the notarial seal and signature of the officer must be attached to each separate affidavit.

          Respectfully,
          SIGNED

          T. B. Needles.
LM 7-23   Commissioner in Charge.

Applications for Enrollment of Choctaw Newborn
Act of 1905   Volume VI

7 NB 308

Muskogee, Indian Territory, April 20, 1905.

James Slinker,
  Durant, Indian Territory.

Dear Sir:

  Receipt is hereby acknowledged of the affidavits of Lizzie Slinker and Robert A. Lively to the birth of William R. Slinker, son of James and Lizzie Slinker, November 4, 1902, and the same have been filed with our records as an application for the enrollment of said child.

  Respectfully,

  Chairman.

Choc New Born 309
  Lottie Loudella Edwards
  (Born Oct. 12, 1902)
  David Jonathan Edwards
  (Born Jan. 27, 1905)

BIRTH AFFIDAVIT.

DEPARTMENT OF THE INTERIOR.
COMMISSION TO THE FIVE CIVILIZED TRIBES.

IN RE APPLICATION FOR ENROLLMENT, as a citizen of the   Choctaw   Nation, of Lottie Loudella Edwards   , born on the 12th   day of   October   , 1902

Name of Father: James Robert Edwards   a citizen of the United States Nation.
Name of Mother: Belle Edwards   a citizen of the   Choctaw   Nation.

  Postoffice   Indianola, I.T.

Applications for Enrollment of Choctaw Newborn
Act of 1905   Volume VI

AFFIDAVIT OF MOTHER.

UNITED STATES OF AMERICA, Indian Territory, }
  Central   DISTRICT.

   I, Belle Edwards , on oath state that I am 23 years of age and a citizen by blood , of the Choctaw Nation; that I am the lawful wife of James Robert Edwards , who is a citizen, ~~by~~ .... of the United States Nation; that a female child was born to me on 12th day of October , 1902; that said child has been named Lottie Loudella Edwards , and was living March 4, 1905.

                                          Belle Edwards
Witnesses To Mark:
  {

   Subscribed and sworn to before me this 21st day of March , 1905

                                          Wirt Franklin
                                          Notary Public.

AFFIDAVIT OF ATTENDING PHYSICIAN OR MID-WIFE.

UNITED STATES OF AMERICA, Indian Territory, }
  Western   DISTRICT.

   I, Mrs Nannie Coker , a mid wife , on oath state that I attended on Mrs. Belle Edwards , wife of James Robert Edwards on the 12th day of October , 1902; that there was born to her on said date a female child; that said child was living March 4, 1905, and is said to have been named Lottie Loudella Edwards

                                          Mrs Nannie Coker
Witnesses To Mark:
  {

   Subscribed and sworn to before me this 22d day of March , 1905

                                          T. T. Caves
                                          Notary Public.

Applications for Enrollment of Choctaw Newborn
Act of 1905   Volume VI

BIRTH AFFIDAVIT.

DEPARTMENT OF THE INTERIOR.
COMMISSION TO THE FIVE CIVILIZED TRIBES.

IN RE APPLICATION FOR ENROLLMENT, as a citizen of the   Choctaw   Nation, of David Jonathan Edwards   , born on the 27th   day of January   , 1905

Name of Father: James Robert Edwards   a citizen of the United States Nation.
Name of Mother: Belle Edwards   a citizen of the Choctaw   Nation.

Postoffice   Indianola, I.T.

AFFIDAVIT OF MOTHER.

UNITED STATES OF AMERICA, Indian Territory, }
   Central   DISTRICT.

I, Belle Edwards   , on oath state that I am   23   years of age and a citizen by   blood   , of the   Choctaw   Nation; that I am the lawful wife of   James Robert Edwards   , who is a citizen, ~~by~~ .... of the   United States   Nation; that a   male   child was born to me on   27th   day of January   , 1905; that said child has been named   David Jonathan Edwards   , and was living March 4, 1905.

Belle Edwards

Witnesses To Mark:
{

Subscribed and sworn to before me this   21st day of   March   , 1905.

Wirt Franklin
Notary Public.

AFFIDAVIT OF ATTENDING PHYSICIAN OR MID-WIFE.

UNITED STATES OF AMERICA, Indian Territory, }
   Western   DISTRICT.

I,   Mrs Alice Hobbs   , a   mid wife   , on oath state that I attended on Mrs.   Belle Edwards   , wife of   James Robert Edwards   on the 27th   day of January   , 1905; that there was born to her on said date a   male   child; that said child was living March 4, 1905, and is said to have been named   David Jonathan Edwards

Mrs Alice Hobbs

Witnesses To Mark:
{

Applications for Enrollment of Choctaw Newborn
Act of 1905 Volume VI

Subscribed and sworn to before me this 22nd day of March , 1905

T. T. Caves
Notary Public.

N. B. 309
COPY
Muskogee, Indian Territory, April 7, 1905.

James Robert Edwards
    Indianola, Indian Territory.

Dear Sir:

    Referring to the affidavits heretofore forwarded to the birth of Lottie Loudella Edwards and David Jonathan Edwards, it is stated in the affidavits of the mother, Belle Edwards, that she is a citizen by blood of the Choctaw Nation.

    If this is correct you are requested to state when, where and under what name she was listed for enrollment, the names of her parents and other members of her family for whom application was made at the same time, and if she has selected an allotment, give her roll number as the same appears upon her allotment certificate.

Respectfully,
SIGNED
T. B. Needles.
Commissioner in Charge.

Choc New Born 310
    James Darrah Catlin, Jr.
    (Born Feb. 20, 1904)

Applications for Enrollment of Choctaw Newborn
Act of 1905   Volume VI

NEW BORN AFFIDAVIT

No ....

CHOCTAW ENROLLING COMMISSION

IN THE MATTER OF THE APPLICATION FOR ENROLLMENT as a citizen of the Choctaw Nation, of   James Darrah Catlin, Jr   born on the 20th day of   February   190 4

Name of father   James Darrah Catlin   a citizen of   Choctaw   Nation, final enrollment No.   837 (Intermarried)
Name of mother   Claude M Catlin   a citizen of   Choctaw   Nation, final enrollment No.   12186

Atoka, I T   Postoffice.

AFFIDAVIT OF MOTHER

UNITED STATES OF AMERICA
INDIAN TERRITORY
DISTRICT   Central

I   Claude M Catlin   , on oath state that I am   27   years of age and a citizen by   Blood   of the   Choctaw   Nation, and as such have been placed upon the final roll of the   Choctaw   Nation, by the Honorable Secretary of the Interior my final enrollment number being   12186   ; that I am the lawful wife of   James Darrah Catlin   , who is a citizen of the   Choctaw   Nation, and as such has been placed upon the final roll of said Nation by the Honorable Secretary of the Interior, his final enrollment number being   837   and that a   male   child was born to me on the   20th day of   February   190 4; that said child has been named   James Darrah Catlin, Jr.   , and is now living.

WITNESSETH: Claude M. Catlin
Must be two witnesses { Leona Turner
who are citizens   (Name Illegible)

Subscribed and sworn to before me this, the   2nd   day of   February   , 190 5

C G Bozarth
Notary Public.

My Commission Expires: July 5- 1908

10

Applications for Enrollment of Choctaw Newborn
Act of 1905 Volume VI

Affidavit of Attending Physician or Midwife

UNITED STATES OF AMERICA,
INDIAN TERRITORY,
Central DISTRICT

I, J. S. Fulton a Physician on oath state that I attended on Mrs. Claude M Catlin wife of James Darrah Catlin on the 20 day of February, 190 4, that there was born to her on said date a male child, that said child is now living, and is said to have been named James Darrah Catlin, Jr.

J. S. Fulton M. D.

Subscribed and sworn to before me this the 3d day of February 1905

W.S. Farmer
Notary Public.

WITNESSETH:
Must be two witnesses who are citizens and know the child.
Joseph G Ralls
Norma E. Smiser

We hereby certify that we are well acquainted with J. S. Fulton a Physician and know him to be reputable and of good standing in the community.

Must be two citizen witnesses.
Joseph G Ralls
Norma E. Smiser

BIRTH AFFIDAVIT.

DEPARTMENT OF THE INTERIOR.
COMMISSION TO THE FIVE CIVILIZED TRIBES.

IN RE APPLICATION FOR ENROLLMENT, as a citizen of the Choctaw Nation, of James Darrah Catlin, Jr. , born on the 20th day of February , 1904

Name of Father: James Darrah Catlin   a citizen of the Choctaw Nation.
Name of Mother: Claude M. Catlin   a citizen of the Choctaw Nation.

Postoffice Atoka, Indian Territory.

Applications for Enrollment of Choctaw Newborn
Act of 1905 Volume VI

AFFIDAVIT OF MOTHER.

UNITED STATES OF AMERICA, Indian Territory, }
Central   DISTRICT.

    I,   Claude M. Catlin   , on oath state that I am   27   years of age and a citizen by   Blood   , of the   Choctaw   Nation; that I am the lawful wife of   James Darrah Catlin   , who is a citizen, by   Intermarriage   of the   Choctaw   Nation; that a   male   child was born to me on   the 20th   day of   February, 1904   , 1......; that said child has been named   James Darrah Catlin, Jr.   , and was living March 4, 1905.

                                              Claude M Catlin

Witnesses To Mark:
{

    Subscribed and sworn to before me this   13th day of   March   , 1905

                                              F. R. Taubner
                                              Notary Public.

AFFIDAVIT OF ATTENDING PHYSICIAN OR MID-WIFE.

UNITED STATES OF AMERICA, Indian Territory, }
Central   DISTRICT.

    I,   J.S. Fulton   , a   Physician   , on oath state that I attended on Mrs.   Claude M. Catlin   , wife of   James Darrah Catlin   on the 20th   day of February, 1904.   , 1.......; that there was born to her on said date a   male   child; that said child was living March 4, 1905, and is said to have been named James Darrah Catlin, Jr.

                                              J.S. Fulton

Witnesses To Mark:
{

    Subscribed and sworn to before me this   13th   day of   February[sic]   , 1905

                                             C G Bozarth
                                            Notary Public.

Applications for Enrollment of Choctaw Newborn
Act of 1905   Volume VI

BIRTH AFFIDAVIT.
DEPARTMENT OF THE INTERIOR.
COMMISSION TO THE FIVE CIVILIZED TRIBES.

IN RE APPLICATION FOR ENROLLMENT, as a citizen of the Choctaw Nation, of James Darrah Catlin, Jr., born on the 20" day of February, 1904

Name of Father: James D Catlin   a citizen of the Choctaw Nation.
Name of Mother: Claude M. Catlin   a citizen of the Choctaw Nation.

Postoffice   Atoka, Ind. Ter.

AFFIDAVIT OF MOTHER.

UNITED STATES OF AMERICA, Indian Territory,}
Central   DISTRICT.

I, Claude M. Catlin, on oath state that I am 27 years of age and a citizen by Blood, of the Choctaw Nation; that I am the lawful wife of James Darrah Catlin, who is a citizen, by Intermarriage of the Choctaw Nation; that a Male child was born to me on the 20" day of February, 1904; that said child has been named James Darrah Catlin, Jr., and was living March 4, 1905.

                                                          Claude M Catlin

Witnesses To Mark:
{

Subscribed and sworn to before me this 13th day of April, 1905

                                                          C G Bozarth
                                                             Notary Public.

AFFIDAVIT OF ATTENDING PHYSICIAN OR MID-WIFE.

UNITED STATES OF AMERICA, Indian Territory,}
Central   DISTRICT.

I, J.S. Fulton, a physician, on oath state that I attended on Mrs. Claude M. Catlin, wife of James D Catlin on the 20" day of February, 1904; that there was born to her on said date a Male child; that said child was living March 4, 1905, and is said to have been named James Darrah Catlin, Jr.

                                                          J.S. Fulton

Witnesses To Mark:
{

Applications for Enrollment of Choctaw Newborn
Act of 1905 Volume VI

Subscribed and sworn to before me this 13th day of April, 1905

C G Bozarth
Notary Public.

N. B. 310

COPY

Muskogee, Indian Territory, April 7, 1905.

James D. Catlin,
    Atoka, Indian Territory.

Dear Sir:

    There is inclosed you herewith for execution application for the enrollment of your infant child, James Darrah Catlin Jr., born February 20, 1904.

    In the affidavits heretofore filed with the Commission, the one of the physician shows the child living on February 24, 1905. It is necessary, for the child to be enrolled, that his affidavit show he was living on March 4, 1905.

    In having these affidavits executed care should be exercised to see that all names are written in full, as they appear in the body of the affidavit, and in the event that either of the persons signing the affidavit are unable to write, signatures by mark must be attested by two witnesses. Each affidavit must be executed before a Notary Public and the notarial seal and signature of the officer must be attached to each separate affidavit.

                          Respectfully,
                            SIGNED
                          T. B. Needles.

LM 7-20.   Commissioner in Charge.

Choctaw N.B. 310.

Muskogee, Indian Territory, April 18, 1905.

James D. Catlin,
    Atoka, Indian Territory.

Dear Sir:

    Receipt is hereby acknowledged of the affidavits of Claude M. Catlin and J. S. Fulton to the birth of James Darrah Catlin, Jr., son of James D. and Claude M. Catlin, February 20, 1904, and the same have been filed with our records in the matter of the enrollment of the above named child.

Applications for Enrollment of Choctaw Newborn
Act of 1905 Volume VI

Respectfully,

Chairman.

Choc New Born 311
    Ruby Mary Betts
    (Born Oct. 5, 1904)

(COPY)

No. 1911.

MARRIAGE LICENSE

==========

United States of America,)
The Indian Territory,   ) ss.
Central District.   )

    To any person authorized by law to solemnize marriage-- Greeting: You are hereby commanded to solemnize the Rite and publish the Banns of Matrimony between Mr. C. A. Betts of Atoka in the Indian Territory, aged 30 years, and Miss Ora Lee York of Atoka in the Indian Territory, aged 16 years, according to law, and do you officially sign and return this License to the parties therein named.

Witness my hand and official seal this 9 day of September, A. D. 1903

                             E. J. Fannin
J. D. Catlin   Clerk of the United States Court.
    Deputy.

CERTIFICATE OF MARRIAGE

Unites States of America,)   I, J. W. Slaten, a minister of the gospel
The Indian Territory,   ) ss. do hereby certify, that

on the 9 day of Sept., A. D. 1903, I did duly and according to law, as commanded in the foregoing license, solemnize the Rite and publish the Banns of matrimony between the parties therein mentioned. Witness my hand this 10 day of Sept A. D. 1903. My

Applications for Enrollment of Choctaw Newborn
Act of 1905   Volume VI

credentials are recorded in the office of the Clerk of the United States Court in the Indian Territory, Central District, Book C, Page 47.

J. W. Slaten
a minister.

ENDORCED[sic] ON BACK:

No. 1911. Certificate of record of Marriage. United States of America, The Indian Territory, Central District. SCT: I, E. J. Fannin, Clerk of the United States Court in the Indian Territory and District aforesaid, do hereby certify that the license for and certificate of the marriage of Mr. C. A. Betts and Miss Ora Lee York was filed in my office in said Territory and District the 21 day of Sept A. D. 1903 and duly recorded in book 2 of Marriage Record, Page 338. Witness my hand and seal of said Court, at Atoka this 21 day of Sept A. D. 1903. E. J. Fannin, Clerk. By J. D. Catlin, Deputy.

Vester W. Rose, after being duly sworn, states that the above and foregoing is a complete and correct copy of the original marriage license filed at this office in the matter of the application for the enrollment of Ruby May Betts as a citizen of the Choctaw Nation.

Vester W Rose

Subscribed and sworn to before me this 15th day of Sept. 1909[sic].

J. L. Gary
Notary Public.

NEW BORN AFFIDAVIT

No ....

CHOCTAW ENROLLING COMMISSION

IN THE MATTER OF THE APPLICATION FOR ENROLLMENT as a citizen of the Choctaw Nation, of   Ruby May Betts   born on the   5th day of   October   190 4

Name of father   Charley A. Betts   a citizen of   Choctaw   Nation, final enrollment No.   12193

Name of mother   Ora Lee Betts   a citizen of   —   ———   Nation, final enrollment No.   ———

Applications for Enrollment of Choctaw Newborn
Act of 1905   Volume VI

Atoka I.T.　　　　　　　　Postoffice.

AFFIDAVIT OF MOTHER

UNITED STATES OF AMERICA
　　INDIAN TERRITORY
DISTRICT　Central

I　Ora Lee Betts　, on oath state that I am　15　years of age and a citizen by —— of the　Choctaw　Nation, and as such have been placed upon the final roll of the ————— Nation, by the Honorable Secretary of the Interior my final enrollment number being ——; that I am the lawful wife of　Charley A Betts　, who is a citizen of the　Choctaw　Nation, and as such has been placed upon the final roll of said Nation by the Honorable Secretary of the Interior, his final enrollment number being　121193　and that a　Female　child was born to me on the　5th　day of October 190 4; that said child has been named　Ruby May Betts　, and is now living.

WITNESSETH:　　　　　　　　　　Ora Lee Betts
Must be two witnesses ⎰　Warneta F Williams
who are citizens　　 ⎱　Elias Thompson

　　Subscribed and sworn to before me this, the　22^d　day of　February　, 190 5

　　　　　　　　　　　　　　　A. E. Folsom
　　　　　　　　　　　　　　　　　　Notary Public.

My Commission Expires:　Jan 9- 1909

Affidavit of Attending Physician or Midwife

UNITED STATES OF AMERICA,
　　INDIAN TERRITORY,
　Central　　DISTRICT

　　I,　J. S. Fulton　a　Physician on oath state that I attended on Mrs. Ora L. Betts　wife of　Charley A. Betts　on the　5th　day of　October　, 190 4, that there was born to her on said date a　Female　child, that said child is now living, and is said to have been named　Ruby May Betts

　　　　　　　　　　　　　　J. S. Fulton　　　M. D.

　　Subscribed and sworn to before me this the　23　day of　February　　1905

　　　　　　　　　　　　　　A. E. Folsom
　　　　　　　　　　　　　　　　Notary Public.

Applications for Enrollment of Choctaw Newborn
Act of 1905   Volume VI

WITNESSETH:

Must be two witnesses who are citizens and know the child. { Warneta F. Williams
Elias Thompson

We hereby certify that we are well acquainted with Dr. J. S. Fulton a Practicing Physician and know him to be reputable and of good standing in the community.

Must be two citizen witnesses. { Warneta F. Williams
Elias Thompson

BIRTH AFFIDAVIT.

DEPARTMENT OF THE INTERIOR.
COMMISSION TO THE FIVE CIVILIZED TRIBES.

IN RE APPLICATION FOR ENROLLMENT, as a citizen of the Choctaw Nation, of Ruby May Betts, born on the 5th day of October, 1904

Name of Father: Charlie A. Betts   a citizen of the Choctaw Nation.
Name of Mother: Ora Lee   "   a citizen of the Non Citz ~~Nation~~.

Postoffice ....

AFFIDAVIT OF MOTHER.

UNITED STATES OF AMERICA, Indian Territory, }
    Central   DISTRICT.

I, Ora Lee Betts, on oath state that I am 18 years of age and a ~~citizen by~~ Non Citizen, of the —— Nation; that I am the lawful wife of Charlie A. Betts, who is a citizen, by blood of the Choctaw Nation; that a female child was born to me on 5th day of October, 1904; that said child has been named Ruby May Betts, and was living March 4, 1905.

                              Ora Lee Betts

Witnesses To Mark:

Subscribed and sworn to before me this 18th day of March, 1905.

                         (Name Illegible)
                            Notary Public.

Applications for Enrollment of Choctaw Newborn
Act of 1905   Volume VI

AFFIDAVIT OF ATTENDING PHYSICIAN OR MID-WIFE.

UNITED STATES OF AMERICA, Indian Territory,　}
　　Central　　　　　　　　DISTRICT.

　　I,　　J S Fulton　　, a　Physician　　, on oath state that I attended on Mrs.　Ora Lee Betts　, wife of　Charlie A. Betts　on the 5th　day of October , 1904; that there was born to her on said date a　female　child; that said child was living March 4, 1905, and is said to have been named　Ruby May Betts

　　　　　　　　　　　　　　　　　　　J.S. Fulton
Witnesses To Mark:
　{

　　Subscribed and sworn to before me this 18th　day of　March　, 1905

　　　　　　　　　　　　　　　　(Name Illegible)
　　　　　　　　　　　　　　　　Notary Public.

Choc New Born 312
　　Fleming P. Clower
　　(Born Feb. 9, 1905)

BIRTH AFFIDAVIT.
DEPARTMENT OF THE INTERIOR.
COMMISSION TO THE FIVE CIVILIZED TRIBES.

　　IN RE APPLICATION FOR ENROLLMENT, as a citizen of the　Choctaw　Nation, of Fleming P. Clower　, born on the　9　day of　February　, 1905

Name of Father: Walter F Clower　　　　a citizen of the　Choctaw　Nation.
Name of Mother: Sallie M Clower　　　　a citizen of the　Choctaw　Nation.

　　　　　　　　　　Postoffice　　Caddo Ind Ty

Applications for Enrollment of Choctaw Newborn
Act of 1905   Volume VI

AFFIDAVIT OF MOTHER.

UNITED STATES OF AMERICA, Indian Territory, }
Central   DISTRICT.

I, Sallie M. Clower, on oath state that I am 37 years of age and a citizen by Blood, of the Choctaw Nation; that I am the lawful wife of Walter F. Clower, who is a citizen, by Marriage of the Choctaw Nation; that a male child was born to me on ninth day of February, 1905; that said child has been named Fleming P. Clower, and was living March 4, 1905.

Sallie M Clower

Witnesses To Mark:
{

Subscribed and sworn to before me this 16th day of March, 1905

Sol. J. Homer
Notary Public.

AFFIDAVIT OF ATTENDING PHYSICIAN OR MID-WIFE.

UNITED STATES OF AMERICA, Indian Territory, }
Central   DISTRICT.

I, Wm Graves, a Physician, on oath state that I attended on Mrs. Sallie M Clower, wife of Walter F Clower on the 9 day of February, 1905; that there was born to her on said date a male child; that said child was living March 4, 1905, and is said to have been named Fleming P. Clower

William Graves, D.O.

Witnesses To Mark:
{

Subscribed and sworn to before me this 16th day of March, 1905

Sol. J. Homer
Notary Public.

Applications for Enrollment of Choctaw Newborn
Act of 1905   Volume VI

7-4394

Muskogee, Indian Territory, March 20, 1905.

Walter F. Clower,
    Caddo, Indian Territory.

Dear Sir:

    Receipt is hereby acknowledged of the affidavits of Sallie M. Clower and William Graves to the birth of Fleming P. Clower, son of Walter F. and Sallie M. Clower, February 9, 1905, and the same have been filed with our records as an application for the enrollment of said child.

                  Respectfully,

                                Chairman.

Choctaw N.B. 312.

Muskogee, Indian Territory, May 1, 1905.

Walter F. Clower,
    Caddo, Indian Territory.

Dear Sir:

    Receipt is hereby acknowledged of your letter of April 26, asking if you will be advised of the approval of the enrollment of your child, Fleming P. Clower. You state that you have an opportunity to buy land for his allotment and wish to know if you can have improved land set aside for him.

    In reply to your letter you are advised that no reservation of land or selection of allotment can be made for children enrolled under the act of Congress approved March 3, 1905, until their enrollment has been approved by the Secretary of the Interior. You will be advised, however, when the enrollment of your child is approved.

                  Respectfully,

                                Chairman.

Choc New Born 313
    Lavinia Albertine Rutherford
    (Born Jan. 28, 1904)

**Applications for Enrollment of Choctaw Newborn
Act of 1905 Volume VI**

No. 233

Certificate of Record of Marriages.

United States of America,
 Indian Territory, } sct:
 Central District.

I, E.J. Fannin , Clerk of the United States Court in the Indian Territory and District aforesaid, do hereby CERTIFY, that the License for and Certificate of the Marriage of

Mr.   Albert B. Rutherford   and

Miss Louvinia Pate   was

filed in my office in said Territory and District the 4 day of May A.D., 190 3 and duly recorded in Book 1 of Marriage Record, Page 111

Witness my hand and seal of said Court, at Durant , this 4 day of May , A.D. 190 3

E. J. Fannin
Clerk.

By WB Stone *Deputy.*

Applications for Enrollment of Choctaw Newborn
Act of 1905 Volume VI

No. 233

FORM NO. 598.

MARRIAGE LICENSE.

UNITES STATES OF AMERICA,
THE INDIAN TERRITORY,   } ss:
Central   DISTRICT.

To any Person Authorized by Law to Solemnize Marriage—Greeting:

You are hereby commanded to solemnize the Rite and publish the Banns of Matrimony between Mr.   Albert B Rutherford
of   Caddo   in the Indian Territory, aged   23   years, and M iss Lovinia Pate   of   Caddo   in the Indian Territory, aged   21 years, according to law, and do you officially sign and return this License to the parties therein named.

WITNESS my hand and official seal, this 24th day of April   A. D. 190 3

EJ Fannin
Clerk of the United States Court.

WB Stone
Deputy

CERTIFICATE OF MARRIAGE.

UNITES STATES OF AMERICA,
THE INDIAN TERRITORY,   } ss:
_____ DISTRICT.

I,   Robt E Talford
a   Minister of the Gospel

do hereby CERTIFY, that on the 29th day of April   A, D. 190 3 ; I did duly and according to law, as commanded in the foregoing License, solemnize the Rite and publish the BANNS OF MATRIMONY between the parties therein named.

Witness my hand this 30th day of April   , A. D. 190 3

My credentials are recorded in the office of the Clerk of the United States Court in the Indian Territory, Central District, Book 6   Page   67

Robt E Talford
a _____

Applications for Enrollment of Choctaw Newborn
Act of 1905 Volume VI

NOTE. -The License and Certificate of Marriage must be returned to the Office of the Clerk of the United States Court of the Indian Territory, from whence it was issued, within sixty days from the date thereof, or the party to whom the License was issued will be liable in the amount of One Hundred Dollars ($100.00).

NEW BORN AFFIDAVIT
No _____

CHOCTAW ENROLLING COMMISSION

IN THE MATTER OF THE APPLICATION FOR ENROLLMENT as a citizen of the Choctaw Nation, of   Albertine L Rutherford   born on the 28th day of January   190 4

Name of father Albert B Rutherford   a citizen of ———— Nation, final enrollment No. ————
Name of mother Lavinia W Pate   a citizen of Choctaw Nation, final enrollment No. 12250

Caddo I.T.   Postoffice.

AFFIDAVIT OF MOTHER

UNITED STATES OF AMERICA }
  INDIAN TERRITORY }
DISTRICT   Central }

Rutherford

I   Lavinia W Pate now _____ , on oath state that I am 23 years of age and a citizen by blood of the Choctaw Nation, and as such have been placed upon the final roll of the Choctaw Nation, by the Honorable Secretary of the Interior my final enrollment number being 12250 ; that I am the lawful wife of Albert B Rutherford , who is a citizen of the ———— Nation, and as such has been placed upon the final roll of said Nation by the Honorable Secretary of the Interior, his final enrollment number being _____ and that a Female child was born to me on the 28 day of January   1903[sic]; that said child has been named Albertine L. Rutherford , and is now living.

WITNESSETH: Lavinia W Rutherford
 Must be two witnesses { Chas Hill
 who are citizens   { W F Clower

Subscribed and sworn to before me this, the 6th day of February , 190 5

A.E. Folsom
Notary Public.

My Commission Expires: Jan 9-1909

Applications for Enrollment of Choctaw Newborn
Act of 1905 Volume VI

Affidavit of Attending Physician or Midwife

UNITED STATES OF AMERICA,
INDIAN TERRITORY,
Central DISTRICT

I, W.J. Melton a Practicing Physician on oath state that I attended on Mrs. Lavinia W Pate now Rutherford wife of Albert B Rutherford on the 28th day of January, 190 4, that there was born to her on said date a Female child, that said child is now living, and is said to have been named Albertine L. Rutherford

W.J. Melton M. D.

Subscribed and sworn to before me this the 11th day of February 1905

A E Folsom
Notary Public.

WITNESSETH:
Must be two witnesses who are citizens and know the child. { Chas Hill
W F Clower

We hereby certify that we are well acquainted with W.J. Melton a Physician and know him to be reputable and of good standing in the community.

Must be two citizen witnesses. { Chas Hill
W.F. Clower

BIRTH AFFIDAVIT.

DEPARTMENT OF THE INTERIOR.
COMMISSION TO THE FIVE CIVILIZED TRIBES.

IN RE APPLICATION FOR ENROLLMENT, as a citizen of the Choctaw Nation, of Lavinia Albertine Rutherford , born on the 28th day of Jan , 1904

Name of Father: Albert B. Rutherford a citizen of the United States xxxxx
nee Pate
Name of Mother: Lavinia W. Rutherford a citizen of the Choctaw Nation.

Postoffice Caddo, Ind. Ter.

Applications for Enrollment of Choctaw Newborn
Act of 1905   Volume VI

AFFIDAVIT OF MOTHER.

UNITED STATES OF AMERICA, Indian Territory, }
Central   DISTRICT.

   I,   Lavinia W. Rutherford nee Pate   , on oath state that I am   23   years of age and a citizen by   blood   , of the   Choctaw   Nation; that I am the lawful wife of   Albert B. Rutherford   , who is a citizen, by .... of the   United States Nation; that a   female   child was born to me on   28th   day of   January   , 1....4; that said child has been named   Lavinia Albertine Rutherford   , and was living March 4, 1905.

                                        Lavinia W. Rutherford

Witnesses To Mark:
{

   Subscribed and sworn to before me this 17th   day of   March   , 1905

                                        Chas E McPherren
                                            Notary Public.

AFFIDAVIT OF ATTENDING PHYSICIAN OR MID-WIFE.

UNITED STATES OF AMERICA, Indian Territory, }
Central   DISTRICT.

   I,   W. J. Melton   , a   physician   , on oath state that I attended on Mrs.   Lavinia W. Rutherford nee Pate   , wife of   Albert B. Rutherford   on the 28th   day of   January   , 1904; that there was born to her on said date a   female   child; that said child was living March 4, 1905, and is said to have been named   Lavinia Albertine Rutherford

                                        W.J. Melton

Witnesses To Mark:
{

   Subscribed and sworn to before me this 17th   day of   March   , 1905

                                        Chas E McPherren
                                            Notary Public.

Applications for Enrollment of Choctaw Newborn
Act of 1905   Volume VI

BIRTH AFFIDAVIT.

DEPARTMENT OF THE INTERIOR.
COMMISSION TO THE FIVE CIVILIZED TRIBES.

IN RE APPLICATION FOR ENROLLMENT, as a citizen of the   Choctaw   Nation, of Lavinia Albertine Rutherford   , born on the 28th day of January   , 1904

Name of Father: Albert B. Rutherford   a citizen of the   U S   Nation
Name of Mother: Lavinia W. Rutherford   a citizen of the   Choctaw   Nation.

Postoffice   Caddo, I.T.

AFFIDAVIT OF MOTHER.

UNITED STATES OF AMERICA, Indian Territory,
Central   DISTRICT.

I,   Lavinia W. Rutherford (Pate)   , on oath state that I am   23   years of age and a citizen by   Blood   , of the   Choctaw   Nation; that I am the lawful wife of Albert B. Rutherford   , who is a citizen, ~~by~~ ——— of the   United States   Nation; that a Female   child was born to me on 28th day of   January   , 1904; that said child has been named   Lavinia Albertine Rutherford   , and was living March 4, 1905.

Lavinia W. Rutherford

Witnesses To Mark:
{

Subscribed and sworn to before me this 24th day of   May   , 1905

Chas E McPherren
Notary Public.

AFFIDAVIT OF ATTENDING PHYSICIAN OR MID-WIFE.

UNITED STATES OF AMERICA, Indian Territory,
Central   DISTRICT.

I,   W. J. Melton   , a   Physician   , on oath state that I attended on Mrs.   Lavinia W. Rutherford (Pate)   , wife of   Albert B. Rutherford   on the 28th day of January   , 1904; that there was born to her on said date a   Female child; that said child was living March 4, 1905, and is said to have been named Lavinia Albertine Rutherford

W.J. Melton

Witnesses To Mark:
{

Applications for Enrollment of Choctaw Newborn
Act of 1905   Volume VI

Subscribed and sworn to before me this 24th day of   May   , 1905

Chas E McPherren
Notary Public.

DEPARTMENT OF THE INTERIOR,
COMMISSION TO THE FIVE CIVILIZED TRIBES.

In the matter of the application	( )	
	( )	Affidavit of
for the enrollment of infant child,	( )	
	( )	Albert B. Rutherford.
Lavinia Albertine Rutherford.	( )	

Be it remembered that on this this[sic] the 17th. day of March 1905, personally appeared before me, the undersigned authority, Albert B. Rutherford, father of Lavinia Albertine Rutherford, who after being duly sworn upon his oath states as follows to-wit:

My name is Albert B. Rutherford, my post office is Caddo, I. T., I am 25 years of age. I am the identical Albert B. Rutherford who married Lavinia W. Pate, on the 29th. day of April 1903; that on the 28th. day of January 1904 my daughter Lavinia Albertine Rutherford was born and is still living. My wife who was Lavinia W. Pate, appears upon the rolls of Choctaw Indians by blood Lavinia W. Pate.

Since our marriage my wife has never appeared before the Commission to the Five Civilized Tribes, and no record has therefore been made by the said Commission as to our marriage.

Witness my hand this the 17th. day of March 1905.

Albert Rutherford

Sworn and subscribed to before me, this the 17th. day of March 1905.

Chas E McPherren

Applications for Enrollment of Choctaw Newborn
Act of 1905   Volume VI

7-4392

Muskogee, Indian Territory, March 22, 1905.

Chas E McPherren,
    Attorney at Law,
        Caddo, Indian Territory.

Dear Sir:

    Receipt is hereby acknowledged of your letter of March 17, 1905, enclosing affidavits of Lavinia W. Rutherford (Pate) and W. J. Melton to the birth of Lavinia Albertine Rutherford, daughter of Albert B. and Lavinia W. Rutherford January 28, 1904; also affidavits of Albert B. Rutherford and marriage license and certificate between Albert B. Rutherford and Lavinia Pate and the same have been filed with our records as an application for the enrollment of Lavinia Albertine Rutherford.

    Respectfully,

    Chairman.

7-NB-313.

Muskogee, Indian Territory, May 22, 1905.

Albert B. Rutherford,
    Caddo, Indian Territory.

Dear Sir:

    There is enclosed you herewith for execution application for the enrollment of your infant child, Lavinia Albertine Rutherford.

    In the affidavits filed in this office on March 18, 1905, the date of the applicants[sic] birth is given as January 28, 1904, while in those filed on the 26th ultimo, the date of birth is given as January 28, 1903. In the enclosed application the date of birth is left blank, which you will please insert and when properly executed return to this office.

    In having these affidavits executed care should be exercised to see that all names are written in full, as they appear in the body of the affidavit, and in the event that either of the persons signing the affidavit are unable to write, signatures by mark must be attested by two witnesses. Each affidavit must be executed before a Notary Public and the notarial seal and signature of the officer must be attached to each separate affidavit.

Applications for Enrollment of Choctaw Newborn
Act of 1905   Volume VI

VR 22-16.

Respectfully,

Chairman.

---

7 N.B. 313.

Muskogee, Indian Territory, May 29, 1905.

Albert B. Rutherford,
    Caddo, Indian Territory.

Dear Sir:

Receipt is hereby acknowledged of the affidavits of Lavinia W. Rutherford and W. J. Melton to the birth of Lavinia Albertine Rutherford, daughter of Albert B. and Lavinia W. Rutherford, January 28, 1904, and the same have been filed with our records in the matter of the enrollment of the above named child.

Respectfully,

Chairman.

7- NB 313

Muskogee, Indian Territory, August 29, 1905.

A. B. Rutherford,
    Caddo, Indian Territory.

Dear Sir:

Receipt is hereby acknowledged of your letter of the 25th instant, asking to be advised if the enrollment of your child, Lavinia Albertine Rutherford, has been approved by the Secretary of the Interior.

In reply to your letter you are advised that on August 22, 1905, the Secretary of the Interior approved the enrollment of Lavinia Albertine Rutherford as a citizen by blood of the Choctaw Nation and the name of the said child appears upon the roll of new born citizens by blood of the Choctaw Nation opposite number 1291.

Respectfully,

Commissioner.

Applications for Enrollment of Choctaw Newborn
Act of 1905 Volume VI

Choc New Born 314
Beulah F. Williams
(Born Jan. 19, 1904)

NEW BORN AFFIDAVIT

No ....

CHOCTAW ENROLLING COMMISSION

IN THE MATTER OF THE APPLICATION FOR ENROLLMENT as a citizen of the Choctaw Nation, of Bulah[sic] F. Williams born on the 19 day of February[sic] 190 4

Name of father   T. R. Williams   a citizen of   United States   ~~Nation~~,
final enrollment No. ....
Name of mother   Warneta F. Williams   a citizen of   Choctaw   Nation,
final enrollment No.   12270

Atoka, Ind. Ter.   Postoffice.

AFFIDAVIT OF MOTHER

UNITED STATES OF AMERICA }
   INDIAN TERRITORY
DISTRICT   Central

I   Warneta F. Williams   , on oath state that I am   25   years of age and a citizen by   blood   of the   Choctaw   Nation, and as such have been placed upon the final roll of the   Choctaw   Nation, by the Honorable Secretary of the Interior my final enrollment number being   12270   ; that I am the lawful wife of   T. R. Williams   , who is a citizen of the .... Nation, and as such has been placed upon the final roll of said Nation by the Honorable Secretary of the Interior, his final enrollment number being .... and that a   Female   child was born to me on the   19th   day of   February[sic]   190 4; that said child has been named   Bulah F Williams   , and is now living.

WITNESSETH: Warneta F. Williams
  Must be two witnesses { CA Betts
  who are citizens   Wm Fronterhouse

Applications for Enrollment of Choctaw Newborn
Act of 1905 Volume VI

Subscribed and sworn to before me this, the 21 day of February , 190 5

                                                A.G. Etheredge
                                                      Notary Public.

My Commission Expires: Oct. 15, 1907

Affidavit of Attending Physician or Midwife

UNITED STATES OF AMERICA,
  INDIAN TERRITORY,
 Central   DISTRICT

    I, J.S. Fulton a Physician
on oath state that I attended on Mrs. Warneta F. Williams wife of T. R. Williams
on the 19th day of February[sic] , 190 4, that there was born to her on said date a
Female child, that said child is now living, and is said to have been named Bulah F. Williams

                                             J.S. Fulton   M. D.

Subscribed and sworn to before me this the 21 day of February 1905

                                          A.G. Etheredge
                                                Notary Public.

WITNESSETH:
- Must be two witnesses who are citizens and know the child.
  - CA Betts
  - R. D. Betts
  - Wm Fronterhouse

    We hereby certify that we are well acquainted with J. S. Fulton
a Physician and know him to be reputable and of good standing in the community.

                                  Must be two citizen witnesses.
- CA Betts
- Elias Thompson

Applications for Enrollment of Choctaw Newborn
Act of 1905   Volume VI

BIRTH AFFIDAVIT.

DEPARTMENT OF THE INTERIOR.
COMMISSION TO THE FIVE CIVILIZED TRIBES.

IN RE APPLICATION FOR ENROLLMENT, as a citizen of the   Choctaw   Nation, of Beulah F. Williams   , born on the 19th day of January, 1904

Name of Father: T. R. Williams   a citizen of the   Non Citz   ~~Nation~~.
Name of Mother: Warneta F. Williams   a citizen of the   Choctaw   Nation.

Postoffice   Atoka I T

AFFIDAVIT OF MOTHER.

UNITED STATES OF AMERICA, Indian Territory, }
Central   DISTRICT. }

I, Warneta F Williams, on oath state that I am 25 years of age and a citizen by blood, of the Choctaw Nation; that I am the lawful wife of T. R. Williams, who is a ~~citizen, by~~ Non Citizen ~~of the~~ ~~Nation~~; that a female child was born to me on 19th day of January, 1904, 1.......; that said child has been named Beulah F. Williams, and was living March 4, 1905.

Warneta F. Williams

Witnesses To Mark:
{

Subscribed and sworn to before me this 18th day of March, 1905

(Name Illegible)
Notary Public.

AFFIDAVIT OF ATTENDING PHYSICIAN OR MID-WIFE.

UNITED STATES OF AMERICA, Indian Territory, }
Central   DISTRICT. }

I, J. S. Fulton, a physician, on oath state that I attended on Mrs. Warneta F. Williams, wife of T. R. Williams on the 19th day of January, 1904; that there was born to her on said date a female child; that said child was living March 4, 1905, and is said to have been named Beulah F Williams

J. S. Fulton

Applications for Enrollment of Choctaw Newborn
Act of 1905   Volume VI

Witnesses To Mark:

{

Subscribed and sworn to before me this 18th day of   March   , 1905

(Name Illegible)
Notary Public.

BIRTH AFFIDAVIT.

DEPARTMENT OF THE INTERIOR.
COMMISSION TO THE FIVE CIVILIZED TRIBES.

IN RE APPLICATION FOR ENROLLMENT, as a citizen of the   Choctaw   Nation, of Beulah F. Williams   , born on the   19   day of   January , 1904

Name of Father: T. R. Williams   a citizen of the   U. S.   Nation.
Name of Mother: Warneta F. Williams   a citizen of the   Choctaw   Nation.

Postoffice   Atoka I T

AFFIDAVIT OF MOTHER.

UNITED STATES OF AMERICA, Indian Territory, }
Central   DISTRICT. }

I,   Warneta F Williams   , on oath state that I am   25   years of age and a citizen by   Blood   , of the   Choctaw   Nation; that I am the lawful wife of   T. R. Williams   , who is a citizen, ~~by~~ ——— of the   United States   Nation; that a   Female   child was born to me on   19th   day of   January , 1904; that said child has been named   Beulah F. Williams   , and was living March 4, 1905.

Warneta F. Williams

Witnesses To Mark:

{

Subscribed and sworn to before me this 24th day of   May   , 1905 at Atoka, IT

My commission expires   A.G. Etheredge
Oct. 15, 1907.   Notary Public.

Applications for Enrollment of Choctaw Newborn
Act of 1905   Volume VI

AFFIDAVIT OF ATTENDING PHYSICIAN OR MID-WIFE.

UNITED STATES OF AMERICA, Indian Territory,
Central   DISTRICT.

I, J. S. Fulton, a Physician, on oath state that I attended on Mrs. Warneta F. Williams, wife of T. R. Williams on the 19th day of January, 1904; that there was born to her on said date a Female child; that said child was living March 4, 1905, and is said to have been named Beulah F Williams

J. S. Fulton

Witnesses To Mark:
{

Subscribed and sworn to before me this 24th day of May, 1905 at Atoka, IT

My commission expires   A.G. Etheredge
    Oct. 15, 1907.   Notary Public.

7-NB-314.

Muskogee, Indian Territory, May 22, 1905.

T. R. Williams,
    Atoka, Indian Territory.

Dear Sir:

There is enclosed you herewith for execution application for the enrollment of your infant child, Beulah F. Williams.

In the affidavits of February 21, 1905, heretofore filed in in[sic] this office, the date of the applicants[sic] birth is given as February 19, 1904, while in the affidavits of March 18, 1905, it is given as January 19, 1904. In the enclosed application the date of birth is left blank, which you will please insert, and when properly executed return to this office.

In having these affidavits executed care should be exercised to see that all names are written in full, as they appear in the body of the affidavit, and in the event that either of the persons signing the affidavit are unable to write, signatures by mark must be attested by two witnesses. Each affidavit must be executed before a Notary Public and the notarial seal and signature of the officer must be attached to each separate affidavit.

Respectfully,

VR 22-15.   Chairman.

Applications for Enrollment of Choctaw Newborn
Act of 1905 Volume VI

7 N.B. 314.

Muskogee, Indian Territory, May 29, 1905.

T. R. Williams,
    Atoka, Indian Territory.

Dear Sir:

    Receipt is hereby acknowledged of the affidavits of Warneta F. Williams and J. S. Fulton to the birth of Beulah F. Williams, daughter of T. R. and Warneta F. Williams, January 19, 1904, and the same have been filed with our records in the matter of the enrollment of the above named child.

               Respectfully,

                             Chairman.

Muskogee, Indian Territory, August 3, 1905.

Chief Clerk,
    Choctaw Land Office,
        Atoka, Indian Territory.

Dear Sir:

    Refer to duplicate Choctaw New Born Roll Card No. 314, in the possession of your office, and change the roll number of the mother thereon to read, "12270" instead of "1227."

               Respectfully,

                             Commissioner.

Applications for Enrollment of Choctaw Newborn
Act of 1905 Volume VI

Muskogee, Indian Territory, August 3, 1905.

Chief Clerk,
    Chickasaw Land Office,
        Ardmore, Indian Territory.

Dear Sir:

    Refer to duplicate Choctaw New Born Roll Card No. 314, in the possession of your office, and change the roll number of the mother thereon to read, "12270" instead of "1227."

                        Respectfully,

                                      Commissioner.

Choc New Born 315
    Autie May Betts
    (Born May 7, 1903)

NEW-BORN AFFIDAVIT.

        Number................

...Choctaw Enrolling Commission...

    IN THE MATTER OF THE APPLICATION FOR ENROLLMENT, as a citizen of the Choctaw Nation, of Autie May Betts

born on the 7th day of May 190 3

Name of father   William W Betts   a citizen of   Choctaw
Nation final enrollment No. 12315
Name of mother   Bettie Betts   a citizen of   Choctaw
Nation final enrollment No. 429

                                Postoffice   Atoka I.T.

Applications for Enrollment of Choctaw Newborn
Act of 1905 Volume VI

AFFIDAVIT OF MOTHER.

UNITED STATES OF AMERICA
INDIAN TERRITORY
Central   DISTRICT

I   Bettie Betts   , on oath state that I am 33   years of age and a citizen by   Marriage   of the   Choctaw Nation, and as such have been placed upon the final roll of the   Choctaw Nation, by the Honorable Secretary of the Interior my final enrollment number being   429   ; that I am the lawful wife of   William W Betts   , who is a citizen of the Choctaw   Nation, and as such has been placed upon the final roll of said Nation by the Honorable Secretary of the Interior, his final enrollment number being   12315   and that a Female   child was born to me on the 7th day of   May   190 3; that said child has been named   Autie May Betts   , and is now living.

Witnesseth.   Bettie Betts
Must be two ⎫   C A Betts
Witnesses who ⎬
are Citizens. ⎭   R.O. Sumter

Subscribed and sworn to before me this 23^d day of   February   190 5

A.E. Folsom
Notary Public.

My commission expires: Jan 9- 1909

Affidavit of Attending Physician or Midwife

UNITED STATES OF AMERICA, ⎫
INDIAN TERRITORY, ⎬
Central   DISTRICT ⎭

I,   J.S. Fulton   a   Practicing Physician on oath state that I attended on Mrs. Bettie Betts   wife of   William W Betts on the 7th day of   May   , 190 3, that there was born to her on said date a   Female child, that said child is now living, and is said to have been named   Autie May Betts

J.S. Fulton   M. D.

Subscribed and sworn to before me this the 23^d day of   February   1905

A.E. Folsom
Notary Public.

Applications for Enrollment of Choctaw Newborn
Act of 1905   Volume VI

WITNESSETH:

Must be two witnesses who are citizens and know the child. { C A Betts
R.O. Sumter

We hereby certify that we are well acquainted with Dr J.S. Fulton a Practicing Physician   and know him   to be reputable and of good standing in the community.

Must be two citizen witnesses. { C A Betts
R.O. Sumter

BIRTH AFFIDAVIT.

DEPARTMENT OF THE INTERIOR.
COMMISSION TO THE FIVE CIVILIZED TRIBES.

IN RE APPLICATION FOR ENROLLMENT, as a citizen of the   Choctaw   Nation, of Autie May Betts   , born on the 7th day of May , 1903

Name of Father: William W Betts   a citizen of the   Choctaw   Nation.
Name of Mother: Bettie   "   a citizen of the   "   Nation.

Postoffice   Atoka IT

AFFIDAVIT OF MOTHER.

UNITED STATES OF AMERICA, Indian Territory,
Central   DISTRICT.

I,   Bettie Betts   , on oath state that I am 33   years of age and a citizen by Intermarriage , of the   Choctaw   Nation; that I am the lawful wife of   William W Betts   , who is a citizen, by blood   of the   Choctaw   Nation; that a female   child was born to me on 7th day of May   , 1903; that said child has been named   Autie May Betts   , and was living March 4, 1905.

Bettie Bets

Witnesses To Mark:
{

Subscribed and sworn to before me this 18th day of March   , 1905

W.H. Angell
Notary Public.

Applications for Enrollment of Choctaw Newborn
Act of 1905 Volume VI

AFFIDAVIT OF ATTENDING PHYSICIAN OR MID-WIFE.

UNITED STATES OF AMERICA, Indian Territory, }
Central   DISTRICT.

I, J.S. Fulton , a physician , on oath state that I attended on Mrs. Bettie Betts , wife of William W Betts on the 7th day of May , 1903; that there was born to her on said date a Female child; that said child was living March 4, 1905, and is said to have been named Autie May Betts

J.S. Fulton

Witnesses To Mark:
{

Subscribed and sworn to before me this 18th day of March , 1905

W.H. Angell
Notary Public.

Choc New Born 316
    Tams Bixby Massey
    (Born Nov. 21, 1902)
    Sillin Walker Massey
    (Born July 21, 1904)

BIRTH AFFIDAVIT.   *After Sept. 25, 1902.*
DEPARTMENT OF THE INTERIOR,
COMMISSION TO THE FIVE CIVILIZED TRIBES.

IN RE Application for Enrollment, as a citizen of the Chocktaw[sic] Nation, of Tams Bixby Massey , born on the 21 day of November , 1902

Name of Father: William Wilson Massey   a citizen of the Chocktaw[sic] Nation.
Name of Mother: Alice Victoria Massey   a citizen of the Chocktaw[sic] Nation.
by Marriage
                        Post-Office: Massey, Ind. Tery

Applications for Enrollment of Choctaw Newborn
Act of 1905   Volume VI

AFFIDAVIT OF MOTHER.

UNITED STATES OF AMERICA,
   INDIAN TERRITORY.
  Central   District.

    I, Alice Victoria Massey , on oath state that I am twenty three years of age and a citizen by Marriage , of the Chocktaw Nation; that I am the lawful wife of William Wilson Massey , who is a citizen, by blood of the Choctaw Nation; that a male child was born to me on 21st day of November , 1902 , that said child has been named Tams Bixby Massey , and is now living.

                                            her
                              Alice Victoria x Massey
WITNESSES TO MARK: mark
{ Sallie Clabron
       her
  Elizziebeth[sic] x Justis
      mark

    Subscribed and sworn to before me this 19th *day of*   December   , 1902
term
expires   W.F. Kelley
June 18th **NOTARY PUBLIC.**
1905

AFFIDAVIT OF ATTENDING PHYSICIAN OR MID-WIFE.

UNITED STATES OF AMERICA,
   INDIAN TERRITORY.
  Central   District.

    I, James H Bristow , a Physician , on oath state that I attended on Mrs. Alice Victoria Massey , wife of William Wilson Massey on the 21st day of November , 1902 ; that there was born to her on said date a male child; that said child is now living and is said to have been named Tams Bixby Massey

                              James H Bristow
WITNESSES TO MARK:
{

    Subscribed and sworn to before me this 19th *day of*   December   , 1902
term
expires   W.F. Kelley
June 18th **NOTARY PUBLIC.**
1902[sic]

Applications for Enrollment of Choctaw Newborn
Act of 1905 Volume VI

NEW BORN AFFIDAVIT

Number---------------------------

CHOCTAW   ENROLLING   COMMISSION.

##############

IN THE MATTER OF THE APPLICATION FOR THE ENROLLMENT as a citizen of the Choctaw Nation of Tams Bixby Massey born on the 22 day of November 190 2. Name of Father William W. Massey a citizen of Choctaw Nation. final roll No. 14419
Name of Mother Alice Victoria Massey a citizen of Choctaw Nation final enrollment No. 435
                                       Post Office Massey   I.T.

AFFIDAVIT OF MOTHER

UNITED STATES OF AMERICA
    Indian Territory
    Central   District.

  I   Alis[sic] Victoria Massey on oath state that I am 25 years of age and a citizen by Intermarriage of the Choctaw Nation and as such have been placed upon the final roll of the Choctaw Nation by the Honorable Secretary of the Interior, my final enrollment No 435 that I am the lawful wife of William W. Massey who is a citizen of the Choctaw Nation and as such has been placed upon the final roll of said Nation by the Honorable Secretary of the Interior his final enrollment No being 14419 , and that a Male child was born to me on the 22 day of November 190 2, and is now living and has been named Tams Bixby Massey

                                              her
                                       Alice x Victoria Massey
Witness.   mark
    Lee P Baldwin
    A Banks

Subscribed and sworn to before me this the 9 day of Jan 190 5

                             O P Swisher
                                    Notary Public
My Commission Expires 14 day of Jan   190 8.

Applications for Enrollment of Choctaw Newborn
Act of 1905   Volume VI

NEW BORN AFFIDAVIT

Number---------------------------

CHOCTAW ENROLLING COMMISSION.

##############

IN THE MATTER OF THE APPLICATION FOR THE ENROLLMENT as a citizen of the Choctaw Nation of Sillin Walker Massey born on the 21 day of July 190 4. Name of Father William W. Massey a citizen of Choctaw Nation. final roll No. 14419
Name of Mother Alice Victoria Massey a citizen of Choctaw Nation final enrollment No. 435

Post Office   Massey   I.T.

AFFIDAVIT OF MOTHER

UNITED STATES OF AMERICA
    Indian Territory
    Central   District.

I Alice Victoria Massey on oath state that I am 25 years of age and a citizen by Intermarriage of the Choctaw Nation and as such have been placed upon the final roll of the Choctaw Nation by the Honorable Secretary of the Interior, my final enrollment No 435 that I am the lawful wife of William W. Massey who is a citizen of the Choctaw Nation and as such has been placed upon the final roll of said Nation by the Honorable Secretary of the Interior his final enrollment No being 14419 , and that a Female child was born to me on the 21 day of July 190 4, and is now living and has been named Sillin Walker Massey

                          her
                     Alice x Victoria Massey
Witness.   mark
    Lee P Baldwin
    A Banks

Subscribed and sworn to before me this the 9 day of Jan 190 5

                        O P Swisher
                          Notary Public
My Commission Expires 14 day of Jan 190 8.

Applications for Enrollment of Choctaw Newborn
Act of 1905   Volume VI

AFFIDAVIT OF ATTENDING PHYSICIAN.
###################

UNITED STATES OF AMERICA
INDIAN TERRITORY
Central   DISTRICT.

I Susanah[sic] Hatfield a Midwife on oath state that I attended on Mrs. Alice Victoria Massey , wife of William W. Massey on the 21 day of July , 1904; that there was born to her on said date a female child; that said child was living March 4, 1905, and is said to have been named Sillin Walker Massey .

witness O P Swisher

Susanah x Hatfield
her / mark

Subscribed and sworn to before me this the 9 day of Jan 190 5

My com expires Jan 14-1908

O P Swisher
Notary Public

Witness
  citizens   Lee P Baldwin
               A Banks

We hereby certify that we are acquainted with Susanah Hatfield a midwife and know that She is reputable and creditable and of good standing in the community.

O P Swisher

Citizens
    Lee P Baldwin
    A Banks

Applications for Enrollment of Choctaw Newborn
Act of 1905   Volume VI

AFFIDAVIT OF ATTENDING PHYSICIAN.
###################

UNITED STATES OF AMERICA
      INDIAN TERRITORY
Central   DISTRICT.

I Lizzie Jestice   a   Midwife   on oath state that I attended on Mrs. Alice Victoria Massey   , wife of   William W. Massey   on the   22 day of November , 1902; that there was born to her on said date a   male   child; that said child was living March 4, 1905, and is said to have been named   Tams Bixby Massey .

Subscribed and sworn to before me this the -------- day of ------------- 190 .

                                      Notary Public

Witness
    Must be citizens   ---

We hereby certify that we are acquainted with -- a --------------------- and know that   She   is reputable and creditable and of good standing in the community.

Witness   ---
Must be citizens

Applications for Enrollment of Choctaw Newborn
Act of 1905   Volume VI

NEW-BORN AFFIDAVIT.

Number..............

...Choctaw Enrolling Commission...

IN THE MATTER OF THE APPLICATION FOR ENROLLMENT, as a citizen of the Choctaw Nation, of   Tams Bixby Massey

born on the 22 day of November 190 2

Name of father   William W Massey   a citizen of   Choctaw
Nation final enrollment No. 14419
Name of mother   Alice Victoria Massey   a citizen of   Choctaw
Nation final enrollment No. 435

Postoffice   Massey I.T.

AFFIDAVIT OF MOTHER.

UNITED STATES OF AMERICA
INDIAN TERRITORY
Central   DISTRICT

I   Alice Victoria Massey   , on oath state that I am 25 years of age and a citizen by Marriage of the Choctaw Nation, and as such have been placed upon the final roll of the Choctaw Nation, by the Honorable Secretary of the Interior my final enrollment number being 435 ; that I am the lawful wife of William W Massey , who is a citizen of the Choctaw Nation, and as such has been placed upon the final roll of said Nation by the Honorable Secretary of the Interior, his final enrollment number being 14419 and that a Male child was born to me on the 22 day of November 190 2; that said child has been named Tams Bixby Massey , and is now living.

Attest O P Swisher   her
Witnesseth.   Alice Victoria x Massey
Must be two ⎱ J.A. LeFlore   mark
Witnesses who ⎰
are Citizens.   Lee P Baldwin

Subscribed and sworn to before me this 1 day of March 190 5

O P Swisher
Notary Public.

My commission expires: Jan 14-1908

Applications for Enrollment of Choctaw Newborn
Act of 1905   Volume VI

AFFIDAVIT OF ATTENDING PHYSICIAN OR MIDWIFE

UNITED STATES OF AMERICA
INDIAN TERRITORY
  Central   DISTRICT

I, Elizabeth Jestice   a   Mid Wife on oath state that I attended on Mrs. Alice Victoria Massey wife of William W. Massey on the 22 day of November , 190 2, that there was born to her on said date a Male child, that said child is now living, and is said to have been named Tams Bixby Massey

Attest O P Swisher

                               her
                      Elizabeth x Jestice   M.D.
                            mark

Subscribed and sworn to before me this, the 1 day of March 190 5

                              O P Swisher
My Com expires Jan 14-1908   Notary Public.

WITNESSETH:

Must be two witnesses who are citizens and know the child.

    J A LeFlore

    Lee P Baldwin

We hereby certify that we are well acquainted with Elizabeth Jestice a Mid Wife and know her to be reputable and of good standing in the community.

                            J A LeFlore

                            Lee P Baldwin

NEW-BORN AFFIDAVIT.

        Number............

...Choctaw Enrolling Commission...

IN THE MATTER OF THE APPLICATION FOR ENROLLMENT, as a citizen of the Choctaw Nation, of Sillin Walker Massey

born on the 21 day of July 190 4

Name of father   William W. Massey   a citizen of   Choctaw
Nation final enrollment No. 14419
Name of mother   Alice Victoria Massey   a citizen of   Choctaw
Nation final enrollment No. 435

                                  Postoffice   Massey I.T.

Applications for Enrollment of Choctaw Newborn
Act of 1905 Volume VI

AFFIDAVIT OF MOTHER.

UNITED STATES OF AMERICA
INDIAN TERRITORY
Central DISTRICT

I Alice Victoria Massey , on oath state that I am 25 years of age and a citizen by Marriage of the Choctaw Nation, and as such have been placed upon the final roll of the Choctaw Nation, by the Honorable Secretary of the Interior my final enrollment number being 435 ; that I am the lawful wife of William W Massey , who is a citizen of the Choctaw Nation, and as such has been placed upon the final roll of said Nation by the Honorable Secretary of the Interior, his final enrollment number being 14419 and that a Female child was born to me on the 21 day of July 190 4; that said child has been named Sillin Walker Massey , and is now living.

Attest O P Swisher

Witnesseth.
Must be two Witnesses who are Citizens. Jackson Burns
James A LeFlore

her
Alice Victoria x Massey
mark

Subscribed and sworn to before me this 1 day of March 190 5

O P Swisher
Notary Public.

My commission expires: Jan 14-1908

AFFIDAVIT OF ATTENDING PHYSICIAN OR MIDWIFE

UNITED STATES OF AMERICA
INDIAN TERRITORY
Central DISTRICT

I, Susanah Hatfield a Midwife on oath state that I attended on Mrs. Alice Victoria Massey wife of William W Massey on the 21 day of July , 190 4, that there was born to her on said date a Female child, that said child is now living, and is said to have been named Sillin Walker Massey

Susanah x Hatfield M.D.

Subscribed and sworn to before me this, the 1 day of March 190 5

O P Swisher
Notary Public.

WITNESSETH:
Must be two witnesses who are citizens and know the child. Jackson Burns
James A LeFlore

Applications for Enrollment of Choctaw Newborn
Act of 1905 Volume VI

We hereby certify that we are well acquainted with .... a   Midwife   and know   her   to be reputable and of good standing in the community.

$\Big\{$ Jackson Burns

James A LeFlore

BIRTH AFFIDAVIT.

DEPARTMENT OF THE INTERIOR.
COMMISSION TO THE FIVE CIVILIZED TRIBES.

IN RE APPLICATION FOR ENROLLMENT, as a citizen of the   Choctaw   Nation, of Tams Bixby Massey   , born on the   22nd   day of   November   , 1902

Name of Father: William W. Massey   a citizen of the   Choctaw   Nation.
Name of Mother: Alice Victoria Massey   a citizen of the   Choctaw   Nation.

Postoffice   Massey, I.T.

AFFIDAVIT OF MOTHER.

UNITED STATES OF AMERICA, Indian Territory, $\Big\}$
Central   DISTRICT.

I,   Alice Victoria Massey   , on oath state that I am   25   years of age and a citizen by   marriage   , of the   Choctaw   Nation; that I am the lawful wife of William W. Massey   , who is a citizen, by   blood   of the   Choctaw   Nation; that a   male   child was born to me on   22nd   day of   November   , 1902; that said child has been named   Tams Bixby Massey   , and was living March 4, 1905.

                                                                her
                                                Alice Victoria x Massey
Witnesses To Mark: mark
$\Big\{$ O P Swisher
  N.A. Crouch

Subscribed and sworn to before me this   22   day of   March   , 1905

                                                O P Swisher
                                                        Notary Public.
My commission expires Jan 14-1908

Applications for Enrollment of Choctaw Newborn
Act of 1905   Volume VI

AFFIDAVIT OF ATTENDING PHYSICIAN OR MID-WIFE.

UNITED STATES OF AMERICA, Indian Territory, }
Central   DISTRICT.

I, Lizzie Justice[sic], a midwife, on oath state that I attended on Mrs. Alice Victoria Massey, wife of William W. Massey on the 22nd day of November, 1902; that there was born to her on said date a male child; that said child was living March 4, 1905, and is said to have been named Tams Bixby Massey

                        her
                    Lizzie x Jestice

Witnesses To Mark: mark
{ O P Swisher
  Sue Swisher

Subscribed and sworn to before me this 25 day of March, 1905

                    O P Swisher
                    Notary Public.

My commission expires Jan 14-1908

BIRTH AFFIDAVIT.

DEPARTMENT OF THE INTERIOR.
COMMISSION TO THE FIVE CIVILIZED TRIBES.

IN RE APPLICATION FOR ENROLLMENT, as a citizen of the Choctaw Nation, of Sillin Walker Massey, born on the 21st day of July, 1904

Name of Father: William W. Massey   a citizen of the Choctaw Nation.
Name of Mother: Alice Victoria Massey   a citizen of the Choctaw Nation.

                Postoffice   Massey, I.T.

AFFIDAVIT OF MOTHER.

UNITED STATES OF AMERICA, Indian Territory, }
Central   DISTRICT.

I, Alice Victoria Massey, on oath state that I am 25 years of age and a citizen by marriage, of the Choctaw Nation; that I am the lawful wife of William W. Massey, who is a citizen, by blood of the Choctaw Nation; that a female child was born to me on 21st day of July, 1904; that said child has been named Sillin Walker Massey, and was living March 4, 1905.

Applications for Enrollment of Choctaw Newborn
Act of 1905 Volume VI

                                                    her
Witnesses To Mark: Alice Victoria x Massey
{ O P Swisher   mark
  N.A. Crouch

Subscribed and sworn to before me this 22 day of March , 1905

                                       O P Swisher
                                       Notary Public.

My commission expires Jan 14-1908

AFFIDAVIT OF ATTENDING PHYSICIAN OR MID-WIFE.

UNITED STATES OF AMERICA, Indian Territory,
    Central   DISTRICT.

      I, Susanna Hatfield , a midwife , on oath state that I attended on Mrs. Alice Victoria Massey , wife of William W. Massey on the 21st day of July , 1904; that there was born to her on said date a female child; that said child was living March 4, 1905, and is said to have been named Sillin Walker Massey

                                                   her
                                      Susanna x Hatfield
Witnesses To Mark: mark
{ O P Swisher
  W.R. Hatfield

Subscribed and sworn to before me this 31 day of March , 1905

                                       O P Swisher
                                       Notary Public.

My commission expires Jan 14-1908

                                                         7-4452

Muskogee, Indian Territory, April 5, 1905.

William W. Massey,
      Massey, Indian Territory.

Dear Sir:

      Receipt is hereby acknowledged of the affidavits of Alice Victoria Massey and Susanna Hatfield to the birth of Sillin Walker Massey daughter of William W. and Alice Victoria Massey, Indian Territory July 21, 1904; also the affidavits of Alice Victoria

Applications for Enrollment of Choctaw Newborn
Act of 1905   Volume VI

Massey and Lizzie Jestice to the birth of Tams Bixby Massey, Indian Territory son of William W. and Alice Victoria Massey, Indian Territory November 22, 1902, and the same have been filed with our records as applications for the enrollment of said children.

Respectfully,

Commissioner in Charge.

Choc New Born 317
    Green M. Walls
    (Born Jan. 14, 1903)

AFFIDAVIT OF ATTENDING PHYSICIAN OR MID-WIFE.

UNITED STATES OF AMERICA, }
   INDIAN TERRITORY,
Western   District.

I, S.E. Mitchell, a Physician, on oath state that I attended on Mrs. Catherine Walls, wife of ~~Enterprise~~ Thomas J. Walls on the 14th day of January, 1903; that there was born to her on said date a male child; that said child is now living and is said to have been named Green M Walls

                          S.E. Mitchell MD

WITNESSES TO MARK:
{

Subscribed and sworn to before me this 21 day of February, 1905.

                          H A Turner
                            NOTARY PUBLIC.

Applications for Enrollment of Choctaw Newborn
Act of 1905 Volume VI

NEW-BORN AFFIDAVIT.

Number................

...Choctaw Enrolling Commission...

IN THE MATTER OF THE APPLICATION FOR ENROLLMENT, as a citizen of the Choctaw Nation, of Green M Walls

born on the 14th day of __January__ 190 3

Name of father   Thomas J Walls   a citizen of   Choctaw
Nation final enrollment No.   12371
Name of mother   Catherine Walls   a citizen of   Choctaw
Nation final enrollment No.   437

Postoffice   Enterprise, I.T.

AFFIDAVIT OF MOTHER.

UNITED STATES OF AMERICA
INDIAN TERRITORY
Western   DISTRICT

I   Catherine Walls   , on oath state that I am 39 years of age and a citizen by   marriage   of the   Choctaw Nation, and as such have been placed upon the final roll of the   Choctaw Nation, by the Honorable Secretary of the Interior my final enrollment number being   437 ; that I am the lawful wife of   Thomas J Walls Sr   , who is a citizen of the   Choctaw Nation, and as such has been placed upon the final roll of said Nation by the Honorable Secretary of the Interior, his final enrollment number being   12371   and that a   Male child was born to me on the   14th day of   January   190 3; that said child has been named   Green M Walls   , and is now living.

Witnesseth.   Catherine Walls
  Must be two ⎤ James Fizer
  Witnesses who ⎦
  are Citizens.   Martha Collier

Subscribed and sworn to before me this   3   day of   Jan   190 5

John M Long
Notary Public.

My commission expires: Nov 27 1907

53

Applications for Enrollment of Choctaw Newborn
Act of 1905   Volume VI

AFFIDAVIT OF ATTENDING PHYSICIAN OR MIDWIFE

UNITED STATES OF AMERICA
INDIAN TERRITORY
Western   DISTRICT

I, Bettie Hamlin a Midwife on oath state that I attended on Mrs. Catherine Walls wife of Thos J Walls, Sr. on the 14 day of January , 190 3, that there was born to her on said date a male child, that said child is now living, and is said to have been named Green M Walls

Bettie Hamlin

Subscribed and sworn to before me this, the 5 day of January   190 5

WITNESSETH: John M Lentz   Notary Public.

Must be two witnesses who are citizens { James Fizer
Jess Walls

We hereby certify that we are well acquainted with Bettie Hamlin a Midwife and know her to be reputable and of good standing in the community.

James Fizer

Jess Walls

BIRTH AFFIDAVIT.

DEPARTMENT OF THE INTERIOR.
COMMISSION TO THE FIVE CIVILIZED TRIBES.

IN RE APPLICATION FOR ENROLLMENT, as a citizen of the Choctaw Nation, of Green M Walls , born on the 14 day of January , 1903

Name of Father: Thomas J Walls, Sr   a citizen of the Choctaw Nation.
Name of Mother: Catherine Walls   a citizen of the Choctaw Nation.

Postoffice   Enterprise, I.T.

Applications for Enrollment of Choctaw Newborn
Act of 1905   Volume VI

AFFIDAVIT OF MOTHER.

UNITED STATES OF AMERICA, Indian Territory,
Western   DISTRICT.

    I, Catherine Walls, on oath state that I am 39 years of age and a citizen by intermarriage, of the Choctaw Nation; that I am the lawful wife of Thomas J Walls, Sr., who is a citizen, by blood of the Choctaw Nation; that a male child was born to me on 14" day of January, 1903; that said child has been named Green M Walls, and was living March 4, 1905.

                                    her
                              Catherine x Walls
Witnesses To Mark: mark
   { W.C. Siemans Brooken, I.T.
     B F Graves Enterprise Ind Tr

    Subscribed and sworn to before me this 14 day of April, 1905
    My commission
    Expires Nov 27 1907   John M Lentz
                                    Notary Public.

AFFIDAVIT OF ATTENDING PHYSICIAN OR MID-WIFE.

UNITED STATES OF AMERICA, Indian Territory,
Central   DISTRICT.

    I, SE Mitchell, a Physician, on oath state that I attended on Mrs. Catherine Walls, wife of Thomas J. Walls, Sr on the 14 day of January, 1903; that there was born to her on said date a male child; that said child was living March 4, 1905, and is said to have been named Green M Walls

                              S.E. Mitchell M.D.
Witnesses To Mark:
   {

    Subscribed and sworn to before me this 27 day of April, 1905

                        (Name Illegible)
                             Notary Public.
My Com. Expires April 20-1909

Applications for Enrollment of Choctaw Newborn
Act of 1905   Volume VI

7-4455.

Muskogee, Indian Territory, February 27, 1903.

Thomas J. Walls, Sr.,
    Enterprise, Indian Territory.

Dear Sir:

    Receipt is hereby acknowledged of the affidavit of S.E. Mitchell relative to the birth of Green M. Walls, infant son of Thomas J. and Catherine Walls, January 14, 1903.

    No letter accompanies the affidavit, but it is presumed that the same has been forwarded as an application for enrollment as a citizen of the Choctaw Nation of the child named therein.

    Your attention is invited to the following provision of section thirty-four of the act of Congress approved July 1, 1902, which was ratified by the citizens of the Choctaw and Chickasaw Nations September 25, 1902:

    "During the ninety days first following the date of the final ratification of this agreement, the Commission to the Five Civilized Tribes may receive applications for enrollment only of persons whose names are on the tribal rolls, but who have not heretofore been enrolled by said Commission, commonly known as "delinquents," and such intermarried white persons as may have married recognized citizens of the Choctaw and Chickasaw Nations in accordance with the tribal laws, customs and usages on or before the date of the passage of this Act by Congress, and such infant children as may have been born to recognized and enrolled citizens on or before the date of the final ratification of this agreement; but the application of no person whomsoever for enrollment shall be received after the expiration of the said ninety days."

    Under the above legislation, the Commission is without authority to enroll this child.

Respectfully,

Chairman.

Applications for Enrollment of Choctaw Newborn
Act of 1905 Volume VI

N. B. 317

Muskogee, Indian Territory, April 6, 1905.

Thomas J. Walls, Sr.,
    Enterprise, Indian Territory.

Dear Sir:

    There is inclosed you herewith for execution application for the enrollment of your infant child, Green M. Walls, born January 14, 1903.

    The affidavit heretofore filed with the Commission shows the child was living on February 21, 1903. It is necessary, for the child to be enrolled, that he was living on March 4, 1905.

    The above mentioned affidavit is of the physician only. You will notice from the inclosed application that the affidavit of the mother is also required. You will please insert the age of the mother in the space for that purpose.

    In the event that the mother is dead, it will be necessary that you procure the affidavits of two persons who have actual knowledge of the fact, that the child was born, was living on March 4, 1905, and that Catherine Walls was his mother.

    In having these affidavits executed care should be exercised to see that all names are written in full, as they appear in the body of the affidavit, and in the event that either of the persons signing the affidavit are unable to write, signatures by mark must be attested by two witnesses. Each affidavit must be executed before a Notary Public and the notarial seal and signature of the officer must be attached to each separate affidavit.

Respectfully,

LM 6-7
                                              Commissioner in Charge.

Choctaw N.B. 317.

Muskogee, Indian Territory, May 2, 1905.

Thomas J. Walls, Sr.,
    Enterprise, Indian Territory.

Dear Sir:

    Receipt is hereby acknowledged of the affidavits of Catherine Walls and S. E. Mitchell to the birth of Green M. Walls, son of Thomas J. and Catherine Walls, January

Applications for Enrollment of Choctaw Newborn
Act of 1905   Volume VI

14, 1903, and the same have been filed with our records in the matter of the enrollment of the above named child.

                Respectfully,

                            Chairman.

Choc New Born 318
    Listy[sic] Thompson
    (Born Aug. 7, 1903)

BIRTH AFFIDAVIT.

DEPARTMENT OF THE INTERIOR,
COMMISSION TO THE FIVE CIVILIZED TRIBES.

In Re Application for Enrollment, as a citizen of the   Choctaw   Nation, of   Listie Thompson , born on the   7th   day of   August   , 1903

Name of Father: Elias Thompson   a citizen of the   Choctaw   Nation.
Name of Mother: Lucy Thompson   a citizen of the   Choctaw   Nation.

                Post-office   Atoka

AFFIDAVIT OF MOTHER.

UNITED STATES OF AMERICA, ⎫
    INDIAN TERRITORY,   ⎬
  Central   District. ⎭

    I, Lucy Thompson , on oath state that I am   21   years of age and a citizen by blood , of the   Choctaw   Nation; that I am the lawful wife of   Elias Thompson , who is a citizen, by blood of the   Choctaw   Nation; that a   female   child was born to me on   7th   day of   August   , 1903, that said child has been named   Listie Thompson   , and is now living.

                            her
                    Lucy x Thompson
WITNESSES TO MARK: main
  ⎰ J M Humphreys
  ⎱ *(Name Illegible)*

Applications for Enrollment of Choctaw Newborn
Act of 1905   Volume VI

Subscribed and sworn to before me this   14th   day of   March   , 1904

E A Newman
NOTARY PUBLIC.

AFFIDAVIT OF ATTENDING PHYSICIAN OR MID-WIFE.

UNITED STATES OF AMERICA, }
INDIAN TERRITORY,
Central   District.

I,   Molcy Folsom   , a   Midwife   , on oath state that I attended on Mrs. Lucy Thompson , wife of Elias Thompson   on the 7th day of August , 1903; that there was born to her on said date a   female   child; that said child is now living and is said to have been named   Listie Thompson

                            her
                        Molcy x Folsom
WITNESSES TO MARK: mark
{ A Hodge
  Saul Folsom

Subscribed and sworn to before me this................ day of   March   , 1904

E A Newman
NOTARY PUBLIC.

NEW BORN AFFIDAVIT

No ....

CHOCTAW ENROLLING COMMISSION

IN THE MATTER OF THE APPLICATION FOR ENROLLMENT   as   a   citizen   of   the   Choctaw Nation, of   Listie Thompson   born on the   7th   day of   August   190 3

    Name of father   Elias Thompson   a citizen of   Choctaw   Nation, final enrollment No.   11756
    Name of mother   Lucy Thompson   a citizen of   Choctaw   Nation, final enrollment No.   11722

                            Atoka I.T.   Postoffice.

Applications for Enrollment of Choctaw Newborn
Act of 1905 Volume VI

AFFIDAVIT OF MOTHER

UNITED STATES OF AMERICA
  INDIAN TERRITORY
DISTRICT   Central

I   Lucy Thompson   , on oath state that I am   21   years of age and a citizen by   blood   of the   Choctaw   Nation, and as such have been placed upon the final roll of the   Choctaw   Nation, by the Honorable Secretary of the Interior my final enrollment number being   11722   ; that I am the lawful wife of   Elias Thompson   , who is a citizen of the   Choctaw   Nation, and as such has been placed upon the final roll of said Nation by the Honorable Secretary of the Interior, his final enrollment number being   11756   and that a   male   child was born to me on the   7th day of   August   190 3; that said child has been named   Listie Thompson   , and is now living.

WITNESSETH:	her
Must be two witnesses { Isaac Folsom	Lucy x Thompson
who are citizens { Wallace Thompson	mark

Subscribed and sworn to before me this, the   22^d day of   February   , 190 5

A.E. Folsom
Notary Public.

My Commission Expires:
Jan 9-1909

Affidavit of Attending Physician or Midwife

UNITED STATES OF AMERICA,
  INDIAN TERRITORY,
  Central   DISTRICT

I,   Malsey McAfee   a   Mid wife   on oath state that I attended on Mrs.   Lucy Thompson   wife of   Elias Thompson   on the   7th day of   August   , 190 3, that there was born to her on said date a   Female   child, that said child is now living, and is said to have been named   Listie Thompson

her
Molsey x McAfee   Mid wife
mark   M. D.

Subscribed and sworn to before me this the   7th day of   August   1905

A E Folsom
Notary Public.

WITNESSETH:
Must be two witnesses   { Isaac Folsom
who are citizens and   {
know the child.   { Wallace Thompson

Applications for Enrollment of Choctaw Newborn
Act of 1905   Volume VI

We hereby certify that we are well acquainted with   Malsey McAfee
a   mid wife   and know   her   to be reputable and of good standing in the community.

Must be two citizen ⎰ Isaac Folsom
witnesses.   ⎱ Wallace Thompson

BIRTH AFFIDAVIT.

DEPARTMENT OF THE INTERIOR.
COMMISSION TO THE FIVE CIVILIZED TRIBES.

IN RE APPLICATION FOR ENROLLMENT, as a citizen of the   Choctaw   Nation, of Listy Thompson   , born on the 7th   day of August   , 1903

Name of Father: Elias Thompson   a citizen of the   blood   Nation.
Name of Mother: Lucy Thompson   a citizen of the   Choctaw   Nation.

Postoffice   Atoka Ind. Ter.

AFFIDAVIT OF MOTHER.

UNITED STATES OF AMERICA, Indian Territory, ⎫
     Central   DISTRICT.   ⎭

I,   Lucy Thompson   , on oath state that I am 22   years of age and a citizen by   blood   , of the   Choctaw   Nation; that I am the lawful wife of   Elias Thompson   , who is a citizen, by blood   of the   Choctaw   Nation; that a female   child was born to me on   7th   day of August   , 1903; that said child has been named   Listy Thompson   , and was living March 4, 1905.

                                          her
                                    Lucy x Thompson
Witnesses To Mark: mark
 ⎰ LG Battiest
 ⎱ Lewis T Martin

Subscribed and sworn to before me this 25th day of   March   , 1905

                                    W.H. Angell
                                        Notary Public.

Applications for Enrollment of Choctaw Newborn
Act of 1905   Volume VI

AFFIDAVIT OF ATTENDING PHYSICIAN OR MID-WIFE.

UNITED STATES OF AMERICA, Indian Territory, }
Central   DISTRICT.

I, Molsey McAfee, a Mid wife, on oath state that I attended on Mrs. Lucy Thompson, wife of Elias Thompson on the 7th day of August, 1903; that there was born to her on said date a female child; that said child was living March 4, 1905, and is said to have been named Listy Thompson

                        her
                  Molsey x McAfee

Witnesses To Mark: mark
{ LG Battiest
{ Lewis T Martin

Subscribed and sworn to before me this 25th day of March, 1905

                   W.H. Angell
                      Notary Public.

                          7-4176
                          7-4203

Muskogee, Indian Territory, March 22, 1904.

Elias Thompson,
    Atoka, Indian Territory.

Dear Sir:

    Receipt is hereby acknowledged of the affidavits of Lucy Thompson and Molcy Folsom, relative to the birth of Listie Thompson, infant daughter of Elias and Lucy Thompson, August 7, 1903, which it is presumed have been forwarded as an application for enrollment of said child as a citizen by blood of the Choctaw Nation.

    You are advised that under the provisions of the act of Congress approved July 1, 1902, the Commission is now without authority to receive or consider the original application of any person whomsoever as a citizen of the Choctaw or Chickasaw Nation.

                  Respectfully,

                  Commissioner in Charge.

Applications for Enrollment of Choctaw Newborn
Act of 1905   Volume VI

Choc New Born 319
(Lydia Byington)
(Born May 6, 1903)

NEW-BORN AFFIDAVIT.

Number..................

...Choctaw Enrolling Commission...

IN THE MATTER OF THE APPLICATION FOR ENROLLMENT, as a citizen of the Choctaw Nation, of Lydia Byington born on the 6th day of May 190 3

Name of father   Henry Byington   a citizen of   Choctaw
Nation final enrollment No.   11850
Name of mother   Lorena Byington   a citizen of   Choctaw
Nation final enrollment No.   11851

Postoffice   Caddo I.T.

AFFIDAVIT OF MOTHER.

UNITED STATES OF AMERICA
INDIAN TERRITORY
   Central   DISTRICT

I   Lorena Byington   , on oath state that I am 23 years of age and a citizen by blood of the Choctaw Nation, and as such have been placed upon the final roll of the Choctaw Nation, by the Honorable Secretary of the Interior my final enrollment number being 11851 ; that I am the lawful wife of   Henry Byington   , who is a citizen of the Choctaw Nation, and as such has been placed upon the final roll of said Nation by the Honorable Secretary of the Interior, his final enrollment number being 11850 and that a Female child was born to me on the 6th day of May 190 3; that said child has been named   Lydia Byington   , and is now living.

Witnesseth.   Lorena Byington
   Must be two ⎫   John *(Illegible)*
   Witnesses who ⎬
   are Citizens. ⎭   RH Byington

Applications for Enrollment of Choctaw Newborn
Act of 1905 Volume VI

Subscribed and sworn to before me this 6th day of May 190 3[sic]

A E Folsom
Notary Public.

My commission expires:
Ja[sic] 9-1909

Affidavit of Attending Physician or Midwife

UNITED STATES OF AMERICA, }
   INDIAN TERRITORY, }
  Central   DISTRICT }

I, Thomas J Long a Practicing Physician on oath state that I attended on Mrs. Lorena Byington wife of Henry Byington on the 6th day of May , 190 3, that there was born to her on said date a Female child, that said child is now living, and is said to have been named Lydia Byington

T. J. Long   M. D.

Subscribed and sworn to before me this the 7 day of Feb 1905

(Name Illegible)
Notary Public.

WITNESSETH:

Must be two witnesses who are citizens and know the child. { O.R. Nicholson
R H Byington

We hereby certify that we are well acquainted with Thomas J Long a Physician and know him to be reputable and of good standing in the community.

Must be two citizen witnesses. { O R Nicholson
R H Byington

Applications for Enrollment of Choctaw Newborn
Act of 1905   Volume VI

BIRTH AFFIDAVIT.

DEPARTMENT OF THE INTERIOR.
COMMISSION TO THE FIVE CIVILIZED TRIBES.

IN RE APPLICATION FOR ENROLLMENT, as a citizen of the Choctaw Nation, of Lydia Byington, born on the 6 day of May, 1903

Name of Father: Henry Byington   a citizen of the Choctaw Nation.
Name of Mother: Lorena Byington   a citizen of the Choctaw Nation.

Postoffice   Caddo, Ind. Ter.

AFFIDAVIT OF MOTHER.

UNITED STATES OF AMERICA, Indian Territory,
Central DISTRICT.

I, Lorena Byington, on oath state that I am 34 years of age and a citizen by blood, of the Choctaw Nation; that I am the lawful wife of Henry Byington, who is a citizen, by blood of the Choctaw Nation; that a female child was born to me on 6 day of May, 1903; that said child has been named Lydia Byington, and was living March 4, 1905.

Lorena Byington

Witnesses To Mark:
{

Subscribed and sworn to before me this 23 day of March, 1905

Chas McPherren
Notary Public.

AFFIDAVIT OF ATTENDING PHYSICIAN OR MID-WIFE.

UNITED STATES OF AMERICA, Indian Territory,
Central DISTRICT.

I, Emily Nicholas, a Mid-wife, on oath state that I attended on Mrs. Lorena Byington, wife of Henry Byington on the 6 day of May, 1903; that there was born to her on said date a female child; that said child was living March 4, 1905, and is said to have been named Lydia Byington

Emily Nicholas

Witnesses To Mark:
{

Applications for Enrollment of Choctaw Newborn
Act of 1905   Volume VI

Subscribed and sworn to before me this 23 day of   March   , 1905

                              Chas McPherren
                              Notary Public.

7-4229

Muskogee, Indian Territory, March 28, 1905.

Henry Byington,
    Caddo, Indian Territory.

Dear Sir:

    Receipt is hereby acknowledged of your letter of March 23, 1905, enclosing affidavits of Lorena Byington and Emily Nicholas to the birth of Lydia Byington, March 4, 1903, and the same have been filed with our records as an application for the enrollment of said child.

    Replying to that part of your letter in which you ask when you can file for your child, you are advised that no allotments can be selected for children enrolled under the provision of the act of Congress approved March 3, 1905, until their enrollment has been approved by the Secretary of the Interior.

                              Respectfully,

                                    Chairman.

<u>Choc New Born 320</u>
    David Noabbi[sic]
    (Born Dec. 17, 1902)

Applications for Enrollment of Choctaw Newborn
Act of 1905   Volume VI

DEPARTMENT OF THE INTERIOR,
Commission to the Five Civilized Tribes.

UNITED STATES OF AMERICA,)
)
INDIAN TERRITORY,)
)
CENTRAL DISTRICT.)

Comes now your petitioner, James Noawbbi, and being first duly sworn deposes and says that he is a citizen of the Choctaw Nation, by blood, and that he xx is 26 years of age, and that his wife's name is Hannah Noawbbi, enrolled as Hannah Austen, and that they were lawfully married on Jan. 6, 1902, and that David Hoawbbi is the child of said marriage, born on the 17th day of December, 1902, and is a citizen by blood of the Choctaw Nation, Indian Territory.

Your petitions states that he is an enrolled citizen of the Choctaw Nation, Indian Territory, and that Hannah Noawbbi, his wife, and mother of said David Noawbbi, is an enrolled citizen of the Choctaw Nation, Indian Territory, and that your said petitioner and his said wife have both filed on their pro rata shares of the public domain as such enrolled citizens, and that there is sufficient surplus lands in the Choctaw Nation to which such child is and ought to be entitled to be allotted to have.

Yours[sic] petitioner therefore prays that the name of Davie[sic] Noawbbi be placed upon the rolls of the Choctaw Nation as a citizen by blood and for such other and further relief as justice may require.

James Noawbbi

Subscribed in my presence and sworn to before me this 23d day of February, 1904.

EA Newman
Notary Public.

BIRTH AFFIDAVIT.

DEPARTMENT OF THE INTERIOR,
COMMISSION TO THE FIVE CIVILIZED TRIBES.

In Re Application for Enrollment, as a citizen of the   Choctaw   Nation, of   David Noawbbi , born on the   17   day of   December , 1902

Name of Father: James Noawbbi   a citizen of the   Choctaw   Nation.
Name of Mother: Hannah Noawbbi   a citizen of the   Choctaw   Nation.
Enrolled Hannah Austin

Post-office   Kosoma I.T.

Applications for Enrollment of Choctaw Newborn
Act of 1905   Volume VI

AFFIDAVIT OF MOTHER.

UNITED STATES OF AMERICA, }
INDIAN TERRITORY,
Central   District.

I, Hannah Noawbbi , on oath state that I am   25   years of age and a citizen by   Blood   , of the   Choctaw   Nation; that I am the lawful wife of David[sic] Noawbbi , who is a citizen, by Blood of the   Choctaw   Nation; that a male   child was born to me on   17   day of December , 1902, that said child has been named   David Noawbbi , and is now living.

Hannah Noawbbi

WITNESSES TO MARK:
{

Subscribed and sworn to before me this   23   day of   February , 1904

EA Newman
NOTARY PUBLIC.

AFFIDAVIT OF ATTENDING PHYSICIAN OR MID-WIFE.

UNITED STATES OF AMERICA, }
INDIAN TERRITORY,
Central   District.

we
We, Jancie Noawbbi and Emma Noawbbi   , on oath state that I attended on Mrs.   Hannah Noawbbi , wife of   James Noawbbi   on the   17 day of December , 1902; that there was born to her on said date a   male   child; that said child is now living and is said to have been named   David Noawbbi that there was no Physician or midwife present

Jancie Noawbbi
Emma Noawbbi

WITNESSES TO MARK:
{

Subscribed and sworn to before me this   23   day of   February , 1904

EA Newman
NOTARY PUBLIC.

Applications for Enrollment of Choctaw Newborn
Act of 1905   Volume VI

BIRTH AFFIDAVIT.

DEPARTMENT OF THE INTERIOR.
COMMISSION TO THE FIVE CIVILIZED TRIBES.

IN RE APPLICATION FOR ENROLLMENT, as a citizen of the Choctaw Nation, of David Nowabbi[sic] , born on the 17 day of December , 1902

Name of Father: James Nowabbi   a citizen of the Choctaw Nation.
Name of Mother: Hannah Nowabbi   a citizen of the Choctaw Nation.

Postoffice   Kosoma I.T.

AFFIDAVIT OF MOTHER.

UNITED STATES OF AMERICA, Indian Territory, }
the 24th   DISTRICT.

I, Hannah Nowabbi , on oath state that I am 25 years of age and a citizen by blood , of the Choctaw Nation; that I am the lawful wife of James Nowabbi , who is a citizen, by blood of the Choctaw Nation; that a male child was born to me on 17 day of December , 1902; that said child has been named David Nowabbi , and was living March 4, 1905.

Hannah Nowabbi

Witnesses To Mark:
{

Subscribed and sworn to before me this 25th day of April , 1905.

Wm Harrison
Notary Public.

My commission expires Dec. 27-1907

AFFIDAVIT OF ATTENDING PHYSICIAN OR MID-WIFE.

UNITED STATES OF AMERICA, Indian Territory, }
the 24th   DISTRICT.

I, Mrs Mary Nowabbi , a ...., on oath state that I attended on Mrs. Hannah Nowabbi , wife of James Nowabbi on the 17 day of December , 1902; that there was born to her on said date a male child; that said child was living March 4, 1905, and is said to have been named David Nowabbi

her
Mary x Nowabbi
mark

Applications for Enrollment of Choctaw Newborn
Act of 1905   Volume VI

Witnesses To Mark:
{ Mike Hamby   Kosoma IT
{ Henry Richey   Hugo IT

Subscribed and sworn to before me this the 25th day of April, 1905

My commission expires Dec. 27-1907

Wm Harrison
Notary Public.

7-4154
7-4213

Muskogee, Indian Territory, January 21, 1905.

James Noabby[sic],
Kosoma, Indian Territory.

Dear Sir:

Receipt is hereby acknowledged of your letter of December 18, 1902, stating that you have a son born December 17, 1902, and request to be furnished with a blank application for the enrollment of an infant child. A blank of such description is enclosed herewith.

Your attention, however, is invited to the following provisions of the act of Congress approved July 1, 1902, which was ratified by the citizens of the Choctaw and Chickasaw Nations September 25, 1902:

"The names of all persons living on the date of the final ratification of this agreement entitled to be enrolled as provided in section 27 hereof shall be placed upon the rolls made by said Commission; and no child born thereafter to a citizen or freedman and no person intermarried thereafter to a citizen shall be entitled to enrollment or to participate in the distribution of the tribal property of the Choctaws and Chickasaws."

And,

"During the ninety days first following the date of the final ratification of this agreement, the Commission to the Five Civilized Tribes may receive applications for enrollment only of persons whose names are on the tribal rolls, but who have not heretofore been enrolled by said Commission, commonly known as "delinquents," and such intermarried white persons as may have married recognized citizens of the Choctaw and Chickasaw Nations in accordance with the tribal laws, customs and usages on or before the date of the passage of this act by Congress, and such infant children as may have been born to recognized and enrolled citizens on or before the

Applications for Enrollment of Choctaw Newborn
Act of 1905   Volume VI

date of the final ratification of this agreement; but the application of no person whomsoever for enrollment shall be received after the expiration of the said ninety days."

Under the above legislation, the Commission is now without authority to enroll this child.

Respectfully,

Commissioner in Charge.

7-4154
7-4231

Muskogee, Indian Territory, February 26, 1904.

J. M. Humphreys,
    Attorney at Law,
        Atoka, Indian Territory.

Dear Sir:

Receipt is hereby acknowledged of your letter of the 23rd inst., enclosing the affidavits of Hannah Noawbbi and Jancie and Emma Noawbby relative to the birth off David Noawbbi, asking for the enrollment of the above named child as a citizen by blood of the Choctaw Nation.

You are informed that under the provisions of the Act of Congress, approved July 1, 1902, the Commission is now without authority to receive or consider the original application for enrollment of any person whomsoever as a citizen of the Choctaw or Chickasaw Nation.

Respectfully,

Commissioner in Charge.

COPY   N.B. 320.

Muskogee, Indian Territory, April 7, 1905.

James Nowabbi,
    Kosoma, Indian Territory.

Dear Sir:

There is enclosed you herewith for execution application for the enrollment of your infant child, David Nowabbi, born December 17, 1902.

Applications for Enrollment of Choctaw Newborn
Act of 1905   Volume VI

The affidavits heretofore filed with the Commission show the child was living on February 23, 1904. It is necessary, for the child to be enrolled, that she[sic] was living on March 4, 1905.

In case there was no physician or mid-wife in attendance it will be necessary that you secure the affidavits of two persons who know the child was born, giving date of birth; was living on March 4, 1905 and that Hanna[sic] Nowabbi is his mother.

In having these affidavits executed care should be exercised to see that all names are written in full, as they appear in the body of the affidavit, and in the event that either of the persons signing the affidavit are unable to write, signatures by mark must be attested by two witnesses. Each affidavit must be executed before a Notary Public and the notarial seal and signature of the officer must be attached to each separate affidavit.

LER 7-5

Respectfully,
SIGNED
T. B. Needles.
Commissioner in Charge.

Choctaw N.B. 320.

Muskogee, Indian Territory, April 28, 1905.

James Nowabbi,
    Kosoma, Indian Territory.

Dear Sir:

Receipt is hereby acknowledged of your letter of April 25, transmitting the affidavits of Hannah Nowabbi and Mary Nowabbi to the birth of David Nowabbi, son of James and Hannah Nowabbi, December 17, 1902, and the same have been filed with our records in the matter of the enrollment of said child.

Respectfully,

Chairman.

Applications for Enrollment of Choctaw Newborn
Act of 1905 Volume VI

7-NB-320

Muskogee, Indian Territory, August 2, 1905.

James L. Noabby[sic],
    Cosoma[sic], Indian Territory.

Dear Sir:

    Receipt is hereby acknowledged of your letter of July 24, 1905, asking when Choctaw infants will be approved.

    In reply to your letter you are advised that on July 22, 1905, the Secretary of the Interior approved the enrollment of David Nowabbi, child of James Nowabbi as a citizen by blood of the Choctaw Nation and selection of allotment may now be made in his behalf in accordance with the rules and regulations governing the selection of allotments and the designation of homesteads in the Choctaw and Chickasaw Nations.

                  Respectfully,

                             Commissioner.

Choc New Born 321
    Marguerite Glenn
    (Born Aug. 25, 1903)

BIRTH AFFIDAVIT.

DEPARTMENT OF THE INTERIOR.
COMMISSION TO THE FIVE CIVILIZED TRIBES.

IN RE APPLICATION FOR ENROLLMENT, as a citizen of the Choctaw Nation, of Marguerite Glenn, born on the 25 day of August, 1903

Name of Father: William T. Glenn   a citizen of the Choctaw Nation.
Name of Mother: Ida B. Glenn   a citizen of the Choctaw Nation.

                Postoffice   Hugo, Ind. Ty.

Applications for Enrollment of Choctaw Newborn
Act of 1905   Volume VI

AFFIDAVIT OF MOTHER.

UNITED STATES OF AMERICA, Indian Territory, }
Central   DISTRICT.

    I,   Ida B Glenn   , on oath state that I am   22   years of age and a citizen by Blood   , of the   Choctaw   Nation; that I am the lawful wife of   William T Glenn, who is a citizen, by Ind Mar   of the   Choctaw   Nation; that a   Female child was born to me on   25   day of   August   , 1903; that said child has been named   Marguerite Glenn   , and was living March 4, 1905.

                                        Ida B Glenn

Witnesses To Mark:
{

    Subscribed and sworn to before me this   24th   day of   March   , 1905

                                        Arthur Adams
                                        Notary Public.

AFFIDAVIT OF ATTENDING PHYSICIAN OR MID-WIFE.

UNITED STATES OF AMERICA, Indian Territory, }
Central   DISTRICT.

    I,   Mandy Peyton   , a   Mid wife   , on oath state that I attended on Mrs.   Ida B Glenn   , wife of   William T Glenn   on the   25 day of   August   , 1903; that there was born to her on said date a   Female   child; that said child was living March 4, 1905, and is said to have been named Marguerite Glenn

                                         her
                                 Mandy x Peyton

Witnesses To Mark: mark
{ J T Forrester
  J Q Carter

    Subscribed and sworn to before me this   24th   day of   March   , 1905

                                        Arthur Adams
                                        Notary Public.

Applications for Enrollment of Choctaw Newborn
Act of 1905   Volume VI

7-4242

Muskogee, Indian Territory, March 31, 1905.

William T. Glenn,
    Hugo, Indian Territory.

Dear Sir:

    Receipt is hereby acknowledged of the affidavits of Ida B. Glenn and Mandy Peyton to the birth of Marguerite Glenn, daughter of William T. and Ida B. Glenn, August 25, 1903, and the same have been filed with our records as an application for the enrollment of said child.

                Respectfully,

                              Chairman.

<u>Choc New Born 322</u>
    Willis Armstrong
    (Born Jan. 26, 1904)

NEW BORN AFFIDAVIT

No ....

CHOCTAW ENROLLING COMMISSION

    IN THE MATTER OF THE APPLICATION FOR ENROLLMENT as a citizen of the Choctaw Nation, of   Willis Armstrong   born on the 26th day of   January   190 3[sic]

    Name of father   Murrow Armstrong   a citizen of   Choctaw   Nation, final enrollment No.   11943

    Name of mother   Annie Armstrong   a citizen of   Choctaw   Nation, final enrollment No.   11944

                          Atoka I.T.   Postoffice.

Applications for Enrollment of Choctaw Newborn
Act of 1905 Volume VI

AFFIDAVIT OF MOTHER

UNITED STATES OF AMERICA }
INDIAN TERRITORY }
DISTRICT   Central }

I   Annie Armstrong   , on oath state that I am   25   years of age and a citizen by   blood   of the   Choctaw   Nation, and as such have been placed upon the final roll of the   Choctaw   Nation, by the Honorable Secretary of the Interior my final enrollment number being   11944 ; that I am the lawful wife of   Murrow Armstrong   , who is a citizen of the   Choctaw   Nation, and as such has been placed upon the final roll of said Nation by the Honorable Secretary of the Interior, his final enrollment number being   11943   and that a   male   child was born to me on the   26th day of   January   190 3[sic]; that said child has been named   Willis Armstrong   , and is now living.

WITNESSETH:

Must be two witnesses { Lewis Armstrong
who are citizens   { A H Homer

her
Annie x Armstrong
mark

Subscribed and sworn to before me this, the   22^d day of   February   , 190 5

A.E. Folsom
Notary Public.

My Commission Expires:
Jan 9-1909

Affidavit of Attending Physician or Midwife

UNITED STATES OF AMERICA, }
INDIAN TERRITORY, }
Central   DISTRICT }

I,   Noel Jones   a   was present as midwife on oath state that I ~~attended on Mrs.~~ was present when child was born   wife of   Murrow Armstrong   on the   26th day of   January   , 190 3[sic], that there was born to her on said date a   male   child, that said child is now living, and is said to have been named   Willis Armstrong

Noel Jones was Present   ~~M. D.~~

Subscribed and sworn to before me this the   22   day of   February   1905

A.E. Folsom
Notary Public.

WITNESSETH:

Must be two witnesses { Lewis Armstrong
who are citizens and {
know the child.   { A.H.Homer

Applications for Enrollment of Choctaw Newborn
Act of 1905   Volume VI

    We hereby certify that we are well acquainted with   Noel Armstrong[sic] a   was present   and know   him   to be reputable and of good standing in the community.

                              Must be two citizen   Lewis Armstrong
                              witnesses.   A H Homer

BIRTH AFFIDAVIT.

DEPARTMENT OF THE INTERIOR.
COMMISSION TO THE FIVE CIVILIZED TRIBES.

        IN RE APPLICATION FOR ENROLLMENT, as a citizen of the   Choctaw   Nation, of Willis Armstrong   , born on the   26th day of   January , 1904

Name of Father: Murrow Armstrong   a citizen of the   Choctaw   Nation.
Name of Mother: Annie Armstrong   a citizen of the   Choctaw   Nation.

                         Postoffice   Atoka, I.T.

                        AFFIDAVIT OF MOTHER.

UNITED STATES OF AMERICA, Indian Territory,
       Central   **DISTRICT.**

    I,   Annie Armstrong   , on oath state that I am   25   years of age and a citizen by   blood   , of the   Choctaw   Nation; that I am the lawful wife of Murrow Armstrong   , who is a citizen, by   blood   of the   Choctaw Nation; that a   male   child was born to me on   26th day of   January   , 1904; that said child has been named   Willis Armstrong   , and was living March 4, 1905.

                                                 her
                                  Annie x Armstrong
Witnesses To Mark: mark
     A.L. Irvine
     HW Cunningham

        Subscribed and sworn to before me this   24th day of   March   , 1905

                                     W.H. Angell
                                     Notary Public.

Applications for Enrollment of Choctaw Newborn
Act of 1905 Volume VI

AFFIDAVIT OF ATTENDING PHYSICIAN OR MID-WIFE.

UNITED STATES OF AMERICA, Indian Territory,
Central DISTRICT.

I, Murrow Armstrong , a——— , on oath state that I attended on Mrs. Murrow Armstrong my , wife of ——— on the 26th day of January , 1904; that there was born to her on said date a male child; that said child was living March 4, 1905, and is said to have been named Willis Armstrong and that no one was present on the date of the birth of said Willis Armstrong except myself and said wife

                                  his
                          Murrow x Armstrong

Witnesses To Mark: mark
  { A.L. Irvine
    HW Cunningham

Subscribed and sworn to before me this 24th day of March , 1905

                          W.H. Angell
                          Notary Public.

United States of America)
    Indian Territory(ss.
Central - - - - District.)

Before me, the undersigned authority, in and for the Central District of the Indian Territory, on this day personally appeared Noel Jones and T. J. Long both of Atoka, Indian Territory after bing[sic] by me first duly sworn state on their oath as follows:

That they are personally acquainted with Murrow Armstrong and Annie Armstrong, his wife, and that they have actual knowledge of the fact that a male child was born to them on the 26th day of January, 1904; that said child was living on the 4th day of March, 1905 and that Annie Armstrong is the mother of said child and that said child is said to have been named Willis Armstrong.

                          his
Witness to mark: Noel x Jones
  R.M. Rainey   mark
  Jno H Linebaugh   Thos J. Long

Subscribed and sworn to before me this the 15th day of April, 1905.

                          Jno H Linebaugh
                          Notary Public.

Applications for Enrollment of Choctaw Newborn
Act of 1905   Volume VI

BIRTH AFFIDAVIT.

DEPARTMENT OF THE INTERIOR.
COMMISSION TO THE FIVE CIVILIZED TRIBES.

IN RE APPLICATION FOR ENROLLMENT, as a citizen of the Choctaw Nation, of Willis Armstrong, born on the .... day of ...., 1.........

Name of Father: Murrow Armstrong   a citizen of the   Choctaw   Nation.
Name of Mother: Annie Armstrong   a citizen of the   Choctaw   Nation.

Postoffice   Atoka, Ind. Ter.

AFFIDAVIT OF MOTHER.

UNITED STATES OF AMERICA, Indian Territory,⎫
   Central   DISTRICT.   ⎬
                                        ⎭

I, Annie Armstrong, on oath state that I am 25 years of age and a citizen by Blood, of the Choctaw Nation; that I am the lawful wife of Murrow Armstrong, who is a citizen, by Blood of the Choctaw Nation; that a male child was born to me on 26th day of January, 1904; that said child has been named Willis Armstrong, and was living March 4, 1905.

                                          her
                                  Annie x Armstrong
Witnesses To Mark: mark
  { WH Martin
    Richard Shanafelt

Subscribed and sworn to before me this 31st day of May, 1905

                                    W.H. Angell
                                      Notary Public.

AFFIDAVIT OF ATTENDING PHYSICIAN OR MID-WIFE.

UNITED STATES OF AMERICA, Indian Territory,⎫
   Central   DISTRICT.   ⎬
                                          ⎭

I, T.J. Long, a physician, on oath state that I attended on Mrs. Annie Armstrong, wife of Murrow Armstrong on the 26th day of January, 1904; that there was born to her on said date a male child; that said child was living March 4, 1905, and is said to have been named Willis Armstrong

                                  T. J. Long M.D.

Applications for Enrollment of Choctaw Newborn
Act of 1905   Volume VI

Witnesses To Mark:

{

    Subscribed and sworn to before me this   31st day of   May   , 1905

                              W.H. Angell
                                Notary Public.

                                    N.B. 322.
                                  COPY
             Muskogee, Indian Territory, April 8, 1905.

Murrow Armstrong,
    Atoka, Indian Territory.

Dear Sir:

    Referring to the application for the enrollment of your infant child, Willis Armstrong, born January 26, 1904, it is noted that there was no physician or mid-wife in attendance upon your wife at the birth of the applicant. In this event it will be necessary that you secure the affidavits of two persons who have actual knowledge of the fat that the child was born, the date of birth, that he was living on March 4, 1905 and that Annie Armstrong is his mother.

    In having these affidavits executed care should be exercised to see that all names are written in full, as they appear in the body of the affidavit, and in the event that either of the persons signing the affidavit are unable to write, signatures by mark must be attested by two witnesses. Each affidavit must be executed before a Notary Public and the notarial seal and signature of the officer must be attached to each separate affidavit.

                            Respectfully,
                            SIGNED
                            T. B. Needles.
LER 8-15   Commissioner in Charge.

Applications for Enrollment of Choctaw Newborn
Act of 1905   Volume VI

Choctaw N.B. 322.

Muskogee, Indian Territory, April 20, 1905.

Murrow Armstrong,
   Atoka, Indian Territory.

Dear Sir:

   Receipt is hereby acknowledged of the joint affidavit of Noel Jones and Thos. J. Long to the birth of Willis Armstrong, son of Murrow and Annie Armstrong, January 26, 1904, and the same has been filed with our records in the matter of the enrollment of the above named child.

   Respectfully,

   Chairman.

7-NB-322.

Muskogee, Indian Territory, May 22, 1905.

Murrow Armstrong,
   Atoka, Indian Territory.

Dear Sir:

   There is enclosed you herewith for execution application for the enrollment of your infant child, Willis Armstrong.

   In the affidavits of March 24, 1905, heretofore filed in this office, the date of birth is given as January 26, 1904, while in the affidavits of February 22, 1905, it is given as January 26, 1903. In the enclosed affidavits the date of birth has been left blank, in which you will please insert the correct date of birth, and when properly executed return to this office.

   In having these affidavits executed care should be exercised to see that all names are written in full, as they appear in the body of the affidavit, and in the event that either of the persons signing the affidavit are unable to write, signatures by mark must be attested by two witnesses. Each affidavit must be executed before a Notary Public and the notarial seal and signature of the officer must be attached to each separate affidavit.

   Respectfully,

VR 22-17.   Chairman.

Applications for Enrollment of Choctaw Newborn
Act of 1905   Volume VI

7-N.B. 322.

Muskogee, Indian Territory, June 5, 1905.

Murrow Armstrong,
   Atoka, Indian Territory.

Dear Sir:

   Receipt is hereby acknowledged of the affidavits of Annie Armstrong and T. J. Long, M. D., to the birth of Willis Armstrong, son of Murrow and Annie Armstrong, January 26, 1904, and the same have been filed with our records in the matter of the application for the enrollment of said child.

Respectfully,

Commissioner in Charge.

Choc New Born 323
   Annie Wood[sic]
   (Born Sep. 14, 1903)

BILL OF DIVORCE.

The Choctaw Nation,

   In *Circuit Court of the Third Judicial District, Regular*   August   *term 190* 1, *a petition of*   Harrison Woods   *being presented by* his   *Attorney in said Court, for a Bill of Divorce, setting forth the facts, etc., and after the Court hearing the Testimony in regard to the petition do order and decree that a Bill of Divorce be issued to the applicant*   Harrison Woods

   THEREFORE I do issue a Bill of Divorce to said applicant   Harrison Woods   *forever releasing* him   *from the Banns of Matrimony heretofore existing between*   Harrison Woods   *and*   Ellen Woods

   Given under my hand and seal of office, this the   21   *day of* August   *A.D. 190* 1

(Name Illegible)
Circuit Clerk, 3d District. C. N.

By .... *Deputy*

Applications for Enrollment of Choctaw Newborn
Act of 1905   Volume VI

This is to certify that I have this *(illegible)* day of January A.D. 1903 united in Marriage Mr. Harrison Woods, a Choctaw citizen and Mrs. Maud Breedlove, a citizen of the United States in accordance with the laws of the Choctaw Nation Indian Terry Atoka Ind. Terry

                          J. S. Murrow
Witnesses by   *(Illegible)*
    Amanda Carnes
    Mrs Louise E Rounds

NEW BORN AFFIDAVIT

No ....

CHOCTAW ENROLLING COMMISSION

IN THE MATTER OF THE APPLICATION FOR ENROLLMENT as a citizen of the Choctaw Nation, of   Annie Woods   born on the   14th day of Sep   190 3

Name of father   Harrison Woods   a citizen of   Choctaw   Nation, final enrollment No. 11955
Name of mother Maud Woods   a citizen of   U S   Nation, final enrollment No. ....

                                          Atoka   Postoffice.

AFFIDAVIT OF MOTHER

UNITED STATES OF AMERICA }
    INDIAN TERRITORY
DISTRICT   Central

    I   Maud Woods , on oath state that I am 24 years of age and a citizen by Marriage of the Choctaw Nation, and as such have been placed upon the final roll of the ———Nation, by the Honorable Secretary of the Interior my final enrollment number being ———; that I am the lawful wife of Harrison Woods , who is a citizen of the Choctaw Nation, and as such has been placed upon the final roll of said Nation by the Honorable Secretary of the Interior, his final enrollment number being 11955 and that a Female child was born to me on the 14th day of Sept 190 3; that said child has been named Annie , and is now living.

                                                Maud Woods

Applications for Enrollment of Choctaw Newborn
Act of 1905   Volume VI

WITNESSETH:

Must be two witnesses who are citizens { Sam Jones
(Name Illegible)

Subscribed and sworn to before me this, the 27th day of Feby, 190 5

Jas H *(Illegible)*
Notary Public.

My Commission Expires:
Mch 5 - 1908

Affidavit of Attending Physician or Midwife

UNITED STATES OF AMERICA,
INDIAN TERRITORY,
Central   DISTRICT

I, Missouri Delana   a   Midwife on oath state that I attended on Mrs. Maud Woods   wife of   Harrison Woods on the 14th day of Sept, 190 3, that there was born to her on said date a Female child, that said child is now living, and is said to have been named Annie Woods

Missouri Delana   ~~M. D.~~
midwife

Subscribed and sworn to before me this the 27th day of February   1905

Jas H *(Illegible)*
Notary Public.

WITNESSETH:

Must be two witnesses who are citizens and know the child. { (Name Illegible)
(Name Illegible)

We hereby certify that we are well acquainted with   Missouri Delana   a mid-wife   and know   her   to be reputable and of good standing in the community.

Must be two citizen witnesses. { Peter Jones
Levi Haskins

84

Applications for Enrollment of Choctaw Newborn
Act of 1905   Volume VI

BIRTH AFFIDAVIT.

DEPARTMENT OF THE INTERIOR.
COMMISSION TO THE FIVE CIVILIZED TRIBES.

IN RE APPLICATION FOR ENROLLMENT, as a citizen of the Choctaw Nation, of Annie Wood[sic] , born on the 14th day of September , 1903

Name of Father: Harrison Wood   a citizen of the Choctaw Nation.
Name of Mother: Maud Wood   a citizen of the Choctaw Nation.

Postoffice Atoka, I.T.

AFFIDAVIT OF MOTHER.

UNITED STATES OF AMERICA, Indian Territory, }
Central   DISTRICT. }

I, Maud Wood , on oath state that I am 24 years of age and a citizen ~~by~~ ——— , of the United States ~~Nation~~; that I am the lawful wife of Harrison Wood, who is a citizen, by blood of the Choctaw Nation; that a female child was born to me on 14th day of September , 1903; that said child has been named Annie Wood , and was living March 4, 1905.

                 Maud Wood
Witnesses To Mark:
{

Subscribed and sworn to before me this 23rd day of March , 1905

                 W.H. Angell
                    Notary Public.

AFFIDAVIT OF ATTENDING PHYSICIAN OR MID-WIFE.

UNITED STATES OF AMERICA, Indian Territory, }
Central   DISTRICT. }

I, Missouri Delana , a midwife , on oath state that I attended on Mrs. Maud Wood , wife of Harrison Wood on the 14th day of September, 1903; that there was born to her on said date a female child; that said child was living March 4, 1905, and is said to have been named Annie Wood

                 Missouri Delana
Witnesses To Mark:
{

Applications for Enrollment of Choctaw Newborn
Act of 1905 Volume VI

Subscribed and sworn to before me this 23rd day of March, 1905

                        W.H. Angell
                        Notary Public.

DEPARTMENT OF THE INTERIOR,
Commission to the Five Civilized Tribes.
CHOCTAW LAND OFFICE,
Atoka, Indian Territory, March 23, 1905.

-- :o: --

In the matter of the application for the enrollment
of Annie Wood as a citizen by blood of the Choctaw Nation.

MAUD WOOD, being first duly sworn, testified as follows:

Examination by the Commission:
Q What is your name? A Maud Wood.
Q What is your post office address? A Atoka.
Q What is your age? A Twenty-four.
Q Are you a citizen by blood of the Choctaw Nation? A No, sir; I am a citizen of the United States.
Q Are you married? A Yes, sir.
Q What is the name of your husband? A Harrison Wood.
Q When were you married? A Married in 1902.
Q In what month? A The 30th day of January.
Q Is your husband a citizen by blood of the Choctaw Nation? A Yes, sir.
Q Have you any children? A Yes, sir.
Q How many? A I have just one by my husband.
Q What is the name of that child? A Annie Wood.
Q When was Annie Wood born? A She was born the 4th[sic] of September, 1903.
Q Who is the father of Annie Wood? A Harrison Wood.
Q Is Annie Wood now living? A Yes, sir.
Q You swear positively that Harrison Wood is the father of this child, Annie Wood?
A Yes, sir.

    The records of the Commission examined, and the name of Harrison Wood, the father of Annie Wood, is found on the approved roll of citizens by blood of the Chocta Nation at No. 11955.

Applications for Enrollment of Choctaw Newborn
Act of 1905   Volume VI

A. L. Irvine, being first duly sworn, states that the above and foregoing is a full, true and correct transcript of his stenographic notes taken in said cause on said date.

A.L. Irvine

Subscribed and sworn to before me, this March 23rd, 1905.

W.H. Angell
Notary Public.

Choc New Born 324
    Benjamin Lawson Taylor
    (Born June 23, 1903)

NEW-BORN AFFIDAVIT.

Number..............

...Choctaw Enrolling Commission...

IN THE MATTER OF THE APPLICATION FOR ENROLLMENT, as a citizen of the Choctaw Nation, of Benjamin Lawson born on the 23 day of June 190 3

Name of father J. T. Taylor	a citizen of	Choctaw
Nation final enrollment No.		
Name of mother Talithia Taylor	a citizen of	Choctaw
Nation final enrollment No. 12547		

Postoffice   McAlester I.T.

AFFIDAVIT OF MOTHER.

UNITED STATES OF AMERICA
INDIAN TERRITORY
Western   DISTRICT

I   Talithia Taylor   , on oath state that I am 36 years of age and a citizen by Blood of the Choctaw Nation, and as such have been placed upon the final roll of the Choctaw Nation, by the Honorable Secretary of the Interior my final enrollment number being 12547; that I am the lawful wife

Applications for Enrollment of Choctaw Newborn
Act of 1905   Volume VI

of   J.T. Taylor   , who is a citizen of the   United States   Nation, and as such has been placed upon the final roll of said Nation by the Honorable Secretary of the Interior, his final enrollment number being .... and that a .... child was born to me on the   23   day of   June   190 3; that said child has been named Benjamin Lawson Taylor   , and is now living.

Witnesseth.   Mrs Talithia Taylor

Must be two ⎫ C.C. Choate
Witnesses who ⎬
are Citizens. ⎭ Robert S. Turner

Subscribed and sworn to before me this   13   day of   March   190 5

My Commission Expires   T.J. Rice
Aug. 1st. 1906
                                                          Notary Public.
My commission expires:

AFFIDAVIT OF ATTENDING PHYSICIAN OR MIDWIFE

UNITED STATES OF AMERICA
INDIAN TERRITORY
  Western   DISTRICT

I,   Amanda Choate   a   midwife
on oath state that I attended on Mrs.   Talithia Taylor   wife of   J. T. Taylor on the 23 day of June , 190 3, that there was born to her on said date a   male   child, that said child is now living, and is said to have been named   Benjamin Lawson Taylor

                                      Amanda Choate   M.W.

WITNESSETH:
Must be two witnesses ⎧ CC Choate
who are citizens and ⎨
know the child.   ⎩ Robert S Turner

               Subscribed and sworn to before me this, the   13   day of
  March   190 5

                        T. J. Rice   Notary Public.

     We hereby certify that we are well acquainted with   Amanda Choate
a   mid wife   and know   her   to be reputable and of good standing in the community.

                                        ⎧ C C Choate
                                        ⎨
                                        ⎩ Robert S Turner

Applications for Enrollment of Choctaw Newborn
Act of 1905   Volume VI

BIRTH AFFIDAVIT.

DEPARTMENT OF THE INTERIOR.
COMMISSION TO THE FIVE CIVILIZED TRIBES.

IN RE APPLICATION FOR ENROLLMENT, as a citizen of the Choctaw Nation, of Benjamin Lawson Taylor, born on the 23rd day of June, 1903

Name of Father: J. T. Taylor   a citizen of the United States Nation.
Name of Mother: Talithia Taylor   a citizen of the Choctaw Nation.

Postoffice   McAlester, I.T.

AFFIDAVIT OF MOTHER.

UNITED STATES OF AMERICA, Indian Territory,
Central DISTRICT.

I, Talithia Taylor, on oath state that I am 36 years of age and a citizen by blood, of the Choctaw Nation; that I am the lawful wife of J. T. Taylor, who is a citizen, ~~by~~ .... of the United States Nation; that a male child was born to me on 23rd day of June, 1903; that said child has been named Benjamin Lawson Taylor, and was living March 4, 1905.

Talithia Taylor

Witnesses To Mark:

Subscribed and sworn to before me this 17th day of March, 1905

Wirt Franklin
Notary Public.

Applications for Enrollment of Choctaw Newborn
Act of 1905   Volume VI

Choc New Born 325
Julia Ann Lester
(Born Jan. 12, 1903)
Ralph Lester
(Born Sep. 30, 1904)

NEW BORN AFFIDAVIT

No ....

CHOCTAW ENROLLING COMMISSION

IN THE MATTER OF THE APPLICATION FOR ENROLLMENT as a citizen of the Choctaw Nation, of   Julia Ann Lester   born on the 12 day of January   190 3

Name of father   Josephes[sic] Lester   a citizen of   White   Nation, final enrollment No. ———
Name of mother   Lucy Lester (nee Rozel)   a citizen of   Choctaw   Nation, final enrollment No.   12548

Crowder I.T.   Postoffice.

AFFIDAVIT OF MOTHER

UNITED STATES OF AMERICA
INDIAN TERRITORY
DISTRICT   Central

I   Lucy Lester (nee Rozel)   , on oath state that I am   18   years of age and a citizen by   blood   of the   Choctaw   Nation, and as such have been placed upon the final roll of the   Choctaw   Nation, by the Honorable Secretary of the Interior my final enrollment number being   12548   ; that I am the lawful wife of   Joseph Lester   , who is a citizen of the   Non   Nation, and as such has been placed upon the final roll of said Nation by the Honorable Secretary of the Interior, his final enrollment number being ——and that a   female   child was born to me on the   12   day of   Jan 190 3; that said child has been named   Julia Ann Lester   , and is now living.

WITNESSETH: Lucy Lester
Must be two witnesses who are citizens { Joseph D *(Illegible)*
....

Applications for Enrollment of Choctaw Newborn
Act of 1905 Volume VI

Subscribed and sworn to before me this, the 16 day of March , 190 5

James Bower
Notary Public.

My Commission Expires:
Sept 23.1907

Affidavit of Attending Physician or Midwife

UNITED STATES OF AMERICA,
INDIAN TERRITORY,
Central DISTRICT

I, Mollie Brinson a midwife on oath state that I attended on Mrs. Lucy Lester wife of Josephus Lester on the 12 day of Jan , 190 3, that there was born to her on said date a female child, that said child is now living, and is said to have been named Julia Ann Lester

Mollie Brinson M. D.

Subscribed and sworn to before me this the 16 day of March 1905

James Bower
Notary Public.

WITNESSETH:

Must be two witnesses who are citizens and know the child. { Joseph D *(Illegible)* ....

We hereby certify that we are well acquainted with Mollie Brinson a midwife and know her to be reputable and of good standing in the community.

Must be two citizen witnesses. { Joseph D *(Illegible)* ....

Applications for Enrollment of Choctaw Newborn
Act of 1905   Volume VI

NEW BORN AFFIDAVIT

No ....

CHOCTAW ENROLLING COMMISSION

IN THE MATTER OF THE APPLICATION FOR ENROLLMENT as a citizen of the Choctaw Nation, of   Ralph Lester   born on the   30   day of   September   190 4

Name of father   Josephus Lester   a citizen of   White   Nation, final enrollment No.   ———

Name of mother   Lucy Lester (nee Rozel)   a citizen of   Choctaw   Nation, final enrollment No.   12548

Crowder I.T.   Postoffice.

AFFIDAVIT OF MOTHER

UNITED STATES OF AMERICA }
INDIAN TERRITORY }
DISTRICT   Central

I   Lucy Lester (nee Rozel)   , on oath state that I am   18   years of age and a citizen by   blood   of the   Choctaw   Nation, and as such have been placed upon the final roll of the   Choctaw   Nation, by the Honorable Secretary of the Interior my final enrollment number being   12548   ; that I am the lawful wife of   Joseph Lester   , who is a citizen of the   Non   Nation, and as such has been placed upon the final roll of said Nation by the Honorable Secretary of the Interior, his final enrollment number being — and that a   male   child was born to me on the   30   day of   Sept   190 4; that said child has been named   Ralph Lester   , and is now living.

WITNESSETH: Lucy Lester

Must be two witnesses { Joseph D *(Illegible)*
who are citizens   { ....

Subscribed and sworn to before me this, the   16   day of   March   , 190 5

James Bower
Notary Public.

My Commission Expires:
Sept 23, 1907

Applications for Enrollment of Choctaw Newborn
Act of 1905   Volume VI

Affidavit of Attending Physician or Midwife

UNITED STATES OF AMERICA,
   INDIAN TERRITORY,
  Central   DISTRICT

I, Annie Southerland a midwife on oath state that I attended on Mrs. Lucy Lester wife of Josephus Lester on the 30 day of Sept, 190 4, that there was born to her on said date a male child, that said child is now living, and is said to have been named Ralph Lester

                      her
              Annie x Southerland   M. D.
                 mark

Subscribed and sworn to before me this the 16 day of March 1905

              James Bower
                    Notary Public.

WITNESSETH:

Must be two witnesses who are citizens and know the child.   { Joseph D *(Illegible)* }

We hereby certify that we are well acquainted with Annie Southerland a midwife and know her to be reputable and of good standing in the community.

        Must be two citizen witnesses. { Joseph D *(Illegible)* }

BIRTH AFFIDAVIT.

DEPARTMENT OF THE INTERIOR.
COMMISSION TO THE FIVE CIVILIZED TRIBES.

IN RE APPLICATION FOR ENROLLMENT, as a citizen of the Choctaw Nation, of Ralph Lester, born on the 30 day of September, 1904

Name of Father: Josephus Lester   a citizen of the Choctaw Nation.
Name of Mother: Lucy Lester (Rozel)   a citizen of the Choctaw Nation.

            Postoffice   Crowder, Ind. Ter.

Applications for Enrollment of Choctaw Newborn
Act of 1905   Volume VI

AFFIDAVIT OF MOTHER.

UNITED STATES OF AMERICA, Indian Territory, }
Western   DISTRICT.

I,   Lucy Lester (Rozel)   , on oath state that I am   18   years of age and a citizen by   Blood   , of the   Choctaw   Nation; that I am the lawful wife of Josephus Lester   , who is a citizen, ~~by~~ ———— of the   United States   Nation; that a Male   child was born to me on   30   day of   September   , 1904; that said child has been named   Ralph Lester   , and was living March 4, 1905.

Lucy Lester (Rozel)

Witnesses To Mark:
{

Subscribed and sworn to before me this   17th day of   April   , 1905

T.J. Rice
Notary Public.

AFFIDAVIT OF ATTENDING PHYSICIAN OR MID-WIFE.

UNITED STATES OF AMERICA, Indian Territory, }
Western   DISTRICT.

I,   Annie Southerland   , a   mid wife   , on oath state that I attended on Mrs.   Lucy Lester (Rozel)   , wife of   Josephus Lester   on the   30   day of September   , 1904; that there was born to her on said date a   male   child; that said child was living March 4, 1905, and is said to have been named   Ralph Lester

Annie Southerland

Witnesses To Mark:
{

Subscribed and sworn to before me this   17   day of   April   , 1905

T.J. Rice
Notary Public.

Applications for Enrollment of Choctaw Newborn
Act of 1905 Volume VI

BIRTH AFFIDAVIT.

DEPARTMENT OF THE INTERIOR.
COMMISSION TO THE FIVE CIVILIZED TRIBES.

IN RE APPLICATION FOR ENROLLMENT, as a citizen of the Choctaw Nation, of Ralph Lester, born on the 30th day of September, 1904

Name of Father: Josephus Lester   a citizen of the Choctaw Nation.
Name of Mother: Lucy Lester   a citizen of the Choctaw Nation.

Postoffice   Crowder, Ind. Ter.

AFFIDAVIT OF MOTHER.

UNITED STATES OF AMERICA, Indian Territory,
Central DISTRICT.

I, Lucy Lester, on oath state that I am 18 years of age and a citizen by blood, of the Choctaw Nation; that I am the lawful wife of Josephus Lester, who is a citizen, ~~by~~ of the United States Nation; that a male child was born to me on 30th day of September, 1904; that said child has been named Ralph Lester, and was living March 4, 1905.

Lucy Lester

Witnesses To Mark:

Subscribed and sworn to before me this 22nd day of March, 1905.

Wirt Franklin
Notary Public.

BIRTH AFFIDAVIT.

DEPARTMENT OF THE INTERIOR.
COMMISSION TO THE FIVE CIVILIZED TRIBES.

IN RE APPLICATION FOR ENROLLMENT, as a citizen of the Choctaw Nation, of Julia Ann Lester, born on the 12th day of January, 1904

Name of Father: Josephus Lester   a citizen of the United States Nation.
Name of Mother: Lucy Lester   a citizen of the Choctaw Nation.

Postoffice   Crowder, I.T.

Applications for Enrollment of Choctaw Newborn
Act of 1905   Volume VI

AFFIDAVIT OF MOTHER.

UNITED STATES OF AMERICA, Indian Territory, }
    Central   DISTRICT.

    I, Lucy Lester, on oath state that I am 18 years of age and a citizen by blood, of the Choctaw Nation; that I am the lawful wife of Josephus Lester, who is a citizen, ~~by~~ of the United States Nation; that a female child was born to me on the 12th day of January, 1903; that said child has been named Julia Ann Lester, and was living March 4, 1905.

                            Lucy Lester

Witnesses To Mark:
  {

    Subscribed and sworn to before me this 22nd day of March, 1905

                            Wirt Franklin
                            Notary Public.

                                      N. B. 325
                          COPY
           Muskogee, Indian Territory, April 7, 1905.

Josephus Lester,
    Crowder, Indian Territory.

Dear Sir:

    There is inclosed you herewith for execution application for the enrollment of your infant child, Ralph Lester, born September 30, 1904.

    Your attention is called to the fact that in the affidavits heretofore filed with the Commission, the signature of Annie Southerland, midwife, was made by mark and attested by only <u>one</u> witness.

    In having these affidavits executed care should be exercised to see that all names are written in full, as they appear in the body of the affidavit, and in the event that either of the persons signing the affidavit are unable to write, signatures by mark <u>must be</u> attested by <u>two</u> witnesses. Each affidavit must be executed before a Notary Public and the notarial seal and signature of the officer must be attached to each separate affidavit.

                        Respectfully,
                        SIGNED
                      T. B. Needles.
LM 7-32.   Commissioner in Charge.

Applications for Enrollment of Choctaw Newborn
Act of 1905 Volume VI

7 NB 325

Muskogee, Indian Territory, April 20, 1905.

Joseph Lester,
    Crowder, Indian Territory.

Dear Sir:

    Receipt is hereby acknowledged of the affidavits of Lucy Lester (Rozel) and Annie Southerland to the birth of Ralph Lester, son of Josephus Lester and Lucy Lester (Rozel) September 30, 1904, and the same have been filed with our records as an application for the enrollment of said child.

Respectfully,

Chairman.

Choc New Born 326
    Lillie M. Lamb
    (Born Dec. 14, 1904)

NEW BORN AFFIDAVIT

No ....

CHOCTAW ENROLLING COMMISSION

IN THE MATTER OF THE APPLICATION FOR ENROLLMENT as a citizen of the Choctaw Nation, of Lillie May Lamb born on the 14 day of December 190 4

Name of father David Lamb a citizen of .... Nation, final enrollment No. ....
Name of mother Addie M. Grubbs now Lamb zen of Choctaw Nation, final enrollment No. 12569

Savanna Postoffice.

Applications for Enrollment of Choctaw Newborn
Act of 1905   Volume VI

AFFIDAVIT OF MOTHER

UNITED STATES OF AMERICA
INDIAN TERRITORY
DISTRICT   Central

I   Addie M Grubbs Lamb   , on oath state that I am   18   years of age and a citizen by   blood   of the   Choctaw   Nation, and as such have been placed upon the final roll of the   Choctaw   Nation, by the Honorable Secretary of the Interior my final enrollment number being   12569   ; that I am the lawful wife of   David Lamb   , who is a citizen of the   Choctaw   Nation, and as such has been placed upon the final roll of said Nation by the Honorable Secretary of the Interior, his final enrollment number being................... and that a   Female   child was born to me on the   14   day of   December   190 4; that said child has been named   Lillie M Lamb   , and is now living.

WITNESSETH: Addie M Lamb

Must be two witnesses { L E Dawson
who are citizens   { Kate Culbertson

Subscribed and sworn to before me this, the   17"   day of   Feby   , 190 5

W.T. Culbertson
Notary Public.

My Commission Expires:
Sept 22-1907

* Married since rolls were closed.

Affidavit of Attending Physician or Midwife

UNITED STATES OF AMERICA,
INDIAN TERRITORY,
Central   DISTRICT

I,   S.P. Ross   a   Physician on oath state that I attended on Mrs. Addie M Lamb   wife of   David Lamb on the   14th day of   Dec   , 190 4, that there was born to her on said date a   Female child, that said child is now living, and is said to have been named   Lillie May

S.P. Ross   M. D.

Subscribed and sworn to before me this the   17th day of   Feby   1905

W.T. Culbertson
Notary Public.

Applications for Enrollment of Choctaw Newborn
Act of 1905   Volume VI

WITNESSETH:

Must be two witnesses who are citizens and know the child. { L E Dawson
Kate Culbertson

We hereby certify that we are well acquainted with Dr S P Ross a Physician and know him to be reputable and of good standing in the community.

Must be two citizen witnesses. { L E Dawson
Kate Culbertson

BIRTH AFFIDAVIT.

DEPARTMENT OF THE INTERIOR,
COMMISSION TO THE FIVE CIVILIZED TRIBES.

In Re Application for Enrollment, as a citizen of the Choctaw Nation, of Lillie M Lamb, born on the 14 day of December, 1904

Name of Father: Dave Lamb   a citizen of the Non-Citizen Nation.
Name of Mother: Addie Lamb   a citizen of the Choctaw Nation.

Post-office   Savanna

AFFIDAVIT OF MOTHER.

UNITED STATES OF AMERICA,
INDIAN TERRITORY,
Central   District.

I, Addie Grubbs now Lamb, on oath state that I am 17 years of age and a citizen by blood, of the Choctaw Nation; that I am the lawful wife of Dave Lamb, who is a citizen, by non-citizen of the —— Nation; that a Female child was born to me on 14 day of Dec, 1904, that said child has been named Lillie M Lamb, and is now living.

Addie Grubbs (now) Lamb

WITNESSES TO MARK:
{ (Name Illegible)
H. A. McVey

Subscribed and sworn to before me this 16th day of March, 1905.

W.T. Culbertson
NOTARY PUBLIC.

Applications for Enrollment of Choctaw Newborn
Act of 1905   Volume VI

AFFIDAVIT OF ATTENDING PHYSICIAN OR MID-WIFE.

UNITED STATES OF AMERICA, }
   INDIAN TERRITORY,
  Central   District.

    I, S.P. Ross , a Physician , on oath state that I attended on Mrs. Addie Lamb , wife of Dave Lamb on the 14 day of December , 1904 ; that there was born to her on said date a Female child; that said child is now living and is said to have been named Lillie M Lamb

                                        S.P. Ross M.D.

WITNESSES TO MARK:
{ WJ McVey
{ H. A. McVey

    Subscribed and sworn to before me this 16 day of March , 1905.

                                        W.T. Culbertson
                                              NOTARY PUBLIC.

                                                      7-4542

                        Muskogee, Indian Territory, March 21, 1905.

Addie M. Lamb (Grubbs),
    Savanna, Indian Territory.

Dear Madam:

    Receipt is hereby acknowledged of the affidavits of Addie Lamb Grubbs and S. P. Ross to the birth of Lillie M. Lamb daughter of Dave and Addie Lamb December 14, 1904, and the same have been filed with our records as an application for the enrollment of said child.

                                    Respectfully,

                                                         Chairman.

<u>Choc New Born 327</u>
    Roy C. Grubbs
    (Born Aug. 29, 1903)

Applications for Enrollment of Choctaw Newborn
Act of 1905 Volume VI

No. 3424

MARRIAGE LICENSE.

UNITED STATES OF AMERICA,   THE INDIAN TERRITORY,
                            CENTRAL DISTRICT, SS.

To any Person Authorized by Law to Solemnize Marriage, Greeting:

You are hereby commanded to Solemnize the Rite and publish the Banns of Matrimony between Mr. Eli Grubbs of McAlester in the Indian Territory, aged 22 years, and Mrs. Susie Stump of McAlester in the Indian Territory, aged 19 years, according to law, and do you officially sign and return this License to the parties therein named.

WITNESS my hand and official seal, this
28th day of Feby A. D. 1903

(SEAL)

E. J. Fannin
Clerk of the United States Court.

W. C. Donnelly
Deputy.

UNITED STATES OF AMERICA,)   Certificate of Marriage.
THE INDIAN TERRITORY,   )ss.
CENTRAL DISTRICT.   )   I, J. H. Lott a Minister of the Gospel

do hereby certify, that on the 28th day of February A. D. 1903, I did, duly and according to law, as commanded in the foregoing License, solemnize the Rite and publish the Banns of Matrimony between the parties therein named.

Witness my hand, this 28th day of February A. D. 1903

J. H. Lott
a M. of Gospel

My credentials are recorded in the office   )
of the Clerk of the United States Court in)
the Indian Territory, Central District,   )
Book B, Page 259   )

NOTE.- This License and Certificate of Marriage must be returned to the office of the Clerk of the United States Court of the Indian Territory from whence it was issued, within sixty days from the date thereof, or the party to whom the License was ssued will be liable in the amount of One Hundred Dollars ($100.00).

Applications for Enrollment of Choctaw Newborn
Act of 1905   Volume VI

No. 3424

CERTIFICATE OF RECORD OF MARRIAGES.

UNITED STATES OF AMERICA,)
THE INDIAN TERRITORY) SCT.
CENTRAL DISTRICT.)

I, E. J. Fannin Clerk of the United States Court in the Indian Territory and District aforesaid, do hereby CERTIFY that the License for and Certificate of the Marriage of Mr. Eli Grubbs and M_____Susie Stump_____was filed in my office in said Territory and District the 7th day of March A. D. 1903, and duly recorded in Book 10 of Marriage Record, Page 419.

WITNESS my hand and seal of said Court, at So. McAlester this 7th day of March A. D. 1903

E. J. Fannin
Clerk

By _____ Deputy.

P. O. _____

DEPARTMENT OF THE INTERIOR,
Commission to the Five Civilized Tribes.
Filed Mar 18, 1905.

NEW BORN AFFIDAVIT

No ....

CHOCTAW ENROLLING COMMISSION

IN THE MATTER OF THE APPLICATION FOR ENROLLMENT as a citizen of the Choctaw Nation, of   Roy C. Grubbs   born on the 29th day of   August   190 4[sic]

Name of father   Eli Grubbs   a citizen of   Choctaw   Nation, final enrollment No. 12565
Name of mother   Susie Grubbs   a citizen of   U.S.   Nation, final enrollment No.........

102

Applications for Enrollment of Choctaw Newborn
Act of 1905 Volume VI

Chambers IT   Postoffice.

AFFIDAVIT OF MOTHER

UNITED STATES OF AMERICA
    INDIAN TERRITORY
DISTRICT   Central

    I   Susie Grubbs   , on oath state that I am   22   years of age and a citizen by   birth   of the   U.S.   Nation, and as such have been placed upon the final roll of the ——Nation, by the Honorable Secretary of the Interior my final enrollment number being ——; that I am the lawful wife of   Eli Grubbs   , who is a citizen of the   Choctaw   Nation, and as such has been placed upon the final roll of said Nation by the Honorable Secretary of the Interior, his final enrollment number being   12565   and that a   male   child was born to me on the   29th   day of   August   190 4[sic]; that said child has been named   Roy C Grubbs   , and is now living.

                                              her
WITNESSETH: Susie x Grubbs
   Must be two witnesses { Phillip Nelson   mark
   who are citizens   Roxy Y Grubbs

    Subscribed and sworn to before me this, the   9th   day of   Feb.   , 190

                                        WG Weimer
Commission expires August 9, 1905.   Notary Public.
My Commission Expires:

Affidavit of Attending Physician or Midwife

UNITED STATES OF AMERICA,
    INDIAN TERRITORY,
  Central   DISTRICT

    I,   Liza Grubbs   a   Midwife
on oath state that I attended on Mrs.   Susie Grubbs   wife of   Eli Grubbs   on the   29th   day of   August   , 190 4[sic], that there was born to her on said date a   male   child, that said child is now living, and is said to have been named   Roy C Grubbs
Witness   her
Phillip Nelson   Liza x Grubbs   Midwife
Roxy Y Grubbs   mark
    Subscribed and sworn to before me this the   9th   day of   Feb   1905

Commission expires August 9, 1905.   WG Weimer
                                               Notary Public.

Applications for Enrollment of Choctaw Newborn
Act of 1905   Volume VI

WITNESSETH:

Must be two witnesses who are citizens and know the child. { Phillip Nelson
Roxy Y Grubbs

We hereby certify that we are well acquainted with   Liza Grubbs   a   Midwife   and know   her   to be reputable and of good standing in the community.

Must be two citizen witnesses. { Phillip Nelson
Roxy Y Grubbs

BIRTH AFFIDAVIT.

DEPARTMENT OF THE INTERIOR.
COMMISSION TO THE FIVE CIVILIZED TRIBES.

IN RE APPLICATION FOR ENROLLMENT, as a citizen of the   Choctaw   Nation, of   Roy C. Grubbs   , born on the   29th   day of   August   , 1903

Name of Father: Eli Grubbs   a citizen of the   Choctaw   Nation.
Name of Mother: Susie Jane Grubbs   a citizen of the United States Nation.

Postoffice   Chambers, I.T.

AFFIDAVIT OF MOTHER.

UNITED STATES OF AMERICA, Indian Territory, }
Central   DISTRICT.

I,   Susie Jane Grubbs   , on oath state that I am   21   years of age and a citizen by ...., of the   United States   Nation; that I am the lawful wife of   Eli Grubbs   , who is a citizen, by blood   of the   Choctaw   Nation; that a   male   child was born to me on   29th   day of   August   , 1903; that said child has been named   Roy C. Grubbs   , and was living March 4, 1905.

                        her
               Susie Jane x Grubbs
Witnesses To Mark: mark
{ John Cole
Jonas Sexton

Subscribed and sworn to before me this   18th   day of   March   , 1905

Wirt Franklin
Notary Public.

Applications for Enrollment of Choctaw Newborn
Act of 1905 Volume VI

AFFIDAVIT OF ATTENDING PHYSICIAN OR MID-WIFE.

UNITED STATES OF AMERICA, Indian Territory, }
Central DISTRICT.

    I, Eliza C. Grubbs , a midwife , on oath state that I attended on Mrs. Susie Jane Grubbs , wife of Eli Grubbs on the 29th day of August , 1903; that there was born to her on said date a male child; that said child was living March 4, 1905, and is said to have been named Roy C. Grubbs

                                                  her
                                       Eliza C. x Grubbs

Witnesses To Mark: mark
{ John Cole
  Jonas Sexton

    Subscribed and sworn to before me this 18th day of March , 1905

                                    Wirt Franklin
                                        Notary Public.

BIRTH AFFIDAVIT.

DEPARTMENT OF THE INTERIOR.
COMMISSION TO THE FIVE CIVILIZED TRIBES.

    IN RE APPLICATION FOR ENROLLMENT, as a citizen of the Choctaw Nation, of Roy C Grubbs , born on the 29 day of August , 1903

Name of Father: Eli Grubbs   a citizen of the Choctaw Nation.
Name of Mother: Susie Jane Grubbs   a citizen of the U.S. Nation.

                      Postoffice Chambers, I.T.

AFFIDAVIT OF MOTHER.

UNITED STATES OF AMERICA, Indian Territory, }
Central DISTRICT.

    I, Susie Jane Grubbs , on oath state that I am 21 years of age and a citizen by ——, of the United States Nation; that I am the lawful wife of Eli Grubbs , who is a citizen, by Blood of the Choctaw Nation; that a Male child was born to me on 29th day of August , 1903; that said child has been named Roy C. Grubbs , and was living March 4, 1905.

                                       her
                                Susie x Jane Grubbs
                                    mark

Applications for Enrollment of Choctaw Newborn
Act of 1905   Volume VI

Witnesses To Mark:
- Roxy Y Grubbs
- S P Ross M.D.

Subscribed and sworn to before me this 17th day of June , 1905

W.T. Culbertson
Notary Public.

AFFIDAVIT OF ATTENDING PHYSICIAN OR MID-WIFE.

UNITED STATES OF AMERICA, Indian Territory,
Central DISTRICT.

I, Mary Lookingbill , a Midwife , on oath state that I attended on Mrs. Susie Jane Grubbs , wife of Eli Grubbs on the 29th day of August , 1903; that there was born to her on said date a male child; that said child was living March 4, 1905, and is said to have been named Roy C. Grubbs

Mary Lookingbill

Witnesses To Mark:
- Roxy Y Grubbs
- S P Ross MD

Subscribed and sworn to before me this 17th day of June , 1905

W.T. Culbertson
Notary Public.

7-NB-327

Muskogee, Indian Territory, May 22, 1905.

Eli Grubbs,
Chambers, Indian Territory.

Dear Sir:

There is enclosed you herewith for execution application for the enrollment of your infant child, Roy C. Grubbs.

In the affidavits of February 9, 1905, heretofore filed with the Commission, the date of birth of the applicant is given as August 29, 1904, while in those of March 18, 1905, it is given as August 29, 1903. In the enclosed application the date of birth is left

Applications for Enrollment of Choctaw Newborn
Act of 1905 Volume VI

blank, in which you will please insert the correct date of birth, and when properly executed return it to this office.

In having these affidavits executed care should be exercised to see that all names are written in full, as they appear in the body of the affidavit, and in the event that either of the persons signing the affidavit are unable to write, signatures by mark must be attested by two witnesses. Each affidavit must be executed before a Notary Public and the notarial seal and signature of the officer must be attached to each separate affidavit.

Respectfully,

VT 22-19.   Chairman.

---

7 NB 327

Muskogee, Indian Territory, June 21, 1905.

Eli Grubbs,
    Chambers, Indian Territory.

Dear Sir:

Receipt is hereby acknowledged of the affidavits of Susie Jane Grubbs and Mary Lookingbill to the birth of Roy C. Grubbs, son of Eli and Susie Jane Grubbs, August 29, 1903, and the same have been filed with our records in the matter of the enrollment of said child.

Respectfully,

Chairman.

Choc New Born 328
    Lena Marie Sumter
    (Born April 13, 1903)
    Milton Leon Sumter
    (Born Feb. 11, 1905)

Applications for Enrollment of Choctaw Newborn
Act of 1905 Volume VI

NEW-BORN AFFIDAVIT.

Number..............

...Choctaw Enrolling Commission...

IN THE MATTER OF THE APPLICATION FOR ENROLLMENT, as a citizen of the Choctaw Nation, of Lena Marie Sumter

born on the 13 day of April 1903

Name of father Joseph Sumter   a citizen of ———
Nation final enrollment No. ———
Name of mother Emma Sumter   a citizen of Choctaw
Nation final enrollment No. 12584

Postoffice   Atoka I.T.

AFFIDAVIT OF MOTHER.

UNITED STATES OF AMERICA
INDIAN TERRITORY
Central   DISTRICT

I   Emma Sumter   , on oath state that I am 24 years of age and a citizen by blood of the Choctaw Nation, and as such have been placed upon the final roll of the Choctaw Nation, by the Honorable Secretary of the Interior my final enrollment number being 12584; that I am the lawful wife of Joseph Sumter, who is a citizen of the ——— Nation, and as such has been placed upon the final roll of said Nation by the Honorable Secretary of the Interior, his final enrollment number being ——— and that a Female child was born to me on the 13th day of April 1903; that said child has been named Lena Marie Sumter, and is now living.

Witnesseth.   Emma Sumter

Must be two ⎫ C.C. Rose
Witnesses who ⎬
are Citizens. ⎭ R.O. Sumter

Subscribed and sworn to before me this 24th day of February 1905

A.E. Folsom
Notary Public.

My commission expires:
Jan 9th 1909

Applications for Enrollment of Choctaw Newborn
Act of 1905   Volume VI

AFFIDAVIT OF ATTENDING PHYSICIAN OR MIDWIFE

UNITED STATES OF AMERICA
INDIAN TERRITORY
   Central   DISTRICT

I,   Thomas Long   a   Practicing Physician on oath state that I attended on Mrs.   Emma Sumter   wife of   Joseph Sumter on the   13th   day of   April, 1903, that there was born to her on said date a   Female   child, that said child is now living, and is said to have been named   Lena Maria Sumter

T. J. Long   M.D.

WITNESSETH:

Must be two witnesses who are citizens and know the child.
{ C. C. Rose
  R.O. Sumter

Subscribed and sworn to before me this, the .... day of .... 190......

.... Notary Public.

We hereby certify that we are well acquainted with   Dr. Thomas Long   a   Practicing Physician   and know   him   to be reputable and of good standing in the community.

{ C C Rose
  R.O. Sumter

BIRTH AFFIDAVIT.

DEPARTMENT OF THE INTERIOR.
COMMISSION TO THE FIVE CIVILIZED TRIBES.

IN RE APPLICATION FOR ENROLLMENT, as a citizen of the   Choctaw   Nation, of   Lena Marie Sumter   , born on the   13   day of   April   , 1903

Name of Father: Joseph M Sumter   a citizen of the   Choctaw   Nation.
Name of Mother: Emma Sumter   a citizen of the   Choctaw   Nation.

Postoffice   Atoka, Ind. Ter.

Applications for Enrollment of Choctaw Newborn
Act of 1905   Volume VI

AFFIDAVIT OF MOTHER.

UNITED STATES OF AMERICA, Indian Territory,
Central   DISTRICT.

I, Emma Sumter, on oath state that I am 24 years of age and a citizen by Blood, of the Choctaw Nation; that I am the lawful wife of Joseph M Sumter, who is a citizen, by ———of the ———Nation; that a female child was born to me on 13th day of April, 1903; that said child has been named Lena Marie Sumter, and was living March 4, 1905.

Emma Sumter

Witnesses To Mark:

Subscribed and sworn to before me this 25th day of March, 1905

W.H. Angell
Notary Public.

AFFIDAVIT OF ATTENDING PHYSICIAN OR MID-WIFE.

UNITED STATES OF AMERICA, Indian Territory,
Central   DISTRICT.

I, Magdale Sumter, a Mid wife, on oath state that I attended on Mrs. Emma Sumter, wife of Joseph M Sumter on the 13th day of April, 1903; that there was born to her on said date a female child; that said child was living March 4, 1905, and is said to have been named Lena Marie Sumter

Magdale Sumter

Witnesses To Mark:

Subscribed and sworn to before me this 25th day of March, 1905

W.H. Angell
Notary Public.

Applications for Enrollment of Choctaw Newborn
Act of 1905   Volume VI

DEPARTMENT OF THE INTERIOR
COMMISSION TO THE FIVE CIVILIZED TRIBES
CHOCTAW LAND OFFICE.
-:-
Atoka, Indian Territory, March 25, 1905.

———

In the matter of the application of Emma Sumter
for the enrollment of her infant child, Milton
Leon Sumter, as a Choctaw by Blood.

———

Emma Sumter, being duly sworn, testified as follows:

Examination by the Commission:

Q What is your name? A Emma Sumter.
Q What is your age? A 24.
Q Are you a citizen by blood of the Choctaw Nation? A Yes, sir.
Q Your purpose in appearing here to-day is to make application for the enrollment of your infant child, Milton Leon Sumter, is it not? A Yes, sir.
Q Are you the mother of Milton Leon Sumter? A Yes, sir.
Q What is the name of his father? A Joseph Sumter.
Q Is he a citizen of the United States? A Yes, sir.
Q When was Milton Leon Sumter born? A 11 of February, 1905.
Q Is he now living? A No, sir.
Q When did he die? A 22nd day of this month.
Q How old was he when he died? A Month and eleven days.
Q Did you have a funeral? A No, sir.
Q Was there any one present when you buried the child? A Yes, sir.
Q Name some persons who were present when you buried the child?
[sic] Mrs. Sumter and Joseph Sumter.

———

Magdaline Sumter, being duly sworn, testified as follows:

Examination by the Commission:

Q What is your name? A Magdaline Sumter.
Q What is your age? A 47.
Q What is your post office address? A Atoka.
Q Are you a citizen of the Choctaw Nation? A No, sir.
Q Are you a United States citizen? A Yes, sir.
Q Are you any kin to Emma Sumter who has just testified? A Yes, sir; she is my son's wife.
Q Did she have a child by the name of Milton Leon Sumter? A Yes, sir.
Q When was that child born? A February 11, 1905.

Applications for Enrollment of Choctaw Newborn
Act of 1905   Volume VI

Q Is that child now living? A No, sir.
Q When did Milton Leon Sumter die? A March 22, 1905.
Q How old was he when he died? A Month and eleven days old.
Q Were you present when the child was born? A Yes, sir.
Q You acted as midwife? A Yes, sir.
Q This child, Milton Leon Sumter, who was born February 11, 1905, and died March 22, 1905, is the identical Milton Leon Sumter whom his mother, Emma Sumter, now makes application for enrollment for, is he? A Yes, sir.

—

Joseph Sumter, being duly sworn, testified as follows:

Examination by the Commission:

Q What is your name? A Joseph Sumter.
Q What is your age? A 24.
Q What is your post office address? A Atoka.
Q Are you a citizen of the United States? A Yes, sir.
Q Are you the husband of Emma Sumter? A Yes, sir.
Q Did she have a child by the name of Milton Leon Sumter? A Yes, sir.
Q When was Milton Leon Sumter born? A February 11, 1905.
Q Is he now living? A No, sir.
Q When did he die? A March 22, 1905.
Q Who was the mother of Milton Leon Sumter? A Emma Sumter.
Q She is your wife? A Yes, sir.
Q This child, Milton Leon Sumter, is the identical child who was born February 11, 1905, and died March 22, 1905, and for whom Emma Sumter is now making application for enrollment? A Yes, sir.

—

I, D. Shelor, on oath, state that the foregoing is a full, true and correct transcript of stenographic notes taken in said cause on said date.

D Shelor

Subscribed and sworn to before me, this March 27, 1905.

W.H. Angell
Notary Public.

Applications for Enrollment of Choctaw Newborn
Act of 1905   Volume VI

NEW-BORN AFFIDAVIT.

Number..............

...Choctaw Enrolling Commission...

IN THE MATTER OF THE APPLICATION FOR ENROLLMENT, as a citizen of the Choctaw Nation, of Milton Leon Sumter

born on the 11th day of February 190 5

Name of father   Joseph Sumter   a citizen of ─────────
Nation final enrollment No.   ─────
Name of mother   Emma Sumter   a citizen of   Choctaw
Nation final enrollment No.   12584

Postoffice   Atoka I.T.

AFFIDAVIT OF MOTHER.

UNITED STATES OF AMERICA
INDIAN TERRITORY
Central   DISTRICT

I   Emma Sumter   , on oath state that I am 24 years of age and a citizen by blood of the Choctaw Nation, and as such have been placed upon the final roll of the Choctaw Nation, by the Honorable Secretary of the Interior my final enrollment number being 12584 ; that I am the lawful wife of Joseph Sumter , who is a citizen of the ───── Nation, and as such has been placed upon the final roll of said Nation by the Honorable Secretary of the Interior, his final enrollment number being ───── and that a Male child was born to me on the 11th day of February 190 5; that said child has been named Milton Leon Sumter , and is now living.

Witnesseth.   Emma Sumter

Must be two ⎫ R.O. Sumter
Witnesses who ⎬
are Citizens. ⎭ C.C. Rose

Subscribed and sworn to before me this 24th day of February 190 5

A.E. Folsom
Notary Public.

My commission expires:
Jan 9-1909

Applications for Enrollment of Choctaw Newborn
Act of 1905   Volume VI

AFFIDAVIT OF ATTENDING PHYSICIAN OR MIDWIFE

UNITED STATES OF AMERICA
INDIAN TERRITORY
Central   DISTRICT

I,   Maggie Sumter   a   Mid wife   on oath state that I attended on Mrs.   Emma Sumter   wife of   Joseph Sumter   on the   11th   day of   February   , 190 5, that there was born to her on said date a   male   child, that said child is now living, and is said to have been named   Milton Leon Sumter

mid wife
Mrs. R.E. Sumter   M.D.

WITNESSETH:
Must be two witnesses who are citizens and know the child.
{ R.O. Sumter
  C.C. Rose

Subscribed and sworn to before me this, the   4"   day of   March   190 5

D N Linebaugh   Notary Public.

We hereby certify that we are well acquainted with   Mrs Maggie Sumter   a   Mid wife   and know   her   to be reputable and of good standing in the community.

{ R.O. Sumter
  C C Rose

BIRTH AFFIDAVIT.

DEPARTMENT OF THE INTERIOR.
COMMISSION TO THE FIVE CIVILIZED TRIBES.

IN RE APPLICATION FOR ENROLLMENT, as a citizen of the   Choctaw   Nation, of   Milton Leon Sumter   , born on the   11   day of   Feby   , 1905

Name of Father: Joseph M Sumter   a citizen of the   ——   Nation.
Name of Mother: Emma Sumter   a citizen of the   Choctaw   Nation.

Postoffice   Atoka, Ind. Ter.

Applications for Enrollment of Choctaw Newborn
Act of 1905   Volume VI

AFFIDAVIT OF MOTHER.

UNITED STATES OF AMERICA, Indian Territory, }
Central   DISTRICT.

I,   Emma Sumter   , on oath state that I am   24   years of age and a citizen by   Blood   , of the   Choctaw   Nation; that I am the lawful wife of   Joseph M Sumter   , who is a citizen, by ——of the ———Nation; that a   Male   child was born to me on   11th   day of   Feby   , 1905; that said child has been named   Milton Leon Sumter   , and was living March 4, 1905.

                                        Emma Sumter

Witnesses To Mark:
{

Subscribed and sworn to before me this   25th   day of   March   , 1905

                                        W.H. Angell
                                          Notary Public.

AFFIDAVIT OF ATTENDING PHYSICIAN OR MID-WIFE.

UNITED STATES OF AMERICA, Indian Territory, }
Central   DISTRICT.

I,   Magdale Sumter   , a   Mid wife   , on oath state that I attended on Mrs.   Emma Sumter   , wife of   Joseph M Sumter   on the   11th day of   Feby , 1905; that there was born to her on said date a   Male   child; that said child was living March 4, 1905, and is said to have been named   Milton Leon Sumter

                                        Magdale Sumter

Witnesses To Mark:
{ Subscribed and sworn to before me this   25th   day of   March   , 1905

                                        W.H. Angell
                                          Notary Public.

Applications for Enrollment of Choctaw Newborn
Act of 1905   Volume VI

Sub.

7-NB-328.

Muskogee, Indian Territory, May 23, 1905.

Commissioner in Charge,
    Choctaw Land Office,
        Atoka, Indian Territory.

Dear Sir:

    There is enclosed herewith affidavit of Emma Sumter and Magdale Sumter to the death of Milton Leon Sumter, executed in your office, in which the notary public omitted the date of execution and his signature.

    Please have the Notary Public, before whom the application was made, to insert the date of execution and affix his signature thereto.

                Respectfully,

                            Chairman.

VR 22-11.

Choc New Born 329
    Clara Belle Cunningham
    (Born Nov. 24, 1902)

Applications for Enrollment of Choctaw Newborn
Act of 1905 Volume VI

BIRTH AFFIDAVIT.

Department of the Interior,
COMMISSION TO THE FIVE CIVILIZED TRIBES.

IN RE APPLICATION FOR ENROLLMENT, as a citizen of the Choctaw Nation, of Clara Belle Cunningham , born on the 24 day of Nov , 190 2

Name of Father: Alfred H Cunningham   a citizen of the Choctaw Nation.
Name of Mother: Martha J Cunningham   a citizen of the Choctaw Nation.

Post-Office: Legal, Ind. Ter.

AFFIDAVIT OF MOTHER.

UNITED STATES OF AMERICA,
   INDIAN TERRITORY,
Central   District.

I, Martha J Cunningham , on oath state that I am 32 years of age and a citizen by blood , of the Choctaw Nation; that I am the lawful wife of Alfred H Cunningham , who is a citizen, by Marriage of the Choctaw Nation; that a female child was born to me on 24 day of Nov , 190 2, that said child has been named Clara Belle Cunningham , and is now living.

Martha J Cunningham

WITNESSES TO MARK:

Subscribed and sworn to before me this 18 day of Dec , 190 2

John D Grubbs
Notary Public.

AFFIDAVIT OF ATTENDING PHYSICIAN OR MID-WIFE.

UNITED STATES OF AMERICA,
   INDIAN TERRITORY,
Central   District.

I, L R Hawkins , a Physician , on oath state that I attended on Mrs. Martha J Cunningham , wife of Alfred H Cunningham on the 24 day of Nov , 190 2; that there was born to her on said date a Girl child; that said child is now living and is said to have been named Clara Belle Cunningham

L R Hawkins

WITNESSES TO MARK:

Applications for Enrollment of Choctaw Newborn
Act of 1905 Volume VI

Subscribed and sworn to before me this 18 day of Dec , 190 2

John D Grubbs
Notary Public.

NEW BORN AFFIDAVIT

No ....

CHOCTAW ENROLLING COMMISSION

IN THE MATTER OF THE APPLICATION FOR ENROLLMENT as a citizen of the Choctaw Nation, of   Clara Belle Cunningham   born on the 24th day of   November   190 2

Name of father   Alfred H Cunningham   a citizen of   Choctaw   Nation, final enrollment No.   573   Choc By Interm.
Name of mother   Martha J Cunningham   a citizen of   Choctaw   Nation, final enrollment No.   12591

Legal Ind. Ter.   Postoffice.

AFFIDAVIT OF MOTHER

UNITED STATES OF AMERICA
INDIAN TERRITORY
DISTRICT   Central

I   Martha J Cunningham   , on oath state that I am   88[sic]   years of age and a citizen by   Blood   of the   Choctaw   Nation, and as such have been placed upon the final roll of the   Choctaw   Nation, by the Honorable Secretary of the Interior my final enrollment number being   12591   ; that I am the lawful wife of   Alfred H Cunningham   , who is a citizen of the   Choctaw   Nation, and as such have been placed upon the final roll of said Nation by the Honorable Secretary of the Interior, his final enrollment number being   573   and that a   Female   child was born to me on the   24   day of   November   190 2; that said child has been named   Clara Belle Cunningham   , and is now living.

Martha J Cunningham

WITNESSETH:
Must be two witnesses   { Mitchell King
who are citizens   { Emma King

118

Applications for Enrollment of Choctaw Newborn
Act of 1905   Volume VI

Subscribed and sworn to before me this, the   9th   day of   Feb   , 1905

Richard E Kemp
Notary Public.

My Commission Expires: Dec 17-1908

Affidavit of Attending Physician or Midwife

UNITED STATES OF AMERICA, }
INDIAN TERRITORY,
Central   DISTRICT

I,   L. R. Hawkins   a   Physician on oath state that I attended on Mrs.   Martha J Cunningham   wife of   Alfred H Cunningham   on the 24   day of   November   , 1902, that there was born to her on said date a   Female   child, that said child is now living, and is said to have been named   Clara Belle Cunningham

L R Hawkins   M. D.

Subscribed and sworn to before me this the   9   day of   Feb   1905

Richard E Kemp
My Commission expires Dec-17-1908   Notary Public.

WITNESSETH:

Must be two witnesses who are citizens and know the child. { Mitchell King
Emma King

We hereby certify that we are well acquainted with   Dr. L. R. Hawkins   a   Physician   and know   him   to be reputable and of good standing in the community.

Must be two citizen witnesses. { Mitchell King
Emma King

Applications for Enrollment of Choctaw Newborn
Act of 1905   Volume VI

BIRTH AFFIDAVIT.

DEPARTMENT OF THE INTERIOR.
COMMISSION TO THE FIVE CIVILIZED TRIBES.

IN RE APPLICATION FOR ENROLLMENT, as a citizen of the Choctaw Nation, of Clara Belle Cunningham, born on the 24 day of Nov, 1902

Name of Father: Alfred H Cunningham   a citizen of the Choctaw Nation.
Name of Mother: Martha J Cunningham   a citizen of the Choctaw Nation.

Postoffice   Legal, Ind. Ter.

AFFIDAVIT OF MOTHER.

UNITED STATES OF AMERICA, Indian Territory, }
Central   DISTRICT.

I, Martha J Cunningham, on oath state that I am 34 years of age and a citizen by Blood, of the Choctaw Nation; that I am the lawful wife of Alfred H Cunningham, who is a citizen, by Intermarriage of the Choctaw Nation; that a Female child was born to me on 24 day of November, 1902; that said child has been named Clara Belle Cunningham, and was living March 4, 1905.

Martha J Cunningham

Witnesses To Mark:
{ O.S. Lawrence
  Mitchell King

Subscribed and sworn to before me this 3 day of April, 1905

Richard E. Kemp
My Commission exp. Dec. 17-1908   Notary Public.

AFFIDAVIT OF ATTENDING PHYSICIAN OR MID-WIFE.

UNITED STATES OF AMERICA, Indian Territory, }
Central   DISTRICT.

I, Sarah P Jenkins, a mid-wife, on oath state that I attended on Mrs. Martha J Cunningham, wife of Alfred H Cunningham on the 24 day of November, 1902; that there was born to her on said date a Female child; that said child was living March 4, 1905, and is said to have been named Clara Belle Cunningham

Sarah P. Jenkins

Applications for Enrollment of Choctaw Newborn
Act of 1905   Volume VI

Witnesses To Mark:
{ O.S. Lawrence
{ Mitchell King

Subscribed and sworn to before me this 3 day of   April   , 1905

My Commission exp. Dec. 17-1908

Richard E. Kemp
Notary Public.

7-4547.

Muskogee, Indian Territory, December 29, 1902.

Alfred H. Cunningham,
Legal, Indian Territory.

Dear Sir:

Receipt is hereby acknowledged of the application for enrollment as a citizen of the Choctaw Nation of Clara Belle Cunningham, infant daughter of Alfred H. and Martha J. Cunningham, born November 24, 1902.

You are advised that the Commission is without authority to enroll this child, it appearing that it was born November 24, 1902, subsequent to the date of the ratification on September 25, 1902, of the act of Congress approved July 1, 1902.

Section twenty-eight thereof provides as follows:

"The names of all persons living on the date of the final ratification of this agreement entitled to be enrolled as provided in section 27 hereof shall be placed upon the rolls made by said Commission; and no child born thereafter to a citizen or freedman and no person intermarried thereafter to a citizen shall be entitled to enrollment or to participate in the distribution of the tribal property of the Choctaws and Chickasaws."

Respectfully,

Acting Chairman.

Applications for Enrollment of Choctaw Newborn
Act of 1905   Volume VI

N. B. 329.
COPY
Muskogee, Indian Territory, April 7, 1905.

Alfred H. Cunningham,
Legal, Indian Territory.

Dear Sir:

There is enclosed you herewith for execution application for the enrollment of your infant child, Clara Belle Cunningham, born November 24, 1902.

The affidavits heretofore filed with the Commission show the child was living on December 18, 1902. It is necessary, for the child to be enrolled, that she was living on March 4, 1905.

In having these affidavits executed care should be exercised to see that all names are written in full, as they appear in the body of the affidavit, and in the event that either of the persons signing the affidavit are unable to write, signatures by mark must be attested by two witnesses. Each affidavit must be executed before a Notary Public and the notarial seal and signature of the officer must be attached to each separate affidavit.

Respectfully,
SIGNED
T. B. Needles.
LER 7-4.   Commissioner in Charge.

Choctaw 4547.

Muskogee, Indian Territory, April 10, 1905.

Alfred H. Cunningham,
Legal, Indian Territory.

Dear Sir:

Receipt is hereby acknowledged of the affidavits of Martha J. Cunningham and Sarah P. Jenkins, to the birth of Clara Belle Cunningham, daughter of Alfred H. and Martha J. Cunningham, November 24, 1902, and the same have been filed with our records as an application for the enrollment of said child.

Respectfully,

Commissioner in Charge.

Applications for Enrollment of Choctaw Newborn
Act of 1905   Volume VI

COPY 7 NB 329

Muskogee, Indian Territory, April 14, 1905.

Alfred H. Cunningham,
    Legal, Indian Territory.

Dear Sir:

    Receipt is hereby acknowledged of your letter of April 11, 1905, referring to the application for the enrollment of your child Clara Bell[sic] Cunningham in which you state that your wife Martha J. Cunningham and Mrs. Jenkins went before a Notary Public and executed affidavits showing that your child was living March 4, 1905; you state if these affidavits have not been received that you will have the ones forwarded you executed.

    In reply to your letter you are advised that it will not be necessary at this time to have other affidavits executed.

                  Respectfully,
                  SIGNED
                  T. B. Needles.
                  Commissioner in Charge.

---

7 NB 329.

Muskogee, Indian Territory, April 19, 1905.

R. C. Kemp,
    Legal, Indian Territory.

Dear Sir:

    Receipt is hereby acknowledged of your letter of April 11, 1905, asking if affidavits have been received to the birth of Clara Bell[sic] Cunningham, child of Martha J. Cunningham, November 24, 1902.

    In reply to your letter you are informed that the affidavits heretofore forwarded to the birth of Clara Bell Cunningham have been filed with our records as an application for her enrollment.

                  Respectfully,

                              Chairman.

Applications for Enrollment of Choctaw Newborn
Act of 1905   Volume VI

Choc New Born 330
   Theodore Tanehill
   (Born March 27, 1903)

BIRTH AFFIDAVIT.

DEPARTMENT OF THE INTERIOR.
COMMISSION TO THE FIVE CIVILIZED TRIBES.

IN RE APPLICATION FOR ENROLLMENT, as a citizen of the   Choctaw   Nation, of Theodore Tanehill   , born on the   27th   day of   March   , 1903

Name of Father: Joseph D. Tanehill   a citizen of the   Choctaw   Nation.
Name of Mother: Mintie Tanehill   a citizen of the   Choctaw   Nation.

   Postoffice   McAlester, I.T.

AFFIDAVIT OF MOTHER.

UNITED STATES OF AMERICA, Indian Territory, ⎫
   Central   DISTRICT. ⎭

   I,   Mintie Tanehill   , on oath state that I am   26   years of age and a citizen by   blood   , of the   Choctaw   Nation; that I am the lawful wife of   Joseph D. Tanehill   , who is a citizen, by   marriage   of the   Choctaw   Nation; that a male   child was born to me on   27th   day of   March   , 1903; that said child has been named   Theodore Tanehill   , and was living March 4, 1905.

   Mintie Tanehill
Witnesses To Mark:
{

   Subscribed and sworn to before me this   22nd   day of   March   , 1905

   Wirt Franklin
      Notary Public.

AFFIDAVIT OF ATTENDING PHYSICIAN OR MID-WIFE.

UNITED STATES OF AMERICA, Indian Territory, ⎫
   Central   DISTRICT. ⎭

   I,   J.C. Robinson   , a   physician   , on oath state that I attended on Mrs.   Mintie Tanehill   , wife of   Joseph D. Tanehill   on the   27th   day of

Applications for Enrollment of Choctaw Newborn
Act of 1905   Volume VI

March   , 1903; that there was born to her on said date a   male   child; that said child was living March 4, 1905, and is said to have been named   Theodore Tanehill

J.C. Robinson

Witnesses To Mark:
{

Subscribed and sworn to before me this   21st   day of   March   , 1905

Wirt Franklin
Notary Public.

Choc New Born 331
    Ruby Holloway
    (Born Sep. 10, 1904)

BIRTH AFFIDAVIT.

DEPARTMENT OF THE INTERIOR.
COMMISSION TO THE FIVE CIVILIZED TRIBES.

IN RE APPLICATION FOR ENROLLMENT, as a citizen of the   Choctaw   Nation, of Ruby Holloway   , born on the   10   day of   Sept   , 1904

Name of Father: Frank Holloway   a citizen of the   Choctaw   Nation.
Name of Mother: Allice[sic] Holloway   a citizen of the   Choctaw   Nation.

Postoffice   Savanna IT

AFFIDAVIT OF MOTHER.

UNITED STATES OF AMERICA, Indian Territory, }
    Central   DISTRICT. }

    I,   Allice Holloway   , on oath state that I am   45   years of age and a citizen by Inter m   , of the   Choctaw   Nation; that I am the lawful wife of   Frank Holloway   , who is a citizen, by   blood   of the   Choctaw   Nation; that a female   child was born to me on   10th   day of   Sept   , 1904, that said child has been named   Ruby Holloway   , and is now living.

Alice Holloway

Applications for Enrollment of Choctaw Newborn
Act of 1905   Volume VI

Witnesses To Mark:
{ Sante Ferrante
{ Isabinda Ferrante

Subscribed and sworn to before me this 20th day of January , 1905.

W.T. Culbertson
Notary Public.

AFFIDAVIT OF ATTENDING PHYSICIAN OR MID-WIFE.

UNITED STATES OF AMERICA, Indian Territory, }
Central   DISTRICT.

I,   Pinie Scott   , a   Midwife   , on oath state that I attended on Mrs. Allice Holloway , wife of Frank Holloway on the 10th day of Sept , 1904; that there was born to her on said date a   Female   child; that said child is now living and is said to have been named Ruby Holloway

Pinie Scott   Midwife

Witnesses To Mark:
{ Sante Ferrante
{ Isabinda Ferrante

Subscribed and sworn to before me this 20th day of January , 1905.

W.T. Culbertson
Notary Public.

NEW-BORN AFFIDAVIT.

Number............

...Choctaw Enrolling Commission...

IN THE MATTER OF THE APPLICATION FOR ENROLLMENT, as a citizen of the Choctaw   Nation, of   Ruby Holloway

born on the 10 day of September   190 4

Name of father   Frank Holloway   a citizen of   Choctaw
Nation final enrollment No.   12605
Name of mother   Allice Holloway   a citizen of   Choctaw
Nation final enrollment No.   1022

Applications for Enrollment of Choctaw Newborn
Act of 1905 Volume VI

Postoffice Celestine IT

AFFIDAVIT OF MOTHER.

UNITED STATES OF AMERICA
INDIAN TERRITORY
Central DISTRICT

I Allice Holloway, on oath state that I am 45 years of age and a citizen by Inter M of the Choctaw Nation, and as such have been placed upon the final roll of the Choctaw Nation, by the Honorable Secretary of the Interior my final enrollment number being 1022 ; that I am the lawful wife of Frank Holloway, who is a citizen of the Choctaw Nation, and as such has been placed upon the final roll of said Nation by the Honorable Secretary of the Interior, his final enrollment number being 12605 and that a Female child was born to me on the 10 day of September 190 4; that said child has been named Ruby Holloway, and is now living.

Witnesseth. Alice Holloway

Must be two Witnesses who are Citizens.
Sante Ferrante
Isabinda Ferrante

Subscribed and sworn to before me this 20 day of Jan 190 5

W.T. Culbertson
Notary Public.

My commission expires:
Sept 22-1907

AFFIDAVIT OF ATTENDING PHYSICIAN OR MIDWIFE

UNITED STATES OF AMERICA
INDIAN TERRITORY
Central DISTRICT

I, Pinie Scott a Midwife on oath state that I attended on Mrs. Allice Holloway wife of Frank Holloway on the 10 day of September , 190 4 , that there was born to her on said date a Female child, that said child is now living, and is said to have been named Ruby Holloway
midwife
Pinie Scott

Subscribed and sworn to before me this, the 20 day of January 190 5

W T Culbertson Notary Public.

WITNESSETH:
Must be two witnesses who are citizens
Sante Ferrante
Isabinda Ferrante

Applications for Enrollment of Choctaw Newborn
Act of 1905 Volume VI

We hereby certify that we are well acquainted with Pinie Scott a Midwife and know her to be reputable and of good standing in the community.

_____   Sante Ferrante

J.W. Culbertson   Frank Holloway

BIRTH AFFIDAVIT.

DEPARTMENT OF THE INTERIOR.
COMMISSION TO THE FIVE CIVILIZED TRIBES.

IN RE APPLICATION FOR ENROLLMENT, as a citizen of the Choctaw Nation, of Ruby Holloway, born on the 10 day of September, 1904

Name of Father: Frank Holloway   a citizen of the Choctaw Nation.
Name of Mother: Alice Holloway   a citizen of the Choctaw Nation.

Postoffice   Savanna, Ind Ter

AFFIDAVIT OF MOTHER.

UNITED STATES OF AMERICA, Indian Territory,
Central DISTRICT.

I, Alice Holloway, on oath state that I am 44 years of age and a citizen by intermarriage, of the Choctaw Nation; that I am the lawful wife of Frank Holloway, who is a citizen, by blood of the Choctaw Nation; that a female child was born to me on 10 day of September, 1904; that said child has been named Ruby Holloway, and was living March 4, 1905.

Alice Holloway

Witnesses To Mark:
My Commission expires
   Mar-17-1909

Subscribed and sworn to before me this 13th day of April, 1905.

Andrew J Turner
Notary Public.

Applications for Enrollment of Choctaw Newborn
Act of 1905   Volume VI

AFFIDAVIT OF ATTENDING PHYSICIAN OR MID-WIFE.

UNITED STATES OF AMERICA, Indian Territory, }
 Central   DISTRICT.

I, Pinnia[sic] Scott, a mid-wife, on oath state that I attended on Mrs. Alice Holloway, wife of Frank Holloway on the 10 day of September, 1904; that there was born to her on said date a female child; that said child was living March 4, 1905, and is said to have been named Ruby Holloway

Pinna Scott

Witnesses To Mark:
{

Subscribed and sworn to before me this 13 day of April, 1905

Andrew J Turner
Notary Public.

7-4550

Muskogee, Indian Territory, March 15, 1905.

Frank Holloway,
 Savanna, Indian Territory.

Dear Sir:

Receipt is hereby acknowledged of the affidavits of Alice Holloway and Piney[sic] Scott to the birth of Ruby Holloway, infant daughter of Frank and Alice Holloway, September 10, 1904, and the same have been filed with our records as an application for the enrollment of said child.

Respectfully,

Chairman.

Applications for Enrollment of Choctaw Newborn
Act of 1905   Volume VI

N.B. 331.
COPY
Muskogee, Indian Territory, April 7, 1904.

Frank Holloway,
    Savanna, Indian Territory.

Dear Sir:

    There is enclosed you herewith for execution application for the enrollment of your infant child, Ruby Holloway, born September 10, 1904.

    The affidavits heretofore filed with the Commission show the child was living January 20, 1905. It is necessary, for the child to be enrolled, that she was living on March 4, 1905. You will please insert the age of the mother in place left blank for that purpose.

    In having these affidavits executed care should be exercised to see that all names are written in full, as they appear in the body of the affidavit, and in the event that either of the persons signing the affidavit are unable to write, signatures by mark must be attested by two witnesses. Each affidavit must be executed before a Notary Public and the notarial seal and signature of the officer must be attached to each separate affidavit.

                  Respectfully,
                  SIGNED
                  T. B. Needles.
LER 7-13   Commissioner in Charge.

Choctaw N.B. 331.

Muskogee, Indian Territory, April 18, 1905.

Frank Holloway,
    Savanna, Indian Territory.

Dear Sir:

    Receipt is hereby acknowledged of the affidavits of Alice Holloway and Pinna Scott to the birth of Ruby Holloway, daughter of Frank and Alice Holloway, September 10, 1904, and the same have been filed with our records in the matter of the enrollment of the above named child.

                  Respectfully,

                  Chairman.

Applications for Enrollment of Choctaw Newborn
Act of 1905 Volume VI

Choc New Born 332
    Zoola May Harkreader
    (Born Dec. 5, 1902)

(The affidavit below typed as written.)

                    Department of the Eter
                    Comission to the five
                    Civatise Tribes, of Muscogee

In the Matter of the Birth of our Infant Girl Baby Born to us on Dec 5-1902
I on oath state that I am the Mother of Zoola May Harkreader
Born on Dec. 5-1902
This Dic 15th 1902

                                Lucy Ann Harkreader

I on My oath state that I am the Father of Zoola May Harkreader
Born on Dec. 5-1902
This Dec 15th 1902

                                SB Harkreader

I on my oath stat that I was the attending phisotion in the Birth of Zoola May Harkreader
Born Dec. 5-1902 to Samuel B and Lucy Ann Harkreader
    This Dec 15th 1902   TT Thornton MD

    I, R.R. Turner a Notary Public in and for Southern District Chickasaw Nation, having duly sworn the parties to the foregoing affidavit, of above date certify that the parties are well to known to me and have this day affixed seal to same this 15th Dec. 1902.

                              R.R. Turner Notary Public.

BIRTH AFFIDAVIT.
                DEPARTMENT OF THE INTERIOR.
    COMMISSION TO THE FIVE CIVILIZED TRIBES.

      IN RE APPLICATION FOR ENROLLMENT, as a citizen of the   Choctaw   Nation, of Zula May Harkreader   , born on the 5th day of December , 1902

Name of Father: Samuel B. Harkreader   a citizen of the Choctaw Nation.
Name of Mother: Lucy Ann Harkreader   a citizen of the Choctaw Nation.

                    Postoffice   Paoli, I.T.

Applications for Enrollment of Choctaw Newborn
Act of 1905 Volume VI

AFFIDAVIT OF MOTHER.

UNITED STATES OF AMERICA, Indian Territory, }
Southern DISTRICT.

I, Lucy Ann Harkreader, on oath state that I am 29 years of age and a citizen by blood, of the Choctaw Nation; that I am the lawful wife of Samuel B Harkreader, who is a citizen, by marriage of the Choctaw Nation; that a female child was born to me on 5th day of December, 1902; that said child has been named Zula May Harkreader, and was living March 4, 1905.

Lucy Ann Harkreader

Witnesses To Mark:
{

Subscribed and sworn to before me this 10th day of April, 1905

JE Williams
Notary Public.

AFFIDAVIT OF ATTENDING PHYSICIAN OR MID-WIFE.

UNITED STATES OF AMERICA, Indian Territory, }
Southern DISTRICT.

I, Stella Florence, a mid-wife, on oath state that I attended on Mrs. Lucy Ann Harkreader, wife of Samuel B Harkreader on the 5th day of December, 1902; that there was born to her on said date a female child; that said child was living March 4, 1905, and is said to have been named Zula May Harkreader

Mary Estella Florence

Witnesses To Mark:
{

Subscribed and sworn to before me this 20th day of April, 1905

Milton M. Bowman
Notary Public.

Applications for Enrollment of Choctaw Newborn
Act of 1905 Volume VI

7-4565.

Muskogee, Indian Territory, December 22, 1902.

Samuel B. Harkreader,
    Paoli, Indian Territory.

Dear Sir:

    Receipt is hereby acknowledged of the application for enrollment as a citizen of the Choctaw Nation of Zoola May Harkreader, infant daughter of S.B. and Lucy M. Harkreader, born December 5, 1902.

    You are advised that the Commission is without authority to enroll this child as a citizen of the Choctaw Nation, it appearing that said child was born December 5, 1902, subsequent to the ratification by the citizens of the Choctaw an Chickasaw Nations on September 25, 1902, of an act of Congress approved July 1, 1902 (32 Stats., 641).

    Section twenty-eight thereof provides as follows:

    "The names of all persons living on the date of the final ratification of this agreement entitled to be enrolled as provided in section 27 hereof shall be placed upon the rolls made by said Commission; and no child born thereafter to a citizen or freedman and no person intermarried thereafter to a citizen shall be entitled to enrollment or to participate in the distribution of the tribal property of the Choctaws and Chickasaws."

    Respectfully,

Acting Chairman.

7-4565

Muskogee, Indian Territory, March 16, 1905.

S. B. Harkreader,
    Paoli, Indian Territory.

Dear Sir:

    Receipt is hereby acknowledged of your letter of March 10, 1905, asking that the application for the enrollment of your child Zula Mary Harkreader be returned to you for the reason that you did not secure the doctor's certificate to the birth of said child.

    In reply to your letter you are advised that the affidavit heretofore forwarded has been filed with our records as an application for the enrollment of your child Zoola May Harkreader, but if you desire to complete the application for the enrollment of this child

Applications for Enrollment of Choctaw Newborn
Act of 1905   Volume VI

there is inclosed herewith another blank form upon which may be forwarded the affidavit of the physician in attendance at the birth of said child.

                            Respectfully,

B.C.   Chairman.

                                                                                      N. B. 332

COPY

Muskogee, Indian Territory, April 6, 1905.

Samuel B. Harkreader,
    Paoli, Indian Territory.

Dear Sir:

    There is inclosed you herewith for execution application for the enrollment of your infant child, Zoola May Harkreader, born December 5, 1902.

    The affidavits heretofore filed with the Commission show the child was living on December 15, 1902. It is necessary, for the child to be enrolled, that she was living on March 4, 1905. You will please insert the mother's age in the place left blank for that purpose.

    In having these affidavits executed care should be exercised to see that all names are written in full, as they appear in the body of the affidavit, and in the event that either of the persons signing the affidavit are unable to write, signatures by mark must be attested by two witnesses. Each affidavit must be executed before a Notary Public and the notarial seal and signature of the officer must be attached to each separate affidavit.

                                            Respectfully,
                                            SIGNED
                                          T. B. Needles.

SEV 4-6.   Commissioner in Charge.

Applications for Enrollment of Choctaw Newborn
Act of 1905   Volume VI

7--N.B. 332.

Muskogee, Indian Territory, May 9, 1905.

Samuel B. Harkreader,
    Paoli, Indian Territory.

Dear Sir:

    Receipt is hereby acknowledged of the affidavits of Lucy Ann Harkreader and Mary Estella Florence to the birth of Zula May Harkreader, daughter of Samuel B. and Lucy Ann Harkreader, December 5, 1902, and the same have been filed with our records in the matter of the enrollment of said child.

Respectfully,

Commissioner in Charge.

Choc New Born 333
    Ina M. Brock
    (Born March 22, 1903)

BIRTH AFFIDAVIT.

DEPARTMENT OF THE INTERIOR.
COMMISSION TO THE FIVE CIVILIZED TRIBES.

IN RE APPLICATION FOR ENROLLMENT, as a citizen of the   Choctaw   Nation, of Ina M. Brock   , born on the 22nd   day of   March   , 1903

Name of Father: Wesley E. Brock   a citizen of the United States Nation.
Name of Mother: Minnie L. Brock   a citizen of the   Choctaw   Nation.

Postoffice   South McAlester, I.T.

AFFIDAVIT OF MOTHER.

UNITED STATES OF AMERICA, Indian Territory,
    Central   DISTRICT.

    I, Minnie L. Brock   , on oath state that I am   27   years of age and a citizen by   blood   , of the   Choctaw   Nation; that I am the lawful wife of   Wesley E.

Applications for Enrollment of Choctaw Newborn
Act of 1905   Volume VI

Brock   , who is a citizen, by .... of the United States   Nation; that a female   child was born to me on   22nd day of   March   , 1903; that said child has been named   Ina M. Brock   , and was living March 4, 1905.

                                        Minnie L. Brock

Witnesses To Mark:
{

    Subscribed and sworn to before me this   17th day of   March   , 1905

                                          Wirt Franklin
                                          Notary Public.

AFFIDAVIT OF ATTENDING PHYSICIAN OR MID-WIFE.

UNITED STATES OF AMERICA, Indian Territory, }
   Central   DISTRICT. }

    I,   J. M. Lester   , a physician   , on oath state that I attended on Mrs. Minnie L. Brock   , wife of   Wesley E. Brock   on the 22nd day of March   , 1903; that there was born to her on said date a   female   child; that said child was living March 4, 1905, and is said to have been named Ina M. Brock

                                          J.M. Lester

Witnesses To Mark:
{

    Subscribed and sworn to before me this   17th day of   March   , 1905

                                          Wirt Franklin
                                          Notary Public.

Applications for Enrollment of Choctaw Newborn
Act of 1905   Volume VI

Choc New Born 334
  (Lotta Hazel)
  (Born July 17, 1904)

BIRTH AFFIDAVIT.

DEPARTMENT OF THE INTERIOR.
COMMISSION TO THE FIVE CIVILIZED TRIBES.

IN RE APPLICATION FOR ENROLLMENT, as a citizen of the   Choctaw   Nation, of Lotta Hazel   , born on the   17   day of   July   , 1904

Name of Father: Seth T Hazel   a citizen of the   Choctaw   Nation.
Name of Mother: Nora Hazel   a citizen of the   Choctaw   Nation.

Postoffice   Lindsay Ind. Ter.

AFFIDAVIT OF MOTHER.

UNITED STATES OF AMERICA, Indian Territory,
  Southern   DISTRICT.

I,   Nora Hazel   , on oath state that I am   26   years of age and a citizen by adoption   , of the   Choctaw   Nation; that I am the lawful wife of   Seth T. Hazel   , who is a citizen, by   Blood   of the   Choctaw   Nation; that a Female   child was born to me on   17   day of   July   , 1904, that said child has been named   Lotta   , and is now living.

                              Nora Hazel
Witnesses To Mark:

Subscribed and sworn to before me this   20   day of   Jan   , 1905.

                              Isaac W. Eagan
                              Notary Public.

AFFIDAVIT OF ATTENDING PHYSICIAN OR MID-WIFE.

UNITED STATES OF AMERICA, Indian Territory,
  Southern   DISTRICT.

I,   S.W. Wilson   , a   Physician   , on oath state that I attended on Mrs.   Nora Hazel   , wife of   Seth T Hazel   on the   17   day of July , 1904; that

Applications for Enrollment of Choctaw Newborn
Act of 1905 Volume VI

there was born to her on said date a   Female   child; that said child is now living and is said to have been named Lotta Hazel

S.W. Wilson M.D.

Witnesses To Mark:
{

Subscribed and sworn to before me this 20 day of Jan , 1905.

Isaac W. Eagan
Notary Public.

BIRTH AFFIDAVIT.

DEPARTMENT OF THE INTERIOR.
COMMISSION TO THE FIVE CIVILIZED TRIBES.

IN RE APPLICATION FOR ENROLLMENT, as a citizen of the   Choctaw   Nation, of Lottie Hazel   , born on the 17th day of July   , 1904

Name of Father: Seth T Hazel   a citizen of the   Choctaw   Nation.
Name of Mother: Nora Hazel   a citizen of the   Intermarried   Nation.

Postoffice   Lindsay I.T.

AFFIDAVIT OF MOTHER.

UNITED STATES OF AMERICA, Indian Territory, }
    Southern   DISTRICT.   }

I, Nora Hazel   , on oath state that I am   26   years of age and a citizen by Inter Marriage   , of the   Choctaw   Nation; that I am the lawful wife of   Seth T Hazel   , who is a citizen, by   blood   of the   Choctaw   Nation; that a Female   child was born to me on   17th day of   July   , 1904; that said child has been named ~~Nora~~   Lottie Hazel   , and was living March 4, 1905.

Norah[sic] Hazel

Witnesses To Mark:
{ W S Thompson
{ R.C. Graham

Subscribed and sworn to before me this 4 day of   April   , 1905

Robt May
Notary Public.

Applications for Enrollment of Choctaw Newborn
Act of 1905   Volume VI

AFFIDAVIT OF ATTENDING PHYSICIAN OR MID-WIFE.

UNITED STATES OF AMERICA, Indian Territory, }
Southern   DISTRICT.

I, S.W. Wilson, a Physician, on oath state that I attended on Mrs. Nora Hazel, wife of Seth T Hazel on the 17th day of July, 1904; that there was born to her on said date a Female child; that said child was living March 4, 1905, and is said to have been named Lottie Hazel

S.W. Wilson

Witnesses To Mark:
{ Geo See
{ Robt. May

Subscribed and sworn to before me this 4" day of   April   , 1905

Robt May
Notary Public.

———

7-4587

Muskogee, Indian Territory, January 26, 1905.

Seth T. Hazel,
    Lindsay, Indian Territory.

Dear Sir:

Receipt is hereby acknowledged of the affidavits of Norah Hazel and S. W. Wilson to the birth of Lotta Hazel, Indian Territory infant daughter of Seth T. and Norah Hazel, Indian Territory July 17, 1904, which it is presumed have been forwarded as an application for the enrollment of said child.

You are advised that under the provisions of the act of Congress approved July 1, 1902, no children born to citizens of the Choctaw and Chickasaw Nations subsequent to September 25, 1902, the date of the ratification of said act, are entitled to enrollment and allotment in the Choctaw and Chickasaw Nations.

Respectfully,

Chairman.

Applications for Enrollment of Choctaw Newborn
Act of 1905 Volume VI

N. B. 334
COPY
Muskogee, Indian Territory, April 7, 1905.

Seth T. Hazel,
    Lindsay, Indian Territory.

Dear Sir:

    There is inclosed you herewith for execution application for the enrollment of your infant child, Lotta Hazel, born July 17, 1904.

    The affidavits heretofore filed with the Commission show the child was living on January 20, 1905. It is necessary, for the child to be enrolled, that she was living on March 4, 1905.

    In having these affidavits executed care should be exercised to see that all names are written in full, as they appear in the body of the affidavit, and in the event that either of the persons signing the affidavit are unable to write, signatures by mark must be attested by two witnesses. Each affidavit must be executed before a Notary Public and the notarial seal and signature of the officer must be attached to each separate affidavit.

                            Respectfully,
                            SIGNED
                            T. B. Needles.
LM 7-31   Commissioner in Charge.

Choc New Born 335
    Hugh Sylvester Taylor
    (Born Feb. 1, 1905)

Applications for Enrollment of Choctaw Newborn
Act of 1905   Volume VI

NEW BORN AFFIDAVIT

No ....

CHOCTAW ENROLLING COMMISSION

IN THE MATTER OF THE APPLICATION FOR ENROLLMENT as a citizen of the Choctaw Nation, of   Hugh Sylvester Taylor   born on the 1 day of February   190 5

Name of father   John W. Taylor   a citizen of   White   Nation, final enrollment No. ——
Name of mother   Ada Taylor nee Walker   a citizen of   Choctaw   Nation, final enrollment No.   12694

Indianola I.T.   Postoffice.

AFFIDAVIT OF MOTHER

UNITED STATES OF AMERICA
INDIAN TERRITORY
DISTRICT   Central

I   Ada Taylor, nee Walker   , on oath state that I am   20   years of age and a citizen by   blood   of the   Choctaw   Nation, and as such have been placed upon the final roll of the   Choctaw   Nation, by the Honorable Secretary of the Interior my final enrollment number being   12694   ; that I am the lawful wife of   John W. Taylor   , who is a citizen of the   Choctaw   Nation, and as such has been placed upon the final roll of said Nation by the Honorable Secretary of the Interior, his final enrollment number being   ——and that a   male   child was born to me on the   1 day of February 190 5; that said child has been named   Hugh Sylvester Taylor   , and is now living.

WITNESSETH: Ada Taylor
Must be two witnesses   Sarah A Harlow
who are citizens   TH Williams

Subscribed and sworn to before me this, the   16   day of   March   , 190 5

James Bower
Notary Public.

My Commission Expires:
Sept 23 1907

Applications for Enrollment of Choctaw Newborn
Act of 1905 Volume VI

Affidavit of Attending Physician or Midwife

UNITED STATES OF AMERICA, }
INDIAN TERRITORY, }
Central DISTRICT }

I, P.S. Johnston a Practicing Physician on oath state that I attended on Mrs. Ada Taylor wife of John W Taylor on the 1 day of February, 190 5, that there was born to her on said date a male child, that said child is now living, and is said to have been named Hugh Sylvester Taylor

P.S. Johnston M. D.

Subscribed and sworn to before me this the 16 day of March 1905

James Bower
Notary Public.

WITNESSETH:
Must be two witnesses who are citizens and know the child. { Sarah A Harlow
T H Williams

We hereby certify that we are well acquainted with P.S. Johnston a Practicing Physician and know him to be reputable and of good standing in the community.

Must be two citizen witnesses. { Sarah A Harlow
T.H. Williams

BIRTH AFFIDAVIT.

DEPARTMENT OF THE INTERIOR.
COMMISSION TO THE FIVE CIVILIZED TRIBES.

IN RE APPLICATION FOR ENROLLMENT, as a citizen of the Choctaw Nation, of Hugh Sylvester Taylor, born on the 1st day of Feby, 1905

Name of Father: John W. Taylor a citizen of the United States Nation.
Name of Mother: Ada Taylor formerly Walker a citizen of the Choctaw Nation.

Postoffice Indianola I.T.

Applications for Enrollment of Choctaw Newborn
Act of 1905   Volume VI

AFFIDAVIT OF MOTHER.

UNITED STATES OF AMERICA, Indian Territory, }
Western   DISTRICT.

    I, Ada Taylor, on oath state that I am 20 years of age and a citizen by Blood, of the Choctaw Nation; that I am the lawful wife of John W. Taylor, who is a citizen, by intermarriage of the Choctaw Nation; that a male child was born to me on 1st day of Feby, 1905; that said child has been named Hugh Sylvester Taylor, and was living March 4, 1905.

                                        Ada Taylor

Witnesses To Mark:
  { G.W. Choate
    L.H. Perkins

    Subscribed and sworn to before me this 25 day of March, 1905

                              T J Rice
                My Commission Expires   Notary Public.
                    Aug. 1st. 1906

AFFIDAVIT OF ATTENDING PHYSICIAN OR MID-WIFE.

UNITED STATES OF AMERICA, Indian Territory, }
.... DISTRICT.

    I, Dr P.S. Johnston, a physician, on oath state that I attended on Mrs. Ada Taylor, wife of John W Taylor on the 1st day of Feby, 1905; that there was born to her on said date a male child; that said child was living March 4, 1905, and is said to have been named Hugh Sylvester Taylor

                                      P.S. Johnston M.D.

Witnesses To Mark:
  { G.W. Choate
    L.H. Perkins

    Subscribed and sworn to before me this 25 day of March, 1905

                              T J Rice
                My Commission Expires   Notary Public.
                    Aug. 1st. 1906

Applications for Enrollment of Choctaw Newborn
Act of 1905 Volume VI

7-4588

Muskogee, Indian Territory, March 31, 1905.

Ada Taylor,
    Indianola, Indian Territory.

Dear Madam:

    Receipt is hereby acknowledged of your letter of March 25, 1905, enclosing the affidavits of Ada Taylor and P. S. Johnston to the birth of Hugh Sylvester Taylor, son of John W. and Ada Taylor, February 1, 1905, and the same have been filed with our records as an application for the enrollment of said child.

        Respectfully,

        Chairman.

<u>Choc New Born 336</u>
    Ada Dickerson
    (Born Aug. 12, 1904)

BIRTH AFFIDAVIT.

DEPARTMENT OF THE INTERIOR,
COMMISSION TO THE FIVE CIVILIZED TRIBES.

IN RE Application for Enrollment, as a citizen of the   Choctaw   Nation, of Ada , born on the 12 day of August , 1904

Name of Father: Jody L Dickerson   a citizen of the United States Nation.
Name of Mother: Rosa E Dickerson   a citizen of the Choctaw Nation.

        Post-Office: Indianola I.T.

Applications for Enrollment of Choctaw Newborn
Act of 1905 Volume VI

AFFIDAVIT OF MOTHER.

UNITED STATES OF AMERICA,
   INDIAN TERRITORY.
   Western District.

I, Rosa E. Dickerson , on oath state that I am 22 years of age and a citizen by Blood , of the Choctaw Nation; that I am the lawful wife of Jody L. Dickerson , who is a citizen, ~~by~~ of the U.S. of ~~the~~ America Nation; that a Girl child was born to me on the 12 day of August , 190 4, that said child has been named Ada Dickerson , and is now living.

                        Rosa E Dickerson

WITNESSES TO MARK:

Subscribed and sworn to before me this 20 day of December , 1904

                        T J Rice
                           NOTARY PUBLIC.

AFFIDAVIT OF ATTENDING PHYSICIAN OR MID-WIFE.

UNITED STATES OF AMERICA,
   INDIAN TERRITORY.
   Western District.

I, P. S. Johnston , a Physician , on oath state that I attended on Mrs. Rosa Dickerson , wife of Jody L Dickerson on the 12 day of August , 1904 ; that there was born to her on said date a Girl child; that said child is now living and is said to have been named Ada Dickerson

                        P.S. Johnston M.D.

WITNESSES TO MARK:

Subscribed and sworn to before me this 20 day of December , 1904

                        T J Rice
                           NOTARY PUBLIC.

Applications for Enrollment of Choctaw Newborn
Act of 1905 Volume VI

BIRTH AFFIDAVIT.

DEPARTMENT OF THE INTERIOR.
COMMISSION TO THE FIVE CIVILIZED TRIBES.

IN RE APPLICATION FOR ENROLLMENT, as a citizen of the Choctaw Nation, of Ada Dickerson, born on the 12th day of August, 1904

Name of Father: Joda[sic] L. Dickerson   a citizen of the United States Nation.
Name of Mother: Rosa E. Dickerson   a citizen of the Choctaw Nation.

Postoffice   Indianola, I.T.

AFFIDAVIT OF MOTHER.

UNITED STATES OF AMERICA, Indian Territory,
Central DISTRICT.

I, Rosa E. Dickerson, on oath state that I am 22 years of age and a citizen by blood, of the Choctaw Nation; that I am the lawful wife of Joda L. Dickerson, who is a citizen, by............... of the United States ~~Nation~~; that a female child was born to me on 12th day of August, 1904; that said child has been named Ada Dickerson, and was living March 4, 1905.

Rosa E Dickerson

Witnesses To Mark:
{

Subscribed and sworn to before me this 21st day of March, 1905.

W.H. Angell
Notary Public.

AFFIDAVIT OF ATTENDING PHYSICIAN OR MID-WIFE.

UNITED STATES OF AMERICA, Indian Territory,
.... DISTRICT.

I, P. S. Johnston, a physician, on oath state that I attended on Mrs. Rosa E. Dickerson, wife of Joda L. Dickerson on the 12th day of August, 1904; that there was born to her on said date a Female child; that said child was living March 4, 1905, and is said to have been named Ada Dickerson

P.S. Johnston M.D.

Witnesses To Mark:
{

Applications for Enrollment of Choctaw Newborn
Act of 1905   Volume VI

Subscribed and sworn to before me this   23rd day of   March   , 1905

T.J. Rice
Notary Public.

Choctaw 4588

Muskogee, Indian Territory, December 23, 1904.

Rosa E. Dickerson,
Indianola, Indian Territory.

Dear Madam:

Receipt is hereby acknowledged of your affidavit and the affidavit of P.S. Johnston to the birth, on August 12, 1904, of Ada Dickerson, infant daughter of Jody and Rosa E. Dickerson, which it is presumed were forwarded as an application for enrollment of said child.

You are advised that under the provisions of the act of Congress approved July 1, 1902, no child born to a recognized and enrolled citizen of the Choctaw or Chickasaw Nation subsequent to September 25, 1902, the date of the final ratification of said act by the Choctaw and Chickasaw Nations, is entitled to enrollment and allotment.

Respectfully,

Chairman.

7-4588

Muskogee, Indian Territory, March 29, 1905.

Joda L. Dickerson,
Indianola, Indian Territory.

Dear Sir:

Receipt is hereby acknowledged of the affidavits of Rhoda[sic] E. Dickerson and P. S. Johnston to the birth of Ada Dickerson daughter of Joda L. and Rhoda E. Dickerson, August 12, 1904, and the same have been filed with our records as an application for the enrollment of said child.

Respectfully,

Chairman.

Applications for Enrollment of Choctaw Newborn
Act of 1905   Volume VI

Choc New Born 337
    Annie Jane Dunn
    (Born Sep. 4, 1904)

NEW-BORN AFFIDAVIT.

    Number..........

...Choctaw Enrolling Commission...

IN THE MATTER OF THE APPLICATION FOR ENROLLMENT, as a citizen of the Choctaw Nation, of   Annie Jane Dunn

born on the 4th day of ___September___ 190 4

Name of father William B Dunn	a citizen of	Choctaw
Nation final enrollment No. 438		
Name of mother Josephine Dunn	a citizen of	Choctaw
Nation final enrollment No. 12381		

                                  Postoffice   South McAlester I.T.

AFFIDAVIT OF MOTHER.

UNITED STATES OF AMERICA
INDIAN TERRITORY
    Central   DISTRICT

        I   Josephine Dunn   , on oath state that I am   30   years of age and a citizen by blood   of the   Choctaw   Nation, and as such have been placed upon the final roll of the Choctaw   Nation, by the Honorable Secretary of the Interior my final enrollment number being   12381 ; that I am the lawful wife of   William B Dunn   , who is a citizen of the   Choctaw Nation, and as such has been placed upon the final roll of said Nation by the Honorable Secretary of the Interior, his final enrollment number being   438   and that a   female child was born to me on the 4th day of   September   190 4; that said child has been named   Annie Jane Dunn   , and is now living.

                                                 her
Witnesseth.   Josephine x Dunn
   Must be two } Alfred W. McClure   mark
   Witnesses who
   are Citizens.   Geo F Bolling

Applications for Enrollment of Choctaw Newborn
Act of 1905 Volume VI

Subscribed and sworn to before me this 3rd day of Feb 190 5

T. R. Dean

Notary Public.

My commission expires: Oct 10" 1905

AFFIDAVIT OF ATTENDING PHYSICIAN OR MIDWIFE

UNITED STATES OF AMERICA }
INDIAN TERRITORY }
..........................DISTRICT }

I, H. E. Williams a Physician on oath state that I attended on Mrs. Josephine Dunn wife of William B. Dunn on the 4th day of September , 190 4, that there was born to her on said date a Female child, that said child is now living, and is said to have been named Annie Jane Dunn

H.E. Williams M.D.

Subscribed and sworn to before me this, the 2^d day of Feby 190 5

BF Jobs

Notary Public.

WITNESSETH:
Must be two witnesses who are citizens and know the child. { Geo F Bolling
J.J. Brown

We hereby certify that we are well acquainted with H. E. Williams a Physician and know him to be reputable and of good standing in the community.

{ Geo F Bolling
J. J. Brown

BIRTH AFFIDAVIT.

DEPARTMENT OF THE INTERIOR.
COMMISSION TO THE FIVE CIVILIZED TRIBES.

IN RE APPLICATION FOR ENROLLMENT, as a citizen of the Choctaw Nation, of Annie Jane Dunn , born on the 4th day of Sept , 1904

Name of Father: William B. Dunn a citizen of the Choctaw Nation.
Name of Mother: Josephine Dunn a citizen of the Choctaw Nation.

Applications for Enrollment of Choctaw Newborn
Act of 1905   Volume VI

Postoffice   South McAlester, I.T.

AFFIDAVIT OF MOTHER.

UNITED STATES OF AMERICA, Indian Territory, }
Central   DISTRICT.

I, Josephine Dunn, on oath state that I am 30 years of age and a citizen by blood, of the Choctaw Nation; that I am the lawful wife of William B Dunn, who is a citizen, by marriage of the Choctaw Nation; that a female child was born to me on 4th day of September, 1904; that said child has been named Annie Jane Dunn, and was living March 4, 1905.

                        her
                Josephine x Dunn

Witnesses To Mark: mark
{ W H Stanton
  Columbus Campelube

Subscribed and sworn to before me this 16th day of March, 1905

                Wirt Franklin
                Notary Public.

AFFIDAVIT OF ATTENDING PHYSICIAN OR MID-WIFE.

UNITED STATES OF AMERICA, Indian Territory, }
Central   DISTRICT.

I, H.E. Williams, a physician, on oath state that I attended on Mrs. Josephine Dunn, wife of William B Dunn on the 4th day of September, 1904; that there was born to her on said date a female child; that said child was living March 4, 1905, and is said to have been named Annie Jane Dunn

                H.E. Williams

Witnesses To Mark:
{

Subscribed and sworn to before me this 16th day of March, 1905

                Wirt Franklin
                Notary Public.

Applications for Enrollment of Choctaw Newborn
Act of 1905 Volume VI

Choc New Born 338
Laura Lucille Mozley
(Born June 24, 1904)

DEPARTMENT OF THE INTERIOR,
Commission to the Five Civilized Tribes.
---o-o---

IN RE APPLICATION FOR ENROLLMENT, as a citizen of the Choctaw Nation of Laura Lucile[sic] Mozley , born on the 24th day of June , 190 4

Name of Father: Benjamin F Mozley , a citizen of the Choctaw Nation.

Name of Mother: Laura E Mozley , a citizen of the Choctaw Nation. by Blood.

Postoffice: Noble, O.T.

---o-oo---
AFFIDAVIT OF MOTHER.
UNITED STATES OF AMERICA, |
INDIAN TERRITORY, | SS.
SOUTHERN DISTRICT. |

I, Laura E Mozley on oath state that I am 33 years of age and a citizen by Blood of the Choctaw Nation; and the lawful wife of Benjamin F. Mozley , who is a citizen by Intermarriage of the Choctaw Nation; that a Female child was born to me on the 24th day of June 190 4; that said child has been named Laura Lucile Mozley and is now living.

        Signature   Laura E Mozley
Witnesses to ~~Mark~~.
B Pybar
G W Sparks

Subscribed and sworn to before me this this 11th day of March , 190 5

        O.H. Loomis
              Notary Public.
---o-o---

Applications for Enrollment of Choctaw Newborn
Act of 1905 Volume VI

AFFIDAVIT OF ATTENDING PHYSICIAN, OR MID-WIFE.

UNITED STATES OF AMERICA, |
INDIAN TERRITORY, | SS.
SOUTHERN DISTRICT. |

I, Dr. J. S. Childs, a Physician on oath state that I attended on Mrs. Laura E Mozley, wife of Benjamin F Mosley[sic] on the 24th day of June, 1904; that there was born to her on said date a Female child; that said child is now living and is said to have been named Laura Lucile Mozley

    Signature   J.S. Childs, MD
Witnesses to ~~Mark~~.
B Pybar
G W Sparks

Subscribed and sworn to before me this this 11th day of March, 1905

                     O.H. Loomis
                     Notary Public.

BIRTH AFFIDAVIT.

DEPARTMENT OF THE INTERIOR,
COMMISSION TO THE FIVE CIVILIZED TRIBES.

IN RE Application for Enrollment, as a citizen of the Choctaw Nation, of Laura Lucille Mozley, born on the 24th day of June, 1904

Name of Father: Benjamin F Mozley   a citizen of the Choctaw Nation.
Name of Mother: Laura E. Mozley   a citizen of the Choctaw Nation.

                 Post-Office: Maysville, I.T.

AFFIDAVIT OF MOTHER.

UNITED STATES OF AMERICA,
INDIAN TERRITORY.
Southern   District.

I, Laura E. Mozley, on oath state that I am 32 years of age and a citizen by blood, of the Choctaw Nation; that I am the lawful wife of Benjamin F. Mozley, who is a citizen, by intermarriage of the Choctaw Nation; that a female child was born to me on 24th day of June, 1904, that said child has been named Laura Lucille Mozley, and is now living.

Applications for Enrollment of Choctaw Newborn
Act of 1905   Volume VI

Laura E Mozley

WITNESSES TO MARK:
{

Subscribed and sworn to before me this 22nd day of December , 1904

My commission
Expires Nov 21st 1906

F C Coon
NOTARY PUBLIC.

AFFIDAVIT OF ATTENDING PHYSICIAN OR MID-WIFE.

UNITED STATES OF AMERICA, ⎫
   INDIAN TERRITORY. ⎬
Southern   District. ⎭

I, J. S. Childs , a physician & surgeon , on oath state that I attended on Mrs. Laura E Mozley , wife of Benjamin F. Mozley on the 24th day of June, 190 4; that there was born to her on said date a female child; that said child is now living and is said to have been named Laura Lucille Mozley

JS Childs MD

WITNESSES TO MARK:
{

Subscribed and sworn to before me this 20th day of December , 1904.

Geo W Miller
NOTARY PUBLIC.

BIRTH AFFIDAVIT.

Mozley

DEPARTMENT OF THE INTERIOR.
COMMISSION TO THE FIVE CIVILIZED TRIBES.

IN RE APPLICATION FOR ENROLLMENT, as a citizen of the Choctaw Nation, of Laura Lucille , born on the 24th day of June , 1904

Name of Father: Benjamin F Mozley   a citizen of the Choctaw Nation.
  by intermarriage
Name of Mother: Laura E Mozley   a citizen of the Choctaw Nation.
  by blood

Postoffice Noble O.T.

Applications for Enrollment of Choctaw Newborn
Act of 1905   Volume VI

AFFIDAVIT OF MOTHER.

UNITED STATES OF AMERICA, Indian Territory, }
Southern   DISTRICT.

I, Laura E Mozley, on oath state that I am 33 years of age and a citizen by blood, of the Choctaw Nation; that I am the lawful wife of Benjamin F Mozley, who is a citizen, by intermarriage of the Choctaw Nation; that a female child was born to me on 24th day of June, 1904; that said child has been named Laura Lucille Mozley, and was living March 4, 1905.

Laura E Mozley

Witnesses To Mark:
{

Subscribed and sworn to before me this 21st day of April, 1905

Geo W Miller
Notary Public.

AFFIDAVIT OF ATTENDING PHYSICIAN OR MID-WIFE.

UNITED STATES OF AMERICA, Indian Territory, }
Southern   DISTRICT.

I, J.S. Childs, a physician, on oath state that I attended on Mrs. Laura E Mozley, wife of Benjamin F Mozley on the 24th day of June, 1904; that there was born to her on said date a female child; that said child was living March 4, 1905, and is said to have been named Laura Lucille Mozley

J.S. Childs MD

Witnesses To Mark:
{

Subscribed and sworn to before me this 21st day of April, 1905

Geo W Miller
Notary Public.

Applications for Enrollment of Choctaw Newborn
Act of 1905   Volume VI

Choctaw 4460

Muskogee, Indian Territory, December 28, 1904.

Benjamin F. Mozley,
    Maysville, Indian Territory.

Dear Sir:

    Receipt is hereby acknowledged of the affidavits of Laura E. Mozley and J. S. Childs, relative to the birth of Laura Lucille Mozley, infant daughter of Benjamin F. and Laura E. Mozley, June 24, 1904, which it is presumed, have been forwarded as an application for enrollment of the above named child.

    You are advised that under the provisions of the act of Congress approved July 1, 1902, no child born to a citizen of the Choctaw or Chickasaw Nation subsequent to September 25, 1902, the date of the ratification of said act by the Choctaw and Chickasaw Nations, is entitled to enrollment and allotment.

Respectfully,

Chairman.

$W^m O.B.$

COMMISSIONERS:
TAMS BIXBY,
THOMAS B. NEEDLES,
C.R. BRECKINBRIDGE.

DEPARTMENT OF THE INTERIOR,
COMMISSIONER TO THE FIVE CIVILIZED TRIBES.

REFER IN REPLY TO THE FOLLOWING:

7-4460

WM. O. BEALL
Secretary

ADDRESS ONLY THE
COMMISSION TO THE FIVE CIVILIZED TRIBES.

Muskogee, Indian Territory, March 16, 1905.

Benjamin F. Mozely[sic],
    Norman, Indian Territory.

Dear Sir:

    Receipt is hereby acknowledged of your letter of March 11, 1905, enclosing the affidavits of Laura E. Mozely and J. H. Childs to the birth of Laura Lucille Mozely, infant daughter of Benjamin F. and Laura E. Mozely and the same have been filed with our records as an application for the enrollment of said child.

Respectfully,
Tams Bixby
Chairman.

Applications for Enrollment of Choctaw Newborn
Act of 1905   Volume VI

Choctaw N.B. 338.

Muskogee, Indian Territory, May 1, 1905.

B. F. Mozley,
  Noble, Indian Territory.

Dear Sir:

Receipt is hereby acknowledged of your letter of April 25, stating that you forwarded an application for the enrollment of Lucile Mozley as a citizen by blood of the Choctaw Nation, and you desire to know if the same has been received.

In reply to your letter you are advised that the affidavits heretofore forwarded to the birth of Laura Lucile Mozley have been filed with our records as an application for the enrollment of said child.

Respectfully,

Chairman.

Choc New Born 339
  Sam Randolph Henderson
  (Born March 25, 1903)

BIRTH AFFIDAVIT.

DEPARTMENT OF THE INTERIOR.
COMMISSION TO THE FIVE CIVILIZED TRIBES.

IN RE APPLICATION FOR ENROLLMENT, as a citizen of the   Choctaw   Nation, of Sam Randolph Henderson   , born on the   25th   day of   March   , 1903

Name of Father: Roy Henderson   a citizen of the   Choctaw   Nation.
                                       By Intermarriage
Name of Mother: Lula Henderson   a citizen of the   Choctaw   Nation.

Postoffice   Story I.T.

Applications for Enrollment of Choctaw Newborn
Act of 1905   Volume VI

AFFIDAVIT OF MOTHER.

UNITED STATES OF AMERICA, Indian Territory, ⎱
  Southern Judicial   DISTRICT.   ⎰

I, Lula Henderson , on oath state that I am 30 years of age and a citizen by Intermarriage , of the Choctaw Nation; that I am the lawful wife of Roy Henderson , who is a citizen, by Blood of the Choctaw Nation; that a male child was born to me on 25th day of March , 1903, that said child has been named Sam Randolph Henderson , and is now living.

                                      Lula Henderson
Witnesses To Mark:
  {

Subscribed and sworn to before me this 7th day of March , 1905.

My commission expires   P.E. High
Jan 19-1908   Notary Public. So Dist.

AFFIDAVIT OF ATTENDING PHYSICIAN OR MID-WIFE.

UNITED STATES OF AMERICA, Indian Territory, ⎱
  Southern   DISTRICT.   ⎰

I, GS Barger , a Physician , on oath state that I attended on Mrs. Lula Henderson , wife of Roy Henderson on the 25 day of March , 1903; that there was born to her on said date a male child; that said child is now living and is said to have been named Sam Randolph Henderson

                                      G.S. Barger M.D.
Witnesses To Mark:
  {

Subscribed and sworn to before me this 8th day of March , 1905.

My Term expires July 22-1907   *(Name Illegible)*
                                      Notary Public.

Applications for Enrollment of Choctaw Newborn
Act of 1905 Volume VI

7-4468

Muskogee, Indian Territory, March 20, 1905.

Roy Henderson,
    Story, Indian Territory.

Dear Sir:

    Receipt is hereby acknowledged of your letter of March 14, 1905, enclosing the affidavits of Lula Henderson and H. S. Barger, M. D., to the birth of Sam Randolph Henderson, son of Roy and Lula Henderson, March 25, 1903, and the same have been filed with our records as an application for the enrollment of said child.

    Respectfully,

    Chairman.

---

7 NB 339

Muskogee, Indian Territory, April 24, 1905.

Roy Henderson,
    Story, Indian Territory.

Dear Sir:

    Receipt is hereby acknowledged of your letter of April 14, 1905, referring to the affidavits heretofore forwarded in the matter of the enrollment of Sam Randolph Henderson, and asking when you will be permitted to file for this child.

    In reply to your letter you are informed that the affidavits forwarded by you to the birth of your son, Sam Randolph Henderson, have been filed with our records as an application for the enrollment of said child, but no selection of allotment can be made for children for whom application has been made under the provisions of the act of Congress approved March 3, 1905, until their enrollment has been approved by the Secretary of the Interior.

    In the event that further evidence be needed to enable the Commission to determine the right of Sam Randolph Henderson to enrollment as a citizen of the Choctaw Nation you will be duly notified.

    Respectfully,

    Chairman.

Applications for Enrollment of Choctaw Newborn
Act of 1905   Volume VI

7-NB-339

Muskogee, Indian Territory, July 18, 1905.

Roy Henderson,
    Story, Indian Territory.

Dear Sir:

Receipt is hereby acknowledged of your letter of July 8, 1905, asking if your child Sam Randolph Henderson appears upon the approved rolls.

In reply to your letter you are advised that the name of your child Sam Randolph Henderson has been placed upon a schedule of citizens by blood of the Choctaw Nation and you will be advised when his enrollment is approved by the Secretary of the Interior.

Respectfully,

Commissioner.

Choc New Born 340
    Henry Jones
    (Born Oct. 11, 1902)

BIRTH AFFIDAVIT.

Department of the Interior,
COMMISSION TO THE FIVE CIVILIZED TRIBES.

IN RE APPLICATION FOR ENROLLMENT, as a citizen of the Choctaw Nation, of Henry Jones, born on the 11 day of October, 1902

Name of Father: T W Jones   a citizen of the U.S.   Nation.
Name of Mother: Louisa Jones   a citizen of the Choctaw Nation.

Post-Office: Owl

Applications for Enrollment of Choctaw Newborn
Act of 1905   Volume VI

AFFIDAVIT OF MOTHER.

UNITED STATES OF AMERICA,
    INDIAN TERRITORY,
Central   District.

    I, Louisa Jones, on oath state that I am 36 years of age and a citizen by blood, of the Choctaw Nation; that I am the lawful wife of T.W. Jones, who is a citizen, by blood of the U.S. Nation; that a male child was born to me on 11 day of October, 190 2, that said child has been named Henry Jones, and is now living.

                                                    her
                                          Louisa x Jones
WITNESSES TO MARK: mark
   { RM Wilson
     W^m C Bunn

    Subscribed and sworn to before me this 21 *day of* November, *190* 2

                                     DN Linebaugh
                                          Notary Public.

AFFIDAVIT OF ATTENDING PHYSICIAN OR MID-WIFE.

UNITED STATES OF AMERICA,
    INDIAN TERRITORY,
Central   District.

    I, T.W. Jones, a husband of Louisa Jones, on oath state that I attended on Mrs. Louisa Jones, wife of T.W. Jones on the 11 day of October, 190 2; that there was born to her on said date a male child; that said child is now living and is said to have been named Henry Jones no midwife or physician being present

                                          T.W. Jones
WITNESSES TO MARK:

   {

    Subscribed and sworn to before me this 21 *day of* November, *190* 2

                                     DN Linebaugh
                                          Notary Public.

Applications for Enrollment of Choctaw Newborn
Act of 1905   Volume VI

NEW-BORN AFFIDAVIT.

Number..................

...Choctaw Enrolling Commission...

IN THE MATTER OF THE APPLICATION FOR ENROLLMENT, as a citizen of the Choctaw Nation, of Henry Jones

born on the 11 day of __Oct__ 190 2

Name of father   T.W. Jones   a citizen of   Choctaw
Nation final enrollment No. ....
Name of mother   Louisa Jones   a citizen of   Choctaw
Nation final enrollment No. 12412

Postoffice   Owl I.T.

AFFIDAVIT OF MOTHER.

UNITED STATES OF AMERICA
INDIAN TERRITORY
Central   DISTRICT

I   Louisa Jones   , on oath state that I am 35 years of age and a citizen by Blood of the Choctaw Nation, and as such have been placed upon the final roll of the Choctaw Nation, by the Honorable Secretary of the Interior my final enrollment number being 12412 ; that I am the lawful wife of T.W. Jones , who is a citizen of the White Nation, and as such has been placed upon the final roll of said Nation by the Honorable Secretary of the Interior, his final enrollment number being .... and that a Male child was born to me on the 11 day of Oct 190 2; that said child has been named Henry Jones , and is now living.

Louisa x Jones
mark

Witnesseth.

Must be two Witnesses who are Citizens.   Elias Harris
Albert *(Illegible)*

Subscribed and sworn to before me this   27   day of   Jan   190 5

John H Cross
Notary Public.

My commission expires:
Sept 24 1908

Applications for Enrollment of Choctaw Newborn
Act of 1905   Volume VI

AFFIDAVIT OF ATTENDING PHYSICIAN OR MIDWIFE

UNITED STATES OF AMERICA
INDIAN TERRITORY
Central   DISTRICT

I,   N. L. Linker   a   midwife on oath state that I attended on Mrs.   Louisa Jones   wife of   T.W. Jones on the   22   day of   Oct   , 190 2, that there was born to her on said date a   male   child, that said child is now living, and is said to have been named   Henry Jones

                                                        her
                                         N. L. x Linker   M.D.

Subscribed and sworn to before me this, the   mark   4   day of Feb   190 5

WITNESSETH: John H Cross   Notary Public.

Must be two witnesses who are citizens { A. L. McCarter

   May Acker

We hereby certify that we are well acquainted with   N. L. Linker   a   Midwife   and know   her   to be reputable and of good standing in the community.

   Lyman Frazier   L. D. Ray

   A. L. McCarter   Maggie Cross

BIRTH AFFIDAVIT.

DEPARTMENT OF THE INTERIOR.
COMMISSION TO THE FIVE CIVILIZED TRIBES.

IN RE APPLICATION FOR ENROLLMENT, as a citizen of the   Choctaw   Nation, of   Henry Jones   , born on the   11   day of   Oct   , 1902

Name of Father: T.W. Jones   a citizen of the   U.S.   Nation.
Name of Mother: Louisa Jones   a citizen of the   Choctaw   Nation.

                            Postoffice   Owl I.T.

Applications for Enrollment of Choctaw Newborn
Act of 1905   Volume VI

AFFIDAVIT OF MOTHER.

UNITED STATES OF AMERICA, Indian Territory, }
   Central   DISTRICT. }

    I, Louisa Jones, on oath state that I am 35 years of age and a citizen by Blood, of the Choctaw Nation; that I am the lawful wife of T.W. Jones, who is a citizen, by of U. S. of the .... Nation; that a Boy child was born to me on 11 day of Oct., 1902; that said child has been named Henry Jones, and was living March 4, 1905.

                                                  her
                                       Louisa x Jones
Witnesses To Mark: mark
{ J G Payte
  S.J. Ethridge

    Subscribed and sworn to before me this 21 day of March, 1905

                                       John H Cross
                                       Notary Public.

AFFIDAVIT OF ATTENDING PHYSICIAN OR MID-WIFE.

UNITED STATES OF AMERICA, Indian Territory, }
   Central   DISTRICT. }

    I, N. L. Linker, a Midwife, on oath state that I attended on Mrs. Louisa Jones, wife of T. W. Jones on the 11 day of Oct, 1902; that there was born to her on said date a male child; that said child was living March 4, 1905, and is said to have been named Henry Jones

                                                her
                                       N. L. x Linker
Witnesses To Mark: mark
{ M O Cross
  J G Payte

    Subscribed and sworn to before me this 21 day of March, 1905

                                       John H Cross
                                       Notary Public.

Applications for Enrollment of Choctaw Newborn
Act of 1905 Volume VI

COPY

Muskogee, Indian Territory, March 29, 1905.

T. W. Jones,
    Owl, Indian Territory.

Dear Sir:

Receipt is hereby acknowledged of the affidavits of Louisa Jones and N. L. Linker to the birth of Henry Jones, son of T. W. and Louisa Jones, October 11, 1902.

It appears from the affidavit of the mother that she is a citizen by blood of the Choctaw Nation and for the purpose of identifying her upon our records you are requested to state the manes of her parents, when, where and under what name application was made for her enrollment and such other information as will enable the Commission to identify her upon its records the affidavits above referred to will then receive further consideration.

Respectfully,
SIGNED
Tams Bixby
Chairman.

7-4470

COPY

Muskogee, Indian Territory, April 7, 1905.

T. W. Jones,
    Owl, Indian Territory.

Dear Sir:

Receipt is hereby acknowledged of your letter of April 1, 1905, in which you refer to the application of Henry Jones and state that his mother Louisa Jones is the daughter of Noel and Mary Jones.

In reply to your letter you are informed that this information has enabled the Commission to identify Louisa Jones as an enrolled citizen of the Choctaw Nation and the affidavit heretofore forwarded to the birth of this child October 11, 1902 has been filed with our records as an application for his enrollment.

Respectfully,
SIGNED
T. B. Needles.
Commissioner in Charge.

Applications for Enrollment of Choctaw Newborn
Act of 1905   Volume VI

Choc New Born 341
    Leroy Tiner
    (Born July 24, 1903)

BIRTH AFFIDAVIT.

DEPARTMENT OF THE INTERIOR,
COMMISSION TO THE FIVE CIVILIZED TRIBES.

IN RE *Application for Enrollment,* as a citizen of the   Choctaw   Nation, of   Leroy Tiner , born on the   24   day of   July   , 1903

Name of Father: N.T. Tiner   a citizen of the   Choctaw   Nation.
Name of Mother: Dora Tiner   a citizen of the   Choctaw   Nation.

                 Post-Office: Pine I.T.

AFFIDAVIT OF MOTHER.

UNITED STATES OF AMERICA,
    INDIAN TERRITORY.
  Centril[sic]   District.

    I,   Dora Tiner   , on oath state that I am   23   years of age and a citizen by marrige[sic] , of the   Choctaw   Nation; that I am the lawful wife of   N.T. Tiner   , who is a citizen, by   blood   of the   Choctaw   Nation; that a   male   child was born to me on   24   day of   July   , 1903 , that said child has been named   Leroy Tiner   , and is now living.

WITNESSES TO MARK:
    { S E Carriger
      Ollie Hanna

       Subscribed and sworn to before me this   15"   *day of*   Sept   , *1903*

                             SD Stephens
                                NOTARY PUBLIC.
                          Centril[sic] district

Applications for Enrollment of Choctaw Newborn
Act of 1905 Volume VI

AFFIDAVIT OF ATTENDING PHYSICIAN OR MID-WIFE.

UNITED STATES OF AMERICA,
INDIAN TERRITORY.
Centril District.

I, Mrs M J George, a midwife, on oath state that I attended on Mrs. Dora Tiner, wife of N T Tiner on the 24 day of July, 1903; that there was born to her on said date a male child; that said child is now living and is said to have been named Leroy Tiner

M J George

WITNESSES TO MARK:
 S E Carriger
 Ollie Hanna

Subscribed and sworn to before me this 15" day of Sept, 1903

SD Stephens
NOTARY PUBLIC.
Centril[sic] district

BIRTH AFFIDAVIT.

DEPARTMENT OF THE INTERIOR.
COMMISSION TO THE FIVE CIVILIZED TRIBES.

IN RE APPLICATION FOR ENROLLMENT, as a citizen of the Choctaw Nation, of Leroy Tiner, born on the 24th day of July 1903

Name of Father: *Newton Tiner*   a citizen of the *Choctaw* Nation.
Name of Mother: *Dora Tiner*   a citizen of the *Choctaw* Nation.

Postoffice   Pine Ind Ter.

AFFIDAVIT OF MOTHER.

UNITED STATES OF AMERICA, Indian Territory,
Central DISTRICT.

I, *Dora Tiner*, on oath state that I am 25 years of age and a citizen by *marriage*, of the *Choctaw* Nation; that I am the lawful wife of *Newton Tiner*, who is a citizen, by *blood* of the *Choctaw* Nation; that a *male* child was born to me on 24th day of *July 1903* (*1903*), 1......; that said child has been named *Leroy Tiner*, and was living March 4, 1905.

Applications for Enrollment of Choctaw Newborn
Act of 1905 Volume VI

Dora Tiner

Witnesses To Mark:
{

Subscribed and sworn to before me this *31st* day of March 1905 , 190....

P E Wilhelm
Notary Public.

AFFIDAVIT OF ATTENDING PHYSICIAN OR MID-WIFE.

UNITED STATES OF AMERICA, Indian Territory,
Southern   DISTRICT.

I, Mary George , a Mid-wife , on oath state that I attended on Mrs. Dora Tiner , wife of Newton Tiner on the 24 day of July , 1903; that there was born to her on said date a male child; that said child was living March 4, 1905, and is said to have been named Leroy Tiner

                                             her
                                       Mary x George
Witnesses To Mark: mark
{ SW Frost
{ A L. Elkins

Subscribed and sworn to before me this 10 day of April , 1905

James T Walter
Notary Public.

7-4477.

Muskogee, Indian Territory, September 19, 1903.

N. T. Tiner,
    Pine, Indian Territory.

Dear Sir:

    Receipt is hereby acknowledged of the affidavits of Dora Tiner and M. J. George, relative to the birth of Leroy Tiner, the infant son of N. T. and Dora Tiner, July 24, 1903, which it is presumed have been forwarded as an application for enrollment of the above named child as a citizen by blood of the Choctaw Nation.

    You are informed that under the provisions of the act of Congress approved July 1, 1902 (32 Stat., 642), which was ratified by the citizens of the Choctaw and

Applications for Enrollment of Choctaw Newborn
Act of 1905   Volume VI

Chickasaw Nations September 25, 1902, this Commission is now without authority to receive or consider the original application for enrollment of any person whomsoever, as a citizen of the Choctaw or Chickasaw Nation.

                Respectfully,

                          Chairman.

                              N.B. 341.
                        COPY
Muskogee, Indian Territory, April 8, 1905.

Newton Tiner,
    Pine, Indian Territory.

Dear Sir:

    There is enclosed you herewith for execution application for the enrollment of your infant child, Leroy Tiner, born July 24, 1903.

    The affidavits heretofore filed with the Commission show the child was living on September 15, 1903. It is necessary, for the child to be enrolled, that she[sic] was living on March 4, 1905. You will please insert the age of the mother in the place left blank for that purpose.

    In having these affidavits executed care should be exercised to see that all names are written in full, as they appear in the body of the affidavit, and in the event that either of the persons signing the affidavit are unable to write, signatures by mark must be attested by two witnesses. Each affidavit must be executed before a Notary Public and the notarial seal and signature of the officer must be attached to each separate affidavit.

                          Respectfully,
                          SIGNED
                        T. B. Needles.
LER 8-2   Commissioner in Charge.

Applications for Enrollment of Choctaw Newborn
Act of 1905   Volume VI

7-4477

Muskogee, Indian Territory, April 17, 1905.

Newton Tiner,
    Pine, Indian Territory.

Dear Sir:

    Receipt is hereby acknowledged of the affidavits of Dora Tiner and Mary George to the birth of Leroy Tiner, son of Newton and Dora Tiner, July 24, 1903, and the same have been filed with our records as an application for the enrollment of said child.

Respectfully,

Chairman.

Choc New Born 342
    Ora T. Gorman
    (Born Nov. 1, 1903)

NEW-BORN AFFIDAVIT.

Number................

...Choctaw Enrolling Commission...

IN THE MATTER OF THE APPLICATION FOR ENROLLMENT, as a citizen of the Choctaw Nation, of Ora T Gorman

born on the 1st day of __November__ 190 3

Name of father   Mike Gorman   a citizen of   Not a Citizen
Nation final enrollment No. ....   D.C. Effie Dawson.
Name of mother   Effie Dawson Gorman   a citizen of   Choctaw
Nation final enrollment No.   12438

Postoffice   Savanna

Applications for Enrollment of Choctaw Newborn
Act of 1905   Volume VI

AFFIDAVIT OF MOTHER.

UNITED STATES OF AMERICA
INDIAN TERRITORY
Central   DISTRICT

I   Effie Dawson Gorman   , on oath state that I am 20   years of age and a citizen by   blood   of the   Choctaw   Nation, and as such have been placed upon the final roll of the Choctaw   Nation, by the Honorable Secretary of the Interior my final enrollment number being   12438 ; that I am the lawful wife of   Mike Gorman   , ~~who is a citizen of the~~   married since enrollment of wife   Nation, and as such has been placed upon the final roll of said Nation by the Honorable Secretary of the Interior, his final enrollment number being .... and that a   Female   child was born to me on the   1st day of   November   190 3; that said child has been named   Ora Tranquie Gorman   , and is now living.

Witnesseth.   Effie Dawson Gorman
Must be two Witnesses who are Citizens.   L E Dawson
I W Harper

Subscribed and sworn to before me this   10   day of   Jan   190 5

W.T. Culbertson
Notary Public.

My commission expires:
Sept ? 1907

AFFIDAVIT OF ATTENDING PHYSICIAN OR MIDWIFE

UNITED STATES OF AMERICA
INDIAN TERRITORY
Central   DISTRICT

I,   S.P. Ross   a   Physician on oath state that I attended on Mrs.   Effie D Gorman   wife of   Mike Gorman on the   1st day of   November   , 190 3, that there was born to her on said date a   Female child, that said child is now living, and is said to have been named   Ora T. Gorman

S. P. Ross   M.D.

WITNESSETH:
Must be two witnesses who are citizens and know the child.   L E Dawson
Kate Culbertson

Subscribed and sworn to before me this, the   17th day of   Feby   190 5

W.T. Culbertson   Notary Public.

Applications for Enrollment of Choctaw Newborn
Act of 1905   Volume VI

We hereby certify that we are well acquainted with   Dr S.P. Ross a   Physician   and know   him   to be reputable and of good standing in the community.

{ L E Dawson
{ Kate Culbertson

BIRTH AFFIDAVIT.

DEPARTMENT OF THE INTERIOR,
COMMISSION TO THE FIVE CIVILIZED TRIBES.

In Re Application for Enrollment, as a citizen of the   Choctaw   Nation, of   Ora T. Gorman , born on the 1st day of   November   , 1903

Name of Father: Mike Gorman   a citizen of the Non-Citizen Nation.
Name of Mother: Effie Dawson now Gorman   a citizen of the   Choctaw   Nation.

Post-office   Savanna I.T.

AFFIDAVIT OF MOTHER.

UNITED STATES OF AMERICA, }
INDIAN TERRITORY,
     Central   District.

I, Effie Dawson Gorman , on oath state that I am 20   years of age and a citizen by   blood   , of the   Choctaw   Nation; that I am the lawful wife of Mike Gorman   , who is a citizen, by non-citizen of the .... Nation; that a   Female   child was born to me on 1st day of   Nov   , 1903 , that said child has been named   Ora Tranque   , and is now living.

Effie Dawson Gorman

WITNESSES TO MARK:
{ Katie Culbertson
{ Mrs E Poe Harriss

Subscribed and sworn to before me this 13th day of   March   , 1905.

W.T. Culbertson
NOTARY PUBLIC.

Applications for Enrollment of Choctaw Newborn
Act of 1905   Volume VI

AFFIDAVIT OF ATTENDING PHYSICIAN OR MID-WIFE.

UNITED STATES OF AMERICA,
INDIAN TERRITORY,
Central District.

I, S.P. Ross, a Physician, on oath state that I attended on Mrs. Effie Gorman, wife of Mike Gorman on the 1st day of November, 1903 ; that there was born to her on said date a Female child; that said child is now living and is said to have been named Ora T.

S.P. Ross M.D.

WITNESSES TO MARK:
Katie Culbertson
Mrs E Poe Harriss

Subscribed and sworn to before me this 13th day of March, 1905.

W.T. Culbertson
NOTARY PUBLIC.

7-4482

Muskogee, Indian Territory, March 16, 1905.

Effie Dawson Gorman,
   Savanna, Indian Territory.

Dear Madam:

Receipt is hereby acknowledged of your affidavit and the affidavit of S. P. Ross to the birth of Ora T. Gorman daughter of Mike and Effie Dawson Gorman, November 1, 1903, and the same have been filed with our records as an application for the enrollment of said child.

Respectfully,

Chairman.

Applications for Enrollment of Choctaw Newborn
Act of 1905   Volume VI

Choc New Born 343
    Esta V. Karl
    (Born April 10, 1903)

BIRTH AFFIDAVIT.

DEPARTMENT OF THE INTERIOR.
COMMISSION TO THE FIVE CIVILIZED TRIBES.

IN RE APPLICATION FOR ENROLLMENT, as a citizen of the   Choctaw   Nation, of Esta V. Karl   , born on the   10   day of   April   , 1903

Name of Father: Frank A. Karl   a citizen of the   Choctaw   Nation.
Name of Mother: Viola Karl   a citizen of the   Choctaw   Nation.

         Postoffice   Pocola, I.T.

AFFIDAVIT OF MOTHER.

UNITED STATES OF AMERICA, Indian Territory,
     Central   DISTRICT.

     I,   Viola Karl   , on oath state that I am   25   years of age and a citizen by Blood   , of the   Choctaw   Nation; that I am the lawful wife of   Frank A. Karl   , who is a citizen, by   Intermarriage   of the   Choctaw   Nation; that a   Girl   child was born to me on   10   day of   April   , 1903, that said child has been named Esta V. Karl   , and is now living.

                               Viola Karl

Witnesses To Mark:

     Subscribed and sworn to before me this   12   day of   November   , 1904

                               W.F. Lester
                                   Notary Public.

AFFIDAVIT OF ATTENDING PHYSICIAN OR MID-WIFE.

UNITED STATES OF AMERICA, Indian Territory,
     Central   DISTRICT.

     I,   Mrs N.A. Carney   , a   mid wife   , on oath state that I attended on Mrs.   Viola Karl   , wife of   Frank A. Karl   on the   10   day of   April, 1903; that there was born to her on said date a   Girl   child; that said child is now living and is said to have been named   Esta V. Karl

Applications for Enrollment of Choctaw Newborn
Act of 1905   Volume VI

Mrs N A Carney

Witnesses To Mark:

{

Subscribed and sworn to before me this 12 day of November , 1904

W.F. Lester
Notary Public.

NEW BORN AFFIDAVIT

No ....

CHOCTAW ENROLLING COMMISSION

IN THE MATTER OF THE APPLICATION FOR ENROLLMENT as a citizen of the Choctaw Nation, of   Esta V. Karl   born on the 10 day of April   190 3

Inter M

Name of father   Frank A. Karl   a citizen of   Choctaw   Nation, final enrollment No. 443

Name of mother   Viola Karl   a citizen of   Choctaw   Nation, final enrollment No. 12440

Pocola I.T.   Postoffice.

AFFIDAVIT OF MOTHER

UNITED STATES OF AMERICA
INDIAN TERRITORY
DISTRICT   Central

I   Viola Karl , on oath state that I am 26 years of age and a citizen by Blood of the Choctaw Nation, and as such have been placed upon the final roll of the Choctaw Nation, by the Honorable Secretary of the Interior my final enrollment number being 443[sic] ; that I am the lawful wife of   A. Frank[sic] Karl Inter M , who is a citizen of the Choctaw Nation, and as such has been placed upon the final roll of said Nation by the Honorable Secretary of the Interior, his final enrollment number being 443 and that a female child was born to me on the 10 day of April 190 3; that said child has been named Esta V. Karl , and is now living.

WITNESSETH: Viola Karl

Must be two witnesses { Mary I McClain
who are citizens   Edwin S Gregory

174

Applications for Enrollment of Choctaw Newborn
Act of 1905   Volume VI

Subscribed and sworn to before me this, the   6 day of   March   , 190 5

W.F. Lester
Notary Public.

My Commission Expires:..

Affidavit of Attending Physician or Midwife

UNITED STATES OF AMERICA,
INDIAN TERRITORY,
Central   DISTRICT

I,   Nancy A Carney   a   midwife   A. Frank Karl
on oath state that I attended on Mrs. Viola Karl   wife of   A. Frank Karl
on the 10   day of   April , 190 3, that there was born to her on said date a   female   child, that said child is now living, and is said to have been named   Esta V. Karl

Nancy A Carney   M. D. *Wife*

Subscribed and sworn to before me this the   6   day of   March   1905

W.F. Lester
Notary Public.

WITNESSETH:

Must be two witnesses who are citizens and know the child. { Mary I McClain

Edwin S Gregory

We hereby certify that we are well acquainted with ....
a   midwife   and know   her   to be reputable and of good standing in the community.

Must be two citizen { Mary I McClain
witnesses.   Edwin S Gregory

Applications for Enrollment of Choctaw Newborn
Act of 1905 Volume VI

BIRTH AFFIDAVIT.

DEPARTMENT OF THE INTERIOR.
COMMISSION TO THE FIVE CIVILIZED TRIBES.

IN RE APPLICATION FOR ENROLLMENT, as a citizen of the Choctaw Nation, of Esta V. Karl, born on the 10 day of April, 1903

Name of Father: Frank A. Karl   a citizen of the Choctaw Nation.
Name of Mother: Viola Karl   a citizen of the Choctaw Nation.

Postoffice   Pocola Ind Ter

AFFIDAVIT OF MOTHER.

UNITED STATES OF AMERICA, Indian Territory,
Central DISTRICT.

I, Viola Karl, on oath state that I am 26 years of age and a citizen by Blood, of the Choctaw Nation; that I am the lawful wife of Frank A Karl, who is a citizen, by Inter Marriage of the Choctaw Nation; that a Female child was born to me on 10 day of April, 1903; that said child has been named Esta V. Karl, and was living March 4, 1905.

Viola Karl

Witnesses To Mark:
{

Subscribed and sworn to before me this 4 day of April, 1905

W.F. Lester
Notary Public.

AFFIDAVIT OF ATTENDING PHYSICIAN OR MID-WIFE.

UNITED STATES OF AMERICA, Indian Territory,
Central DISTRICT.

I, Nancy A Carney, a midwife, on oath state that I attended on Mrs. Viola Karl, wife of Frank A Karl on the 10 day of April, 1903; that there was born to her on said date a female child; that said child was living March 4, 1905, and is said to have been named Esta V. Karl

Nancy A Carney

Witnesses To Mark:
{

Applications for Enrollment of Choctaw Newborn
Act of 1905   Volume VI

Subscribed and sworn to before me this 4 day of April , 1905

W.F. Lester
Notary Public.

7-4484

Muskogee, Indian Territory, November 17, 1904.

Frank A. Karl,
Pocola, Indian Territory.

Dear Sir:-

Receipt is hereby acknowledged of the affidavits of Viola Karl and N. A. Carney relative to the birth of your infant daughter Esta V. Karl April 10, 1903, which it is presumed have been forwarded to this office as an application for enrollment of said child as a citizen by blood of the Choctaw Nation.

The Act of Congress approved July 1, 1902, which was ratified by the citizens of the Choctaw and Chickasaw Nations, on September 25, 1902, among other things provides that no child born to a citizen of the Choctaw or Chickasaw Nation subsequent to the date of said ratification shall be entitled to enrollment or to participate in the distribution of the tribal property of the Choctaw and Chickasaws.

Respectfully,

Chairam[sic]

N.B. 343.
COPY
Muskogee, Indian Territory, April 7, 1905.

Frank A. Karl,
Pocola, Indian Territory.

Dear Sir:

There is enclosed you herewith for execution application for the enrollment of your infant child, Esta V. Karl, born April 10, 1903.

The affidavits heretofore filed with the Commission show the child was living on November 12, 1904. It is necessary, for the child to be enrolled, that she was living on March 4, 1905.

Applications for Enrollment of Choctaw Newborn
Act of 1905   Volume VI

In having these affidavits executed care should be exercised to see that all names are written in full, as they appear in the body of the affidavit, and in the event that either of the persons signing the affidavit are unable to write, signatures by mark must be attested by two witnesses. Each affidavit must be executed before a Notary Public and the notarial seal and signature of the officer must be attached to each separate affidavit.

Respectfully,
SIGNED
T. B. Needles.

LER 7-1   Commissioner in Charge.

Choctaw 4484.

Muskogee, Indian Territory, April 18, 1905.

Frank A. Carl[sic],
   Pocola, Indian Territory.

Dear Sir:

Receipt is hereby acknowledged of the affidavits of Viola Karl and Nancy A. Carney to the birth of Esta V. Karl, daughter of Frank A. and Viola Karl, April 10, 1903, and the same have been filed with our records as an application for the enrollment of said child.

Respectfully,

Chairman.

Choc New Born 344
   Arthur Floid Vail
   (Born Oct. 19, 1902)
   Gilbert Vail
   (Born Aug. 17, 1904)

Applications for Enrollment of Choctaw Newborn
Act of 1905 Volume VI

BIRTH AFFIDAVIT.

Department of the Interior,
COMMISSION TO THE FIVE CIVILIZED TRIBES.

IN RE APPLICATION FOR ENROLLMENT, as a citizen of the   Choctaw   Nation, of   Arthur Floyd Vails[sic]   , born on the   19   day of   Oct   , 190 2

Name of Father: John F Vails   a citizen of the   Choctaw   Nation.
Name of Mother: Sophia Vails   a citizen of the   Choctaw   Nation.

Post-Office: Durant, I.T.

AFFIDAVIT OF MOTHER.

UNITED STATES OF AMERICA,
   INDIAN TERRITORY,
   Central   District.

I,   Sophia Vails   , on oath state that I am   35   years of age and a citizen by   Blood   , of the   Choctaw   Nation; that I am the lawful wife of   John F. Vails   , who is a citizen, by   marriage   of the   Choctaw   Nation; that a male   child was born to me on   19 day of   October   , 190 2, that said child has been named   Arthur Floid   , and is now living.

Mrs Sophia Vails

WITNESSES TO MARK:
{

Subscribed and sworn to before me this   7   day of   November   , 190 2

L.D. Horton
Notary Public.

AFFIDAVIT OF ATTENDING PHYSICIAN OR MID-WIFE.

UNITED STATES OF AMERICA,
   INDIAN TERRITORY,
   Central   District.

I,   W.A. Horton   , a physician   , on oath state that I attended on Mrs.   Sophia Vails   , wife of   John F. Vails   on the   19   day of   October   , 190 2; that there was born to her on said date a   Male   child; that said child is now living and is said to have been named   Arthur Floid

W.A. Horton M.D.

Applications for Enrollment of Choctaw Newborn
Act of 1905   Volume VI

WITNESSES TO MARK:
{ (Name Illegible)
  M E Turner

Subscribed and sworn to before me this   7   day of   November   , 190 2

L.D. Horton
Notary Public.

DEPARTMENT OF THE INTERIOR.
COMMISSION TO THE FIVE CIVILIZED TRIBES.

In the matter of the death of   Arthur Floyd Vail   a citizen of the Chocktaw[sic]   Nation, who formerly resided at or near   Pirtle   , Ind. Ter., and died on the   22^d day of   March , 1904

AFFIDAVIT OF RELATIVE.

UNITED STATES OF AMERICA, Indian Territory, }
Central   DISTRICT.

I,   Sophia Vail   , on oath state that I am   28   years of age and a citizen by Blood   , of the   Chocktaw   Nation; that my postoffice address is   Durant   , Ind. Ter.; that I am   the mother   of   Arthur Floyd Vail   who was a citizen, by   Blood   , of the   Chocktaw   Nation and that said   Arthur Floyd Vail   died on the   22^d day of   March   , 1904

Sophia Vail

Witnesses To Mark:
{

Subscribed and sworn to before me this   12th   day of   August   , 1905.

Charles A Phillips
Notary Public.
Central Dist

AFFIDAVIT OF ACQUAINTANCE.

UNITED STATES OF AMERICA, Indian Territory, }
Central   DISTRICT.

I,   Joseph E Nelson   , on oath state that I am   55   years of age, and a citizen by Blood   of the   Chocktaw   Nation; that my postoffice address is   Durant   , Ind. Ter.; that I was personally acquainted with   Arthur Floyd Vail   who was a citizen, by

Applications for Enrollment of Choctaw Newborn
Act of 1905   Volume VI

Blood , of the Chocktaw Nation; and that said Arthur Floyd Vail died on the 22^d day of March , 1904

Joseph E Nelson

Witnesses To Mark:
{

Subscribed and sworn to before me this 12th day of August , 1905.

Charles A Phillips
Notary Public.
Central Dist

NEW-BORN AFFIDAVIT.

Number...........

Choctaw Enrolling Commission.

IN THE MATTER OF THE APPLICATION FOR ENROLLMENT, as a citizen of the Choctaw Nation, of Gilbert Vail

born on the 17th day of August 190 4

Name of father   John Vail   a citizen of ....
Nation final enrollment No ....
Name of mother   Sophia Vail   a citizen of   Choctaw
Nation final enrollment No 14168

Postoffice   Durant I.T.

AFFIDAVIT OF MOTHER.

UNITED STATES OF AMERICA, ⎫
   INDIAN TERRITORY,   ⎬
   Central   DISTRICT   ⎭

I   Sophia Vail   on oath state that I am 38 years of age and a citizen by blood of the Choctaw Nation, and as such have been placed upon the final roll of the Choctaw Nation, by the Honorable Secretary of the Interior my final enrollment number being 14168 ; that I am the lawful wife of John Vail , who is a citizen of the .... Nation, and as such has been placed upon the final roll of said Nation by the Honorable Secretary of the Interior, his final enrollment number being .... and that a male child was born to me on the 17th day of August 190 4; that said child has been named Gilbert Vail , and is now living.

Sophia Vail

Applications for Enrollment of Choctaw Newborn
Act of 1905   Volume VI

WITNESSETH:
Must be two Witnesses who are Citizens.   Cyrus Byington
Jesse Robinson

Subscribed and sworn to before me this   20th   day of   February   190 5

Charles A Phillips
Notary Public.

My commission expires   Feb 8th 1908

AFFIDAVIT OF ATTENDING PHYSICIAN OR MIDWIFE

UNITED STATES OF AMERICA
INDIAN TERRITORY
Central   DISTRICT

I,   W. F. Clifton   a   Physician on oath state that I attended on Mrs.   Sophia Vail   wife of   John Vail   on the   17th day of   August   , 190 4, that there was born to her on said date a   male   child, that said child is now living, and is said to have been named   Gilbert Vail

W.F. Clifton   M.D.

Subscribed and sworn to before me this, the   2 day of   February   190 5

(Name Illegible)
Notary Public.

WITNESSETH:
Must be two witnesses who are citizens and know the child.   Cyrus Byington
Jesse Robinson

We hereby certify that we are well acquainted with   W. F. Clifton   a   Physician   and know   him   to be reputable and of good standing in the community.

Cyrus Byington
Dick Morgan

Applications for Enrollment of Choctaw Newborn
Act of 1905   Volume VI

BIRTH AFFIDAVIT.

DEPARTMENT OF THE INTERIOR.
COMMISSION TO THE FIVE CIVILIZED TRIBES.

IN RE APPLICATION FOR ENROLLMENT, as a citizen of the   Chocktaw[sic]   Nation, of   Gilbert Vail   , born on the 17th day of   August   , 1904

Name of Father: John F Vail   a citizen of the   Chocktaw   Nation.
Name of Mother: Sophia Vail   a citizen of the   Chocktaw   Nation.

Postoffice   Durant, Indian Territory

AFFIDAVIT OF MOTHER.

UNITED STATES OF AMERICA, Indian Territory,
   Central   DISTRICT.

   I,   Sophia Vail   , on oath state that I am   Thirty Eight   years of age and a citizen by   blood   , of the   Choctaw   Nation; that I am the lawful wife of   John F Vail   , who is a citizen, by Intermarriage   of the   Choctaw Nation; that a   male   child was born to me on   Seventeenth day of August   , 1904; that said child has been named   Gilbert Vail   , and was living March 4, 1905.

Mrs Sophia Vail

Witnesses To Mark:
{

   Subscribed and sworn to before me this   25th   day of   March   , 1905

Com Ex   Charles A Phillips
Feb 8th 1908   Notary Public.

AFFIDAVIT OF ATTENDING PHYSICIAN OR MID-WIFE.

UNITED STATES OF AMERICA, Indian Territory,
   Central   DISTRICT.

   I,   W.F. Clifton   , a   Physician   , on oath state that I attended on Mrs.   Sophia Vail   , wife of   Jno F. Vail   on the 17th day of   August   , 1904; that there was born to her on said date a   male   child; that said child was living March 4, 1905, and is said to have been named Gilbert Vail

W.F. Clifton M.D.

Witnesses To Mark:
{

Applications for Enrollment of Choctaw Newborn
Act of 1905   Volume VI

Subscribed and sworn to before me this 27 day of   March   , 1905

J M Routh
Notary Public.

Choctaw 4486.

Muskogee, Indian Territory, April 4, 1904.

John F. Vail,
    Durant, Indian Territory.

Dear Sir:

    Receipt is hereby acknowledged of the affidavits of Mrs. Sophia Vail and W. F. Clifton to the birth of Gilbert Vail, son of John F. and Sophia Vail, August 17, 1904, and the same have been filed with our records as an application for the enrollment of said child.

Respectfully,

Commissioner in Charge.

Sub.   7-NB-344.

Muskogee, Indian Territory, May 25, 1905.

John F. Vail,
    Durant, Indian Territory.

Dear Sir:

    There is enclosed you herewith for execution application for the enrollment of your infant child, Arthur Floid Vail, born October 19, 1902.

    The affidavits heretofore filed with the Commission show the child was living on November 7, 1902. It is necessary, for the child to be enrolled, that he was living on March 4, 1905.

    In having these affidavits executed care should be exercised to see that all names are written in full, as they appear in the body of the affidavit, and in the event that either of the persons signing the affidavit are unable to write, signatures by mark must be attested by two witnesses. Each affidavit must be executed before a Notary Public and the notarial seal and signature of the officer must be attached to each separate affidavit.

Applications for Enrollment of Choctaw Newborn
Act of 1905   Volume VI

Respectfully,

Chairman.

VR 24-1.

7-NB-344

Muskogee, Indian Territory July 29, 1905.

John Vail,
    Durant, Indian Territory.

Dear Sir:

    Your attention is called to a communication addressed to you by the Commission to the Five Civilized Tribes, dated May 25, 1905, with which there was inclosed for execution application for the enrollment of your infant child, Arthur Floid Vail, born October 19, 1902.

    In said letter you were advised that the affidavits heretofore filed in this office show that the child was living November 7, 1902, and that it was necessary for the child to be enrolled, that he was living March 4, 1905. No reply to this letter has been received.

    In the event that the child has died prior to March 4, 1905, you are requested to erase the words "was living March 4, 1905, and insert instead the date of his death' in the event that he was living March 4, 1905 have the affidavits properly executed and return to this office immediately, as no further action can be taken relative to the enrollment of your said child until the application heretofore forwarded you if filed in this office showing either the date of death or that he was living on March 4, 1905.

Respectfully,

Commissioner.

Applications for Enrollment of Choctaw Newborn
Act of 1905 Volume VI

7-NB-344.

Muskogee, Indian Territory, August 8, 1905.

John F. Vail,
Durant, Indian Territory.

Dear Sir:

Receipt is hereby acknowledged of your letter of August 5, 1905, stating that your son Arthur Floyd Vail was born October 19, 1902, and died March 22, 1904, and that you have been under the impression he was not entitled to enrollment, but if he is you state you would like to file for him.

In reply to your letter you are advised that by the provision of the act of Congress approved March 3, 1905, the Commission to the Five Civilized Tribes was authorized to enroll children born to enrolled citizens by blood of the Choctaw and Chickasaw Nations subsequent to September 25, 1902, and prior to March 4, 1905, and living on the latter date; you will therefore see that there is no provision for the enrollment of children born subsequent to September 25, 1902, who were not living on March 4, 1905.

For the purpose of making the death of your son Arthur Floyd Vail a matter of record there is inclosed herewith proof of death which please have executed and returned to this office as early as practicable.

Respectfully,

DC *(End of letter)*

7-NB-344

Muskogee, Indian Territory, August 15, 1905.

Sophia Vail,
Durant, Indian Territory.

Dear Madam:

Receipt is hereby acknowledged of your affidavit and the affidavit of Joseph E. Nelson to the death of your son, Arthur Floyd Vail, which occurred March 22, 1904, and the same have been filed with the records as evidence of death of the above named child.

Respectfully,

Acting Commissioner.

Applications for Enrollment of Choctaw Newborn
Act of 1905   Volume VI

7-NB-344

Muskogee, Indian Territory, August 23, 1905.
COPY

John F. Vail,
    Durant, Indian Territory.

Dear Sir:

    You are hereby advised that it appearing from the records of this office that your child, Arthur Floyd Vail, died prior to March 4, 1905, the Commissioner to the Five Civilized Tribes on August 23, 1905, dismissed the application for the enrollment of said child as a citizen by blood of the Choctaw Nation.

Respectfully,
SIGNED

Tams Bixby
Commissioner.

7-NB-344

Muskogee, Indian Territory, August 23, 1905.
COPY

Mansfield, McMurray & Cornish,
    Attorneys for Choctaw and Chickasaw Nations,
        South McAlester, Indian Territory.

Gentlemen:

You are hereby advised that it appearing from the records of this office that your child, Arthur Floyd Vail, died prior to March 4, 1905, the Commissioner to the Five Civilized Tribes on August 23, 1905, dismissed the application for the enrollment of said child as a citizen by blood of the Choctaw Nation.

Respectfully,
SIGNED

Tams Bixby
Commissioner.

Applications for Enrollment of Choctaw Newborn
Act of 1905   Volume VI

Choc New Born 345
Clittie Elizabeth Holleman
(Born Jan. 11, 1905)

BIRTH AFFIDAVIT.

DEPARTMENT OF THE INTERIOR.
COMMISSION TO THE FIVE CIVILIZED TRIBES.

IN RE APPLICATION FOR ENROLLMENT, as a citizen of the Choctaw Nation, of Clittie Elizabeth Holleman, born on the 11th day of Jan, 1905

Name of Father: William G Holleman   a citizen of the Choctaw Nation.
Name of Mother: Gillie A. Holleman   a citizen of the Choctaw Nation.

Postoffice   Savanna Ind. Ter.

AFFIDAVIT OF MOTHER.

UNITED STATES OF AMERICA, Indian Territory, }
Central   DISTRICT.

I, Gillie A. Holleman, on oath state that I am 33 years of age and a citizen by Blood, of the Choctaw Nation; that I am the lawful wife of William G. Holleman, who is a citizen, by Intermarriage of the Choctaw Nation; that a Female child was born to me on 11th day of Jan, 1905; that said child has been named Clittie Elizabeth Holleman, and was living March 4, 1905.

Gillie A Holleman
Witnesses To Mark:
{

Subscribed and sworn to before me this 18th day of March, 1905

My commission expires   Andrew J. Turner
March 17th 1909   Notary Public.

AFFIDAVIT OF ATTENDING PHYSICIAN OR MID-WIFE.

UNITED STATES OF AMERICA, Indian Territory, }
Central   DISTRICT.

I, E.L. Graham, a Mid-wife, on oath state that I attended on Mrs. Gillie A Holleman, wife of William G. Holleman on the 11th day of Jan, 1905; that there was born to her on said date a Female child; that said

Applications for Enrollment of Choctaw Newborn
Act of 1905   Volume VI

child was living March 4, 1905, and is said to have been named   Clittie Elizabeth Holleman

                                      E.L. Graham

Witnesses To Mark:

{

    Subscribed and sworn to before me this 18th day of   March   , 1905

My commission expires   Andrew J. Turner
March 17th 1909   Notary Public.

7-4493

Muskogee, Indian Territory, March 24, 1905.

W. J[sic]. Holliman,
    Savanna, Indian Territory.

Dear Sir:

    Receipt is hereby acknowledged of your letter of March 19, 1905, enclosing affidavits of Gillie A. Holleman and E. L. Graham to the birth of Clittie Elizabeth Holleman, daughter of W. J[sic]. and Gillie A. Holleman, January 11, 1905, and the same have been filed as an application for the enrollment of this child.

    You are informed that you will be notified when the enrollment of this child is approved by the Secretary of the Interior.

                Respectfully,

                            Chairman.

7-4493

Muskogee, Indian Territory, April 4, 1905.

William G. Holleman,
    Savanna, Indian Territory.

Dear Sir:

    Receipt is hereby acknowledged of your letter of March 28, 1905, calling attention to the fact that your name appears as William J. Holleman in the letter of the Commission acknowledging receipt of the affidavits to the birth of Clittie Elizabeth Holleman.

Applications for Enrollment of Choctaw Newborn
Act of 1905   Volume VI

In reply to your letter you are advised that this is a clerical error and your name should have appeared as William G. Holleman.

Respectfully,

Chairman.

Choc New Born 346
    Clide Bushnell Ryan
    (Born Aug. 23, 1903)

BIRTH AFFIDAVIT.

DEPARTMENT OF THE INTERIOR.
COMMISSION TO THE FIVE CIVILIZED TRIBES.

IN RE APPLICATION FOR ENROLLMENT, as a citizen of the   Choctaw   Nation, of Clide Bushnell Ryan   , born on the 23rd   day of   Aug   , 1903

Name of Father: Theron J Ryan   a citizen of the   Choctaw   Nation.
Name of Mother: Annie L. Ryan   a citizen of the   Choctaw   Nation.

Postoffice   Savanna, I.T.

AFFIDAVIT OF MOTHER.

UNITED STATES OF AMERICA, Indian Territory,
    Central   **DISTRICT.**

    I,   Annie L. Ryan   , on oath state that I am   32   years of age and a citizen by   blood   , of the   Choctaw   Nation; that I am the lawful wife of   Theron J Ryan   , who is a citizen, by blood   of the   Choctaw   Nation; that a male   child was born to me on   23rd   day of   August   , 1903; that said child has been named   Clide Bushnell Ryan   , and was living March 4, 1905.

                            Annie L. Ryan

Witnesses To Mark:

Applications for Enrollment of Choctaw Newborn
Act of 1905 Volume VI

Subscribed and sworn to before me this 21st day of March , 1905

                                    Wirt Franklin
                                    Notary Public.

AFFIDAVIT OF ATTENDING PHYSICIAN OR MID-WIFE.

UNITED STATES OF AMERICA, Indian Territory,
    Central   DISTRICT.

    I, Lela E. Dawson , a mid-wife , on oath state that I attended on Mrs. Annie L Ryan , wife of Theron J Ryan on the 23rd day of August , 1903; that there was born to her on said date a male child; that said child was living March 4, 1905, and is said to have been named Clide Bushnell Ryan

                                    Lela E Dawson

Witnesses To Mark:

Subscribed and sworn to before me this 21st day of March , 1905

                                    Wirt Franklin
                                    Notary Public.

Choc New Born 347
    Roy Ruth Luper
    (Born May 7, 1904)

DEPARTMENT OF THE INTERIOR,
Commission to the Five Civilized Tribes.
--- o-o----

    IN RE Application for enrollment, as a citizen of the Choctaw Nation, of Roy Ruth Luper, born May 7, 1904.

Name of father: D. R. Luper, a citizen of the United States.
Name of Mother: Ruth L. Luper, nee Boatwright, a citizen of the Choctaw Nation.

Postoffice: Wayne, Indian Territory.

Applications for Enrollment of Choctaw Newborn
Act of 1905   Volume VI

AFFIDAVIT OF MOTHER.
---o-o---

Indian Territory,
        ss.
Southern District.

I, Ruth L. Luper, on oath, states that I am 17 years of age, and a citizen by blood of the Choctaw Nation; that I am the lawful wife of D. R. Luper, a citizen of the United States: that a male child was born to me on the 7th day of May, 1904; that said child has been named Roy Ruth Luper and is now living.

Ruth L Luper

Subscribed and sworn to before me this this the 11th day of November, 1904.

BH Love
Notary Public.

AFFIDAVIT OF ATTENDING PHYSICIAN.

UNITED STATES OF AMERICA,
    INDIAN TERRITORY,   ss.
SOUTHERN   DISTRICT.

I, JB Maples, a physician, on oath, state that I attended on Mrs. Ruth L. Luper, wife of D. R. Luper, on the 7th day of May, 1904; that there was born to her on said date, a male child that child is now living and is said to have been named, Roy Ruth Luper.

J B Maples, M.D.

Subscribed and sworn to before me this this the 17th day of November, 1904.

A.S. Kelley
Notary Public.

Applications for Enrollment of Choctaw Newborn
Act of 1905   Volume VI

BIRTH AFFIDAVIT.

DEPARTMENT OF THE INTERIOR.
COMMISSION TO THE FIVE CIVILIZED TRIBES.

IN RE APPLICATION FOR ENROLLMENT, as a citizen of the   Choctaw   Nation, of Roy Ruth Luper   , born on the 7th day of   May , 1904

Name of Father: Dee Luper   a citizen of the   U. S.   ~~Nation~~.
                                  nee Ruth L. Boatwright
Name of Mother: Ruth L. Luper   a citizen of the   Choctaw   Nation.

Postoffice   Wayne I.T.

AFFIDAVIT OF MOTHER.

UNITED STATES OF AMERICA, Indian Territory, }
   Southern   DISTRICT.

I, Ruth L Luper nee Ruth L Boatwright   , on oath state that I am 18 years of age and a citizen by   blood , of the   Choctaw   Nation; that I am the lawful wife of   Dee Luper   , who is a citizen, of the United States ~~of the~~ residing in the Chickasaw Nation; that a   male   child was born to me on   7th day of May   , 1904; that said child has been named   Roy Ruth Luper   , and was living March 4,17 1905.

                                                Ruth L Luper
Witnesses To Mark:
   {

Subscribed and sworn to before me this 18 day of   March   , 1905

                                                A S Kelley
                                                   Notary Public.

AFFIDAVIT OF ATTENDING PHYSICIAN OR MID-WIFE.

UNITED STATES OF AMERICA, Indian Territory, }
   Southern   DISTRICT.

I, Mary Carper   , a   Midwife   , on oath state that I attended on Mrs. Ruth L Luper   , wife of   Dee Luper   on the   7th day of   May   , 1904; that there was born to her on said date a   male   child; that said child was living March 4, 1905, and is said to have been named Roy Ruth Luper

                                                Mary Carper

193

Applications for Enrollment of Choctaw Newborn
Act of 1905   Volume VI

Witnesses To Mark:

{

    Subscribed and sworn to before me this 18 day of   March   , 1905

                                  A S Kelley
                                      Notary Public.

My Com expires Mch 12-1908

                                      7-4508

            Muskogee, Indian Territory, November 26, 1904.

J. F. Sharp,
        Attorney at Law,
                Purcell, Indian Territory.

Dear Sir:-

    Receipt is hereby acknowledged of your letter of November 21, 1904, enclosing the affidavits of Ruth L. Luper nee Boatwright and J. B. Maples relative to the birth of Roy Ruth Luper, infant son of D. R. and Ruth L. Luper May 7, 1904.

    In reply to your letter you are advised that under the provisions of the Act of Congress approved July 1, 1902, no child born to a citizen or freedman of the Choctaw or Chickasaw Nations[sic] subsequent to September 25, 1902 is entitled to enrollment or allotment in the Choctaw or Chickasaw Nations[sic].

                          Respectfully,

                                      Commissioner in Charge.

                                      7-4508

              Muskogee, Indian Territory, March 23, 1905.

Dee Luper,
        Wayne, Indian Territory.

Dear Sir:

    Receipt is hereby acknowledged of the affidavits of Ruth L. Luper (Boatwright) and Mary Carter[sic] to the birth of Roy Ruth Luper son of Dee and Ruth L. Luper May 7, 1904, and the same have been filed with our records as an application for the enrollment of said child.

Applications for Enrollment of Choctaw Newborn
Act of 1905   Volume VI

Respectfully,

Chairman.

7-NB-347

Muskogee, Indian Territory, July 28, 1905.

D. R. Luper,
    Wayne, Indian Territory.

Dear Sir:

    Receipt is hereby acknowledged of your letter of July 20, 1905, asking if the name of Ray R. Luper has been sent to the Secretary of the Interior for approval.

    In reply to your letter you are advised that the name of Ray Ruth Luper has been placed upon a schedule of citizens by blood of the Choctaw Nation, which has been forwarded the Secretary of the Interior and you will be notified when his enrollment has been approved by the Department.

Respectfully,

Commissioner.

Choc New Born 348
    Nina Pearl Ansley
    (Born Feb. 16, 1904)

BIRTH AFFIDAVIT.

DEPARTMENT OF THE INTERIOR,
COMMISSION TO THE FIVE CIVILIZED TRIBES.

    IN RE Application for Enrollment, as a citizen of the Choctaw Nation, of Nina Pearl Ansley, born on the 16th day of February, 1904

Name of Father: Gilbert Ansley   a citizen of the Choctaw Nation.
Name of Mother: Dolly May Ansley   a citizen of the Choctaw Nation.

Post-Office: McAlester I.T.

Applications for Enrollment of Choctaw Newborn
Act of 1905 Volume VI

AFFIDAVIT OF MOTHER.

UNITED STATES OF AMERICA,
 INDIAN TERRITORY.
 Central   District.

I, Dolly May Ansley, on oath state that I am 22 years of age and a citizen by Marriage, of the Choctaw Nation; that I am the lawful wife of Gilbert Ansley, who is a citizen, by Blood of the Choctaw Nation; that a female child was born to me on 16th day of February, 1904, that said child has been named Nina Pearl Ansley, and is now living.

Dolly May Ansley

WITNESSES TO MARK:

Subscribed and sworn to before me this 16th day of March, 1905.

S.F. Brown
NOTARY PUBLIC.

AFFIDAVIT OF ATTENDING PHYSICIAN OR MID-WIFE.

UNITED STATES OF AMERICA,
 INDIAN TERRITORY.
 Central   District.

I, Dr. J. O. Grubbs, a Physician, on oath state that I attended on Mrs. Dolly May Ansley, wife of Gilbert Ansley on the 16th day of February, 1904; that there was born to her on said date a Female child; that said child is now living and is said to have been named Nina Pearl Ansley

J O Grubbs M.D.

WITNESSES TO MARK:

Subscribed and sworn to before me this 17th day of March, 1905.

S.F. Brown
NOTARY PUBLIC.

Applications for Enrollment of Choctaw Newborn
Act of 1905 Volume VI

Choc New Born 349
Irene Inez Richards
(Born July 31, 1903)

NEW BORN AFFIDAVIT

No ....

CHOCTAW ENROLLING COMMISSION

IN THE MATTER OF THE APPLICATION FOR ENROLLMENT as a citizen of the Choctaw Nation, of Inez Irene Richards born on the 31 day of July 190 3

Name of father Edward Richards a citizen of Choctaw Nation, final enrollment No..........................
Name of mother Irena Richards a citizen of Choctaw Nation, final enrollment No. 12517

McAlester I.T.   Postoffice.

AFFIDAVIT OF MOTHER

UNITED STATES OF AMERICA
INDIAN TERRITORY
DISTRICT Central

I   Irena A. Richards   , on oath state that I am   30   years of age and a citizen by   blood   of the   Choctaw   Nation, and as such have been placed upon the final roll of the   Choctaw   Nation, by the Honorable Secretary of the Interior my final enrollment number being   12517 ; that I am the lawful wife of   Edward Richards , who is a citizen of the   Choctaw   Nation, and as such has been placed upon the final roll of said Nation by the Honorable Secretary of the Interior, his final enrollment number being .... and that a   female   child was born to me on the   31   day of   July   190 3; that said child has been named   Inez Irene Richards , and is now living.

WITNESSETH: Irena A Richards
Must be two witnesses { W C Bolling
who are citizens   { N.B. Ainsworth

Applications for Enrollment of Choctaw Newborn
Act of 1905   Volume VI

Subscribed and sworn to before me this, the 16 day of   March   , 190 5

>James Bower
>Notary Public.

My Commission Expires:
Sept 23 1907

Affidavit of Attending Physician or Midwife

UNITED STATES OF AMERICA,
INDIAN TERRITORY,
Central   DISTRICT

I,   W.E. Abbott   a ....
on oath state that I attended on Mrs. E.T. Richard[sic]   wife of   Edward Richard[sic]
on the 31   day of   July , 190 3, that there was born to her on said date a   female   child,
that said child is now living, and is said to have been named   Inez Irene Richards

>W.E. Abbott   M. D.

Subscribed and sworn to before me this the   16   day of March   1905

>James Bower
>Notary Public.

WITNESSETH:
Must be two witnesses
who are citizens and
know the child.
{ W C Bolling
  N. B. Ainsworth

We hereby certify that we are well acquainted with   W.E. Abbott
a Practicing Physician   and know   him   to be reputable and of good
standing in the community.

Must be two citizen { W C Bolling
witnesses.   N.B. Ainsworth

Applications for Enrollment of Choctaw Newborn
Act of 1905   Volume VI

BIRTH AFFIDAVIT.

DEPARTMENT OF THE INTERIOR.
COMMISSION TO THE FIVE CIVILIZED TRIBES.

IN RE APPLICATION FOR ENROLLMENT, as a citizen of the Choctaw Nation, of Irene Inez Richards, born on the 31st day of July, 1903

Name of Father: Edwin T. Richards   a citizen of the Choctaw Nation.
Name of Mother: Irene A. Richards   a citizen of the Choctaw Nation.

Postoffice   McAlester, I.T.

AFFIDAVIT OF MOTHER.

UNITED STATES OF AMERICA, Indian Territory,
Central   DISTRICT.

I, Irene A. Richards, on oath state that I am 30 years of age and a citizen by blood, of the Choctaw Nation; that I am the lawful wife of Edwin T. Richards, who is a citizen, by marriage of the Choctaw Nation; that a female child was born to me on 31st day of July, 1903; that said child has been named Irene Inez Richards, and was living March 4, 1905.

Irene A. Richards

Witnesses To Mark:
{

Subscribed and sworn to before me this 20th day of March, 1905

Wirt Franklin
Notary Public.

AFFIDAVIT OF ATTENDING PHYSICIAN OR MID-WIFE.

UNITED STATES OF AMERICA, Indian Territory,
Central   DISTRICT.

I, Dr W.E. Abbott, a physician, on oath state that I attended on Mrs. Irene A. Richards, wife of Edwin T Richards on the 31st day of July, 1903; that there was born to her on said date a female child; that said child was living March 4, 1905, and is said to have been named Irene Inez Richards

W.E. Abbott M.D.

Witnesses To Mark:
{

Applications for Enrollment of Choctaw Newborn
Act of 1905 Volume VI

Subscribed and sworn to before me this 20th day of March , 1905

S. F. Brown
Notary Public.

Choc New Born 350
    Albert Roy Patterson
    (Born Jan. 15, 1904)

No. 3057

Certificate of Record of Marriages.

𝕌nited 𝔖tates of 𝔄merica,
The Indian Territory, } sct.
Central *District.*

I,   EJ Fannin   Clerk of the United States Court, in the Indian Territory and District aforesaid, do hereby CERTIFY, that the License for and Certificate of the Marriage of Mr.   Robert Patterson   and M iss Alice Loughridge   was filed in my office in said Territory and District the   16   day of   Oct A.D., 190 2 , and duly recorded in Book   10 of Marriage Record, Page 286

WITNESS my hand and Seal of said Court, at   So McAlester this   18   day of   March A.D. 190 5

    EJ Fannin
                  Clerk.
By   W.C. Donnelly   Deputy.

P. O.

Applications for Enrollment of Choctaw Newborn
Act of 1905   Volume VI

No. 3057

MARRIAGE LICENSE

United States of America,   The Indian Territory,
                             Central District, SS.

To any Person Authorized by Law to Solemnize Marriage, Greeting:

You are hereby commanded to Solemnize the Rite and publish the Banns of Matrimony between Mr. Robert Patterson *of* Alderson *in the Indian Territory, aged* 22 *years, and M* iss Alice Loughridge *of* Alderson *in the Indian Territory., aged* 19 *years, according to law, and do you officially sign and return this License to the parties therein named.*

WITNESS my hand and official seal, this 16 day of Oct. A. D. 190 2

E. J. Fannin
Clerk of the United States Court.

WC Donnelly   *Deputy*

Certificate of Marriage.

United States of America, ⎫
 The Indian Territory,   ⎬ ss.
 Central   District.   ⎭

I, EJ Fannin *a* U.S. Clerk *, do hereby certify, that on the* 16 *day of* Oct. *A. D. 190* , *I did, duly and according to law, as commanded in the foregoing License, solemnize the Rite and publish the Banns of Matrimony between the parties therein named.*

Witness my hand, this 16 day of Oct A. D. 190 2

My credentials are recorded in the office of the Clerk of ⎫ EJ Fannin US Clk
the United States Court in the Indian Territory,   ⎬
Central District, Book ...., Page ....   ⎭ *by* WC Donnelly DC

Note—This License and Certificate of Marriage must be returned to the Office of the Clerk of the United States Court of the Indian Territory, from whence it was issued, within sixty days from the date thereof, or the party to whom the License was issued will be liable in the amount of the One Hundred Dollars ($100.00)

Applications for Enrollment of Choctaw Newborn
Act of 1905 Volume VI

BIRTH AFFIDAVIT.

DEPARTMENT OF THE INTERIOR.
COMMISSION TO THE FIVE CIVILIZED TRIBES.

IN RE APPLICATION FOR ENROLLMENT, as a citizen of the Choctaw Nation, of Albert Roy Patterson, born on the 15th day of January, 1904

Name of Father: Robert E. Lee Patterson   a citizen of the Choctaw Nation.
Name of Mother: Alice May Patterson   a citizen of the Choctaw Nation.

Postoffice   Alderson, I T

AFFIDAVIT OF MOTHER.

UNITED STATES OF AMERICA, Indian Territory, }
Central   DISTRICT.

I, Alice May Patterson, on oath state that I am 22 years of age and a citizen by ...., of the United States ~~Nation~~; that I am the lawful wife of Robert E. Lee Patterson, who is a citizen, by blood of the Choctaw Nation; that a male child was born to me on 15th day of January, 1904; that said child has been named Albert Roy Patterson, and was living March 4, 1905.

                         Alice May Patterson

Witnesses To Mark:
{

Subscribed and sworn to before me this 18th day of March, 1905

                       Wirt Franklin
                           Notary Public.

AFFIDAVIT OF ATTENDING PHYSICIAN OR MID-WIFE.

UNITED STATES OF AMERICA, Indian Territory, }
Central   DISTRICT.

I, J.C. Robinson, a physician, on oath state that I attended on Mrs. Alice May Patterson, wife of Robert E. Lee Patterson on the 15th day of January, 1904; that there was born to her on said date a male child; that said child was living March 4, 1905, and is said to have been named Albert Roy Patterson

                       J C Robinson

Witnesses To Mark:
{

Applications for Enrollment of Choctaw Newborn
Act of 1905   Volume VI

Subscribed and sworn to before me this 18th day of March, 1905

                         Wirt Franklin
                         Notary Public.

<u>Choc New Born 351</u>
    Everett Edwards
    (Born Dec. 10, 1902)
    Ruth Edwards
    (Born Dec. 13, 1904)

(The affidavit below typed as given.)

Indian Territory)
) ss
Central District)

    IN RE)) Application of Routh Edwards to be enrolled as a member of the Choctaw Tribe of Indians, under the act of Congress of March 3, 1905.

AFFIDAVIT

    Be it remembered that on this the 22st day of July, 1905, personally appeared before me the undersigned notary public in and for the Central District of the Indian Territory, R. P. Colbert of Caddo, Indian Territory personally known to me as a reputible person, who being by me first duly sworn, on his oath states:

    My name is R.P. Colbert, I am __33__ years old, and I reside eight miles east of Caddo, Indian Territory. I am personally acquainted with Eli Edwards and his wife Sallie Edwards. I have been personally acquainted with Eli Edwards for about 18 years, and his wife Sallie Edwards about the same lenght of time.

    I was present when the rights of matrimony was celebrated between them. They were married by a man by the name of Hill at Atoka Indian Territory on February the 21st, 1896. The ceremony was performed at the home of Sophia Wagoner in the town of Atoka.

                         R.P. Colbert

Subscribed and sworn to before me this the 26 day of July, 1905.

                         Chas E McPherren
                         Notary Public.

Applications for Enrollment of Choctaw Newborn
Act of 1905   Volume VI

(The affidavit below typed as given.)

Indian Territory)
) ss
Central District)

IN RE--Application of Routh Edwards to be enrolled as a member of the Choctaw Tribe of Indians, under the Act of Congress of March 3, 1905.

AFFIDAVIT

On this the 21st day of July, personally appeared before me, Dwight Brown, a notary public in and for the Central District of the Indian Territory, Eli Edwards, personally known to me, who being by me duly sworn, on his oath sates: My name is Eli Edwards, I am a Choctaw by blood my enrollment number being 12958; I was duly married to Sallie Edwards in the town of Atoka, Indian Territory, on the 21st day of February 1896 by one Rev. P.H. Hill.

The marriage license was never returned to me by him, and I have made dilligent enquiry to locate him, but as yet have not succeeded. I have also made dilligent effort to procure a certified copy of said marriage license, but thus far have been unable to find where same was recorded.

                                    Eli Edwards

Subscribed and sworn to before me this the 21st day of July, 1905.

                                      Dwight Brown
                                      Notary Public.

Indian Territory)
) ss
Central District)

IN RE --Application of Routh Edwards to be enrolled as a member of the Choctaw Tribe of Indians, under the Act of Congress of March 3, 1905.

AFFIDAVIT

Be it remembered that on this 22nd day of July, 1905, personally appeared before me the undersigned a notary public in and for the Central District of the Indian Territory, Dee Colbert of Caddo, Indian Territory, personally known to me as a reputible person, who being by me first duly sworn as the law directs on her oath deposes and says:

My name is Dee Colbert, I am __27__ years old, and I reside at eight miles east of Caddo, Indian Territory.

Applications for Enrollment of Choctaw Newborn
Act of 1905   Volume VI

I am personally acquainted with Ely Edwards and his wife Sallie Edwards. and have known them for the last past eighteen years. I was present at their marriage which took place in the town of Atoka in the winter of 1896. They were married by Reverand Hill at the home of Sophia Wagoner of the town of Atoka.

Dee Colbert

Subscribed and sworn to before me this the 26th day of July, 1905.

Chas E. McPherren
Notary Public.

BIRTH AFFIDAVIT.

DEPARTMENT OF THE INTERIOR.
COMMISSION TO THE FIVE CIVILIZED TRIBES.

IN RE APPLICATION FOR ENROLLMENT, as a citizen of the   Choctaw   Nation, of Everette[sic] Edwards   , born on the 10   day of Dec , 1902

Name of Father: Eli Edwards   a citizen of the   Choctaw   Nation.
Name of Mother: Sallie Edwards   a citizen of the   Choctaw   Nation.

Postoffice ....

AFFIDAVIT OF MOTHER.

UNITED STATES OF AMERICA, Indian Territory, }
    Central   DISTRICT.

I, Salle[sic] Edwards   , on oath state that I am 26 years of age and a citizen by   intermarriage   , of the   Choctaw   Nation; that I am the lawful wife of Eli Edwards   , who is a citizen, by   blood   of the   Choctaw   Nation; that a male   child was born to me on   10th   day of   Dec   , 1902, that said child has been named   Everette Edwards   , and is now living.

Sallie Edwards

Witnesses To Mark:
{

Subscribed and sworn to before me this 10 day of Jan.   , 1905.

Dwight Brown
Notary Public.

Applications for Enrollment of Choctaw Newborn
Act of 1905   Volume VI

AFFIDAVIT OF ATTENDING PHYSICIAN OR MID-WIFE.

UNITED STATES OF AMERICA, Indian Territory, }
Central   DISTRICT.

I,   J. M. Bentley   , a   physician   , on oath state that I attended on Mrs. Sallie Edwards   , wife of   Eli Edwards   on the   10   day of   Dec , 1902; that there was born to her on said date a   male   child; that said child is now living and is said to have been named   Everette Edwards

Witnesses To Mark:
{

J. M. Bentley MD

Subscribed and sworn to before me this 10   day of   Jan.   , 1905.

Dwight Brown
Notary Public.

BIRTH AFFIDAVIT.

DEPARTMENT OF THE INTERIOR.
COMMISSION TO THE FIVE CIVILIZED TRIBES.

IN RE APPLICATION FOR ENROLLMENT, as a citizen of the   Choctaw   Nation, of Everette[sic] Edwards   , born on the 10   day of December , 1902

Name of Father: Eli Edwards   a citizen of the   Choctaw   Nation.
Name of Mother: Sallie Edwards   a citizen of the   Choctaw   Nation.

Postoffice   Lehigh, I.T.

AFFIDAVIT OF MOTHER.

UNITED STATES OF AMERICA, Indian Territory, }
Central   DISTRICT.

I,   Sallie Edwards   , on oath state that I am 26   years of age and a citizen by ...., of the   U.S.   Nation; that I am the lawful wife of   Eli Edwards   , who is a citizen, by   blood   of the   Choctaw   Nation; that a   male   child was born to me on 10   day of   December   , 1902; that said child has been named Everette Edwards   , and was living March 4, 1905.

Sallie Edwards

Witnesses To Mark:
{

Applications for Enrollment of Choctaw Newborn
Act of 1905   Volume VI

Subscribed and sworn to before me this 29 day of   April   , 1905

Dwight Brown
Notary Public.

AFFIDAVIT OF ATTENDING PHYSICIAN OR MID-WIFE.

UNITED STATES OF AMERICA, Indian Territory, }
    Central   DISTRICT.

I,   John M. Bentley   , a   physician   , on oath state that I attended on Mrs. Sallie Edwards   , wife of Eli Edwards   on the 10 day of December , 1902; that there was born to her on said date a   male   child; that said child was living March 4, 1905, and is said to have been named Everette Edwards

John M Bentley

Witnesses To Mark:
{

Subscribed and sworn to before me this 29 day of   April   , 1905

Dwight Brown
Notary Public.

BIRTH AFFIDAVIT.

DEPARTMENT OF THE INTERIOR,
COMMISSION TO THE FIVE CIVILIZED TRIBES.

In Re Application for Enrollment, as a citizen of the   Choctaw   Nation, of Ruth Edwards , born on the 13   day of December , 1904

Name of Father: Eli Edwards   a citizen of the   Choctaw   Nation.
Name of Mother: Sallie Edwards   a citizen of the .... Nation.

Post-office   Lehigh, I.T.

AFFIDAVIT OF MOTHER.

UNITED STATES OF AMERICA, }
    INDIAN TERRITORY,
    Central   District.

I, Sallie Edwards , on oath state that I am 26   years of age and a citizen by   intermarriage , of the   Choctaw   Nation; that I am the lawful wife of   Eli

Applications for Enrollment of Choctaw Newborn
Act of 1905   Volume VI

Edwards   , who is a citizen, by blood of the   Choctaw   Nation; that a   female child was born to me on   13 day of   December , 1904 , that said child has been named   Ruth Edwards , and is now living.

                                        Sallie Edwards

WITNESSES TO MARK:

{

Subscribed and sworn to before me this 10   day of   January , 1905.

                                        Dwight Brown
                                        NOTARY PUBLIC.

AFFIDAVIT OF ATTENDING PHYSICIAN OR MID-WIFE.

UNITED STATES OF AMERICA,
   INDIAN TERRITORY,
.... District.

I,   J.L. Cass M.D.   , a   Physician , on oath state that I attended on Mrs.   Sallie Edwards , wife of   Eli ~~Eli~~ Edwards on the 13th day of December , 1904 ; that there was born to her on said date a   female   child; that said child is now living and is said to have been named Ruth Edwards

                                        J.L. Cass, M.D.

WITNESSES TO MARK:

{

Subscribed and sworn to before me this 10   day of   January , 1905.

                                        Dwight Brown

My Commission Expires Dec 2, 1904   **NOTARY PUBLIC.**

BIRTH AFFIDAVIT.

DEPARTMENT OF THE INTERIOR.
COMMISSION TO THE FIVE CIVILIZED TRIBES.

    IN RE APPLICATION FOR ENROLLMENT, as a citizen of the   Choctaw   Nation, of Ruth Edwards , born on the 13   day of December , 1904

Name of Father: Eli Edwards   a citizen of the   Choctaw   Nation.
Name of Mother: Sallie Edwards   a citizen of the   Choctaw   Nation.

                            Postoffice   Lehigh, I.T.

Applications for Enrollment of Choctaw Newborn
Act of 1905   Volume VI

AFFIDAVIT OF MOTHER.

UNITED STATES OF AMERICA, Indian Territory,
Central   DISTRICT.

I,   Sallie Edwards   , on oath state that I am   26   years of age and a citizen by ...., of the   U.S. Nation; that I am the lawful wife of   Eli Edwards   , who is a citizen, by blood   of the   Choctaw   Nation; that a   female   child was born to me on   13   day of   December   , 1904; that said child has been named Ruth Edwards   , and was living March 4, 1905.

Sallie Edwards

Witnesses To Mark:
{

Subscribed and sworn to before me this 20th day of   April   , 1905

Dwight Brown
Notary Public.

AFFIDAVIT OF ATTENDING PHYSICIAN OR MID-WIFE.

UNITED STATES OF AMERICA, Indian Territory,
Central   DISTRICT.

I,   J.L. Cass   , a   physician   , on oath state that I attended on Mrs. Sallie Edwards   , wife of   Eli Edwards   on the 13 day of   December , 1904; that there was born to her on said date a   female   child; that said child was living March 4, 1905, and is said to have been named Ruth Edwards

J.L. Cass M.D.

Witnesses To Mark:
{

Subscribed and sworn to before me this   21   day of   April   , 1905

My Com Expires Dec 27-1905

Dwight Brown
Notary Public.

Applications for Enrollment of Choctaw Newborn
Act of 1905 Volume VI

COPY

Muskogee, Indian Territory, January 18, 1905.

Eli Edwards,
Lehigh, Indian Territory.

Dear Sir:

Receipt is hereby acknowledged of the affidavits of Sallie Edwards and J. N[sic]. Bentley to the birth of Everett minor son of Eli and Sallie Edwards December 10, 1902. Also the affidavits of Sallie Edwards and J. S[sic]. Cass relative to the birth of Ruth Edwards, infant daughter of Eli and Sallie Edwards December 13, 1904, which it is presumed have been forwarded as an application for enrollment of the above named children. It is stated in the affidavit of the mother that you are a citizen by blood of the Choctaw Nation and that she is a citizen by intermarriage of said Nation.

If this is true you are requested to state when and where application was made for your enrollment, your age, the names of your parents, and any other information which will enable the Commission to identify you upon its records. If you have married Sallie Edwards since the time you were listed for enrollment this should also be stated.

Upon receipt of the information above requested the matter will then receive further consideration.

Respectfully,
SIGNED

(End of letter)

7-4693

Muskogee, Indian Territory, January 25, 1905.

Eli Edwards,
Lehigh, Indian Territory.

Dear Sir:

Receipt is hereby acknowledged of your letter of January 21, 1905, giving your roll number on the Choctaw roll in the matter of the enrollment of your two children Everette[sic] and Ruth Edwards.

In reply to your letter you are advised that the information contained therein has enabled the Commission to identify you upon its records as having been enrolled as a citizen by blood of the Choctaw Nation.

Referring to the affidavits forwarded by you relative to the birth of your children Everette and Ruth Edwards December 10, 1902 and December 13, 1904, respectively,

Applications for Enrollment of Choctaw Newborn
Act of 1905   Volume VI

you are advised that under the provisions of the act of Congress approved July 1, 1902, the provisions of the act of Congress approved July 1, 1902, no children born to citizens of the Choctaw and Chickasaw Nations subsequent to September 25, 1902, the date of the ratification of said act, are entitled to enrollment and allotment in the Choctaw and Chickasaw Nations.

Respectfully,

Chairman.

N.B. 351.
COPY
Muskogee, Indian Territory, April 8, 1905.

Eli Edwards,
Lehigh, Indian Territory.

Dear Sir:

There is enclosed you herewith for execution application for the enrollment of your infant children, Everette[sic] Edwards, born December 10, 1902, and Ruth Edwards born December 13, 1904.

The affidavits heretofore filed with the Commission show the children were living on January 10, 1905. It is necessary, for the children to be enrolled, that they were living on March 4, 1905.

In having these affidavits executed care should be exercised to see that all names are written in full, as they appear in the body of the affidavit, and in the event that either of the persons signing the affidavit are unable to write, signatures by mark must be attested by two witnesses. Each affidavit must be executed before a Notary Public and the notarial seal and signature of the officer must be attached to each separate affidavit.

Respectfully,

SIGNED

Commissioner in Charge.

LER 8-1

Applications for Enrollment of Choctaw Newborn
Act of 1905 Volume VI

7 N.B. 351.

Muskogee, Indian Territory, May 3, 1905.

Eli Edwards,
    Lehigh, Indian Territory.

Dear Sir:

    Receipt is hereby acknowledged of the affidavits of Sallie Edwards and J. L. Cass to the birth of Ruth Edwards, daughter of Eli and Sallie Edwards, December 13, 1904, and the same have been filed with our records in the matter of the enrollment of said child.

Respectfully,

Chairman.

---

7 NB 351

Muskogee, Indian Territory, May 5, 1905.

Eli Edwards,
    Lehigh, Indian Territory.

Dear Sir:

    Receipt is hereby acknowledged of the affidavits of Sallie Edwards and John M. Bentley to the birth of Everette[sic] Edwards son of Eli and Sallie Edwards, December 10, 1902, and the same have been filed with our records as an application for the enrollment of said child.

Respectfully,

Commissioner in Charge.

Applications for Enrollment of Choctaw Newborn
Act of 1905   Volume VI

7-4693

Muskogee, Indian Territory, May 12, 1905.

Eli Edwards,
    Lehigh, Indian Territory.

Dear Sir:

    Receipt is hereby acknowledged of your letter of May 6, 1905, asking if application for the enrollment of your two children Everett and Ruth Edwards have been received.

    I reply to your letter you are advised that the affidavits heretofore forwarded to the birth of your children Everett and Ruth Edwards have been filed with our records as an application for their enrollment.

    If further evidence is necessary to enable us to determine the right of these children to enrollment you will be duly notified.

    Respectfully,

    Chairman.

7-NB-351/

Muskogee, Indian Territory, May 22, 1905.

Eli Edwards,
    Lehigh, Indian Territory.

Dear Sir:

    Referring to the application for the enrollment of your infant child, Everette[sic] Edwards, born December 10, 1902, it is noted from the affidavits heretofore filed in this office that the applicant claims through you.

    If this is correct it will be necessary that you file in this office either the original or a certified copy of the license and certificate of your marriage to the applicants[sic] mother, Sallie Edwards.

    Respectfully,

    Chairman.

Applications for Enrollment of Choctaw Newborn
Act of 1905   Volume VI

7-NB-351

Muskogee, Indian Territory, July 29, 1905.

Eli Edwards,
   Lehigh, Indian Territory.

Dear Sir:

Referring to the application for the enrollment of your infant children, Everette[sic] and Ruth Edwards, born December 10, 1902, and December 13, 1904, respectively, it is noted from the affidavits heretofore filed in this office, that the applicants claim through you.

In this event it will be necessary for the enrollment of the children that you file in this office either the original or a certified copy of the license and certificate of your marriage to Sallie Edwards, the mother of the applicants.

This matter should receive your immediate attention as no further action can be taken relative to the enrollment of your said children until this evidence is supplied.

          Respectfully,

                    Commissioner.

---

7 N B 351

Muskogee, Indian Territory, August 30, 1905.

Eli Edwards,
   Lehigh, Indian Territory.

Dear Sir:

Receipt is hereby acknowledged of the affidavits of R. P. Colbert, Dee Colbert and Eli Edwards in reference to the marriage of Eli Edwards and Sallie Edwards on February 21. 1896, and the same have been filed with the records of this office and will receive consideration in the disposition of the application for the enrollment of Everette[sic] and Ruth Edwards as new-born citizens by blood of the Choctaw Nation.

          Respectfully,

                    Commissioner.

Applications for Enrollment of Choctaw Newborn
Act of 1905   Volume VI

Choc New Born 352
    Annie Traut[sic]
    (Born Feb. 17, 1903)

NEW-BORN AFFIDAVIT.

Number..............

...Choctaw Enrolling Commission...

IN THE MATTER OF THE APPLICATION FOR ENROLLMENT, as a citizen of the Choctaw Nation, of Annie Trout

born on the 17 day of February 190 3

Name of father   Henry Trout   a citizen of   Choctaw
Nation final enrollment No. 931
Name of mother   Minney[sic] Trout   a citizen of   Choctaw
Nation final enrollment No. 12971

                      Postoffice   South McAlester

AFFIDAVIT OF MOTHER.

UNITED STATES OF AMERICA
INDIAN TERRITORY
   Central   DISTRICT

I   Minnie Trout   , on oath state that I am 43   years of age and a citizen by   blood   of the   Choctaw   Nation, and as such have been placed upon the final roll of the Choctaw   Nation, by the Honorable Secretary of the Interior my final enrollment number being   12971 ; that I am the lawful wife of   Henry Trout   , who is a citizen of the   Choctaw   Nation, and as such has been placed upon the final roll of said Nation by the Honorable Secretary of the Interior, his final enrollment number being   931   and that a   Female   child was born to me on the   17th day of   February   190 3; that said child has been named   Annie Trout   , and is now living.

Witnesseth.   Minnie Trauth[sic]
  Must be two   } Ellen Smallfield
  Witnesses who
  are Citizens.   Minnie Ott

Applications for Enrollment of Choctaw Newborn
Act of 1905   Volume VI

Subscribed and sworn to before me this   25th   day of   February   190 5

Edgar L. Stegall
Notary Public.

My commission expires: January 10, 1907

AFFIDAVIT OF ATTENDING PHYSICIAN OR MIDWIFE

UNITED STATES OF AMERICA
INDIAN TERRITORY
  Central   DISTRICT

I,   Henry Trout   the Husband & father on oath state that I attended on Mrs.   Minnie Trout   wife of   Henry Trout   on the   17th   day of   February , 190 3, that there was born to her on said date a   Female   child, that said child is now living, and is said to have been named   Annie Trout

Father
Henry Trauth   the   ~~M.D.~~

WITNESSETH:
Must be two witnesses who are citizens and know the child.
{ Ellen Smallfield
  Minnie Ott

Subscribed and sworn to before me this, the   24th   day of   February   190 5

A E Folsom   Notary Public.

We hereby certify that we are well acquainted with   Henry Trout   the Father of Annie Trout   and know   him   to be reputable and of good standing in the community.

{ EL Stegall
  A Bollinger

Applications for Enrollment of Choctaw Newborn
Act of 1905   Volume VI

BIRTH AFFIDAVIT.

DEPARTMENT OF THE INTERIOR.
COMMISSION TO THE FIVE CIVILIZED TRIBES.

IN RE APPLICATION FOR ENROLLMENT, as a citizen of the   Choctaw   Nation, of Annie Trauth   , born on the   18th [sic]   day of   February , 1903

Name of Father: Henry Trauth   a citizen of the   Choctaw   Nation.
Name of Mother: Minnie Trauth   a citizen of the   Choctaw   Nation.

Postoffice   South McAlester, I.T.

AFFIDAVIT OF MOTHER.

UNITED STATES OF AMERICA, Indian Territory, }
    Central   DISTRICT.   }

I,   Minnie Trauth   , on oath state that I am   43   years of age and a citizen by   blood   , of the   Choctaw   Nation; that I am the lawful wife of   Henry Trauth   , who is a citizen, by   marriage   of the   Choctaw   Nation; that a female   child was born to me on   18th[sic]   day of   February   , 1903; that said child has been named   Annie Trauth   , and was living March 4, 1905.

          her
        Minnie x Trauth
Witnesses To Mark: mark
 { Peter Maytubby Jr
 { Green Taylor

Subscribed and sworn to before me this 20th   day of   March   , 1905

        Wirt Franklin
         Notary Public.

AFFIDAVIT OF ATTENDING PHYSICIAN OR MID-WIFE.

UNITED STATES OF AMERICA, Indian Territory, }
    Central   DISTRICT.   }

I,   Ellen Smallfield   , a   mid-wife   , on oath state that I attended on Mrs.   Minnie Trauth   , wife of   Henry Trauth   on the   18th[sic] day of February , 1903; that there was born to her on said date a   female   child; that said child was living March 4, 1905, and is said to have been named   Annie Trauth

        her
      Ellen x Smallfield
       mark

Applications for Enrollment of Choctaw Newborn
Act of 1905 Volume VI

Witnesses To Mark:
- Peter Maytubby Jr
- Green Taylor

Subscribed and sworn to before me this 20th day of March , 1905

Wirt Franklin
Notary Public.

BIRTH AFFIDAVIT.

DEPARTMENT OF THE INTERIOR.
COMMISSION TO THE FIVE CIVILIZED TRIBES.

IN RE APPLICATION FOR ENROLLMENT, as a citizen of the   Choctaw   Nation, of Annie Traut , born on the 18[sic] day of February , 1903

Name of Father: Henry Traut   a citizen of the Choctaw   Nation.
Name of Mother: Minnie Traut   a citizen of the Choctaw   Nation.

Postoffice   South McAlester, I.T.

AFFIDAVIT OF MOTHER.

UNITED STATES OF AMERICA, Indian Territory, }
    Central   DISTRICT.

I, Minnie Traut , on oath state that I am 43 years of age and a citizen by blood , of the Choctaw Nation; that I am the lawful wife of Henry Traut , who is a citizen, by intermarriage of the Choctaw Nation; that a female child was born to me on 18[sic] day of February , 1903; that said child has been named Annie Traut , and was living March 4, 1905.

                                                  her
                                            Minnie x Trauth

Witnesses To Mark: mark
- EL Stegall
- R.L. Gates

Subscribed and sworn to before me this 11th day of April , 1905

Edgar L. Stegall
My Commission expires January 15, 1907   Notary Public.

Applications for Enrollment of Choctaw Newborn
Act of 1905   Volume VI

AFFIDAVIT OF ATTENDING PHYSICIAN OR MID-WIFE.

UNITED STATES OF AMERICA, Indian Territory, }
    Central   DISTRICT.

    I, Henry Traut, a Physician, on oath state that I attended on Mrs. Minnie Traut, wife of Henry Traut on the 18[sic] day of February, 1903; that there was born to her on said date a female child; that said child was living March 4, 1905, and is said to have been named Annie Traut

                            Henry Traut

Witnesses To Mark:
  { EL Stegall
    R.L. Gates

    Subscribed and sworn to before me this 11th day of April, 1905

                        Edgar L. Stegall
My Commission expires January 15, 1907   Notary Public.

BIRTH AFFIDAVIT.

DEPARTMENT OF THE INTERIOR.
COMMISSION TO THE FIVE CIVILIZED TRIBES.

    IN RE APPLICATION FOR ENROLLMENT, as a citizen of the Choctaw Nation, of Annie Traut, born on the 17th day of February, 1903 about 11 P.M.

Name of Father: Henry Traut   a citizen of the Choctaw Nation.
Name of Mother: Minnie Traut   a citizen of the Choctaw Nation.

                Postoffice   South McAlester, I.T.

AFFIDAVIT OF MOTHER.

UNITED STATES OF AMERICA, Indian Territory, }
    Central   DISTRICT.

    I, Minnie Traut, on oath state that I am 43 years of age and a citizen by Blood, of the Choctaw Nation; that I am the lawful wife of Henry Traut, who is a citizen, by intermarriage of the Choctaw Nation; that a Female child was born to me on 17" day of February, 1903; that said child has been named Annie Traut, and was living March 4, 1905.

                              her
                      Minnie x Traut
                         mark

Applications for Enrollment of Choctaw Newborn
Act of 1905 Volume VI

Witnesses To Mark:
{ EL Stegall
{ O.C. Cooper

Subscribed and sworn to before me this 26th day of May , 1905

Edgar L. Stegall
My Commission expires January 10, 1907   Notary Public.

AFFIDAVIT OF ATTENDING PHYSICIAN OR MID-WIFE.

UNITED STATES OF AMERICA, Indian Territory, }
    Central   DISTRICT. }

I, Henry Traut , a Physician , on oath state that I attended on Mrs. Minnie Traut , wife of Henry Traut on the 17th day of February, 1903; that there was born to her on said date a Female child; that said child was living March 4, 1905, and is said to have been named Annie Traut

                          his
                     Henry x Traut
Witnesses To Mark: mark
{ EL Stegall
{ O.C. Cooper

Subscribed and sworn to before me this 26th day of May , 1905

Edgar L. Stegall
My Commission expires January 10, 1907   Notary Public.

---

7 𝑛𝐵 352
BIRTH AFFIDAVIT.

DEPARTMENT OF THE INTERIOR.
COMMISSION TO THE FIVE CIVILIZED TRIBES.

IN RE APPLICATION FOR ENROLLMENT, as a citizen of the Choctaw Nation, of Annie Traut , born on the 17 day of Feby , 1903

Name of Father: Henry Traut   a citizen of the Choctaw Nation.
Name of Mother: Minnie Traut   a citizen of the Choctaw Nation.

                  Postoffice   South McAlester, I.T.

Applications for Enrollment of Choctaw Newborn
Act of 1905   Volume VI

AFFIDAVIT OF MOTHER.

UNITED STATES OF AMERICA, Indian Territory, }
.... DISTRICT. }

I, ..., on oath state that I am ...... years of age and a citizen by ...., of the .... Nation; that I am the lawful wife of ...., who is a citizen, by .... of the .... Nation; that a .... child was born to me on ...... day of ...., 1......, that said child has been named ...., and was living March 4, 1905.

....

Witnesses To Mark:
{ ....
  .... }

Subscribed and sworn to before me this ...... day of ...., 1905.

....
Notary Public.

AFFIDAVIT OF ATTENDING PHYSICIAN OR MID-WIFE.

UNITED STATES OF AMERICA, Indian Territory, }
  Central   DISTRICT. }

I, Ellen Smallfield, a midwife, on oath state that I attended on Mrs. Minnie Traut, wife of Henry Traut on the 17th day of Feby, 1903; that there was born to her on said date a Female child; that said child was living March 4, 1905, and is said to have been named Annie Traut

                                          her
                               Ellen x Smallfield
Witnesses To Mark: mark
{ *(Name Illegible)*
  (Name Illegible) }

Subscribed and sworn to before me this 7th day of July, 1907[sic]

My Commission expires Jan 10 1907   Edgar L Stegall
                                        Notary Public.

Applications for Enrollment of Choctaw Newborn
Act of 1905 Volume VI

COMMISSIONERS:
TAMS BIXBY,
THOMAS B. NEEDLES,
C.R. BRECKINRIDGE.

WM. O. BEALL
Secretary

DEPARTMENT OF THE INTERIOR,
COMMISSIONER TO THE FIVE CIVILIZED TRIBES.

Wm O.B.

REFER IN REPLY TO THE FOLLOWING:

N.B. 352.

ADDRESS ONLY THE
COMMISSION TO THE FIVE CIVILIZED TRIBES.

Muskogee, Indian Territory, April 8, 1905.

Henry Traut,
    South McAlester, Indian Territory.

Dear Sir:

    There is enclosed you herewith for execution application for the enrollment of your infant child, Annie Traut, born February 18, 1903.

    In the application heretofore filed with the Commission your surname is written "Trauth" while it appears on the records of this office as "Traut", in conformity with which the application is made out.

    In having these affidavits executed care should be exercised to see that all names are written in full, as they appear in the body of the affidavit, and in the event that either of the persons signing the affidavit are unable to write, signatures by mark must be attested by two witnesses. Each affidavit must be executed before a Notary Public and the notarial seal and signature of the officer must be attached to each separate affidavit.

                         Respectfully,
                           T.B. Needles
LER 8-16   Commissioner in Charge.

Choctaw N.B. 352.

Muskogee, Indian Territory, April 14, 1905.

Henry Traut,
    South McAlester, Indian Territory.

Dear Sir:

    Receipt is hereby acknowledged of the affidavits of Minnie Traut and Henry Traut to the birth of Annie Traut, daughter of Henry and Minnie Traut, February 18, 1903, and the same have been filed with our records in the matter of the enrollment of said child.

Applications for Enrollment of Choctaw Newborn
Act of 1905 Volume VI

Respectfully,

Commissioner in Charge.

7-NB-352.

Muskogee, Indian Territory, May 23, 1905.

Henry Traut,
    South McAlester, Indian Territory.

Dear Sir:

    There is enclosed you herewith for execution application for the enrollment of your infant child, Annie Traut.

    In the affidavits filed in the office of March 15, 1905, and April 15, 1905, the date of the childs[sic] birth is given as February 18, 1903, while in those filed April 26, 1905, the date of birth is given as February 17, 1903. In the enclosed application the date of birth has been left blank, in which you will insert the correct date of birth, and, when the affidavits are properly executed, return them to this office.

    In having these affidavits executed care should be exercised to see that all names are written in full, as they appear in the body of the affidavit, and in the event that either of the persons signing the affidavit are unable to write, signatures by mark must be attested by two witnesses. Each affidavit must be executed before a Notary Public and the notarial seal and signature of the officer must be attached to each separate affidavit.

Respectfully,

VR 23-3.   Chairman.

7-N.B. 352.

Muskogee, Indian Territory, June 2, 1905.

Henry Traut,
    South McAlester, Indian Territory.

Dear Sir:

    Receipt is hereby acknowledged of the affidavits of Minnie Traut and Henry Traut to the birth of Annie Traut, daughter of Henry and Minnie Traut, February 17, 1903, and the same have been filed with our records in the matter of the enrollment of said child.

Applications for Enrollment of Choctaw Newborn
Act of 1905   Volume VI

(End of letter) Respectfully,

---

7 NB 352

Muskogee, Indian Territory, July 21, 1905.

McKennon & Dean,
    Attorneys at Law,
        South McAlester, Indian Territory.

Gentlemen:

    Replying to that portion of your letter of July 11, 1905, in which you ask if an allotment may now be selected for Annie Traut.

    In reply to your letter you are advised that the affidavits heretofore forwarded to the birth of Annie Traut, child of Henry and Minnie Traut, has been filed as an application for the enrollment of said child but her name has not yet been placed upon a schedule of citizens by blood of the Choctaw Nation, prepared for forwarding to the Secretary of the Interior, and pending her approval, no selection of allotment can be made in her behalf.

        Respectfully,

            Commissioner.

Substitute

7-NB-352

Muskogee, Indian Territory, July 26, 1905.

Henry Traut,
    South McAlester, Indian Territory.

Dear Sir:

    There is inclosed you herewith for execution by Ellen Smallfield, midwife, an affidavit to the birth of your infant child, Annie Traut, born February 17, 1903.

    In the affidavit of Ellen Smallfield, to the birth of this child, heretofore filed in this office, the date of birth was given as February 18, 1903, as February 17, 1903, appears from the record of this case to be the correct date of birth, you will please have this affidavit properly executed and return to this office as soon as possible, as no further action can be taken relative to the enrollment of your infant child, until the evidence requested is supplied.

Applications for Enrollment of Choctaw Newborn
Act of 1905 Volume VI

Respectfully,

LM 25/3   Commissioner.

7-NB-352

Muskogee, Indian Territory, August 10, 1905.

Henry Traut,
    South McAlester, Indian Territory.

Dear Sir:

    Receipt is hereby acknowledged of the affidavit of Ellen Smallfield to the birth of Annie Traut, February 17, 1903, and the same has been filed in the matter of the enrollment of said child.

Respectfully,

Acting Commissioner.

Choc New Born 353
    Katherine Culbertson
    (Born Aug. 15, 1903)

NEW-BORN AFFIDAVIT.

Number...............

...Choctaw Enrolling Commission...

    IN THE MATTER OF THE APPLICATION FOR ENROLLMENT, as a citizen of the Choctaw   Nation, of   Katherine Culbertson

born on the 15   day of __August__   190 3

Name of father   Jesse W Culbertson   a citizen of   Choctaw
Nation final enrollment No. 772
Name of mother   Katie Culbertson   a citizen of   Choctaw
Nation final enrollment No. 13015

Applications for Enrollment of Choctaw Newborn
Act of 1905   Volume VI

Postoffice   Savanna

AFFIDAVIT OF MOTHER.

UNITED STATES OF AMERICA
INDIAN TERRITORY
Central   DISTRICT

I   Katie Culbertson   , on oath state that I am 31 years of age and a citizen by Blood of the Choctaw Nation, and as such have been placed upon the final roll of the Choctaw Nation, by the Honorable Secretary of the Interior my final enrollment number being 13015 ; that I am the lawful wife of Jesse W Culbertson , who is a citizen of the Choctaw Nation, and as such has been placed upon the final roll of said Nation by the Honorable Secretary of the Interior, his final enrollment number being 772 and that a Female child was born to me on the 15 day of August 190 3; that said child has been named Katherine Culbertson , and is now living.

Witnesseth.   Katie Culbertson

Must be two Witnesses who are Citizens.   } F E Dawson
                                            I W Harper

Subscribed and sworn to before me this 10 day of Jan   190.........

W.T. Culbertson
Notary Public.

My commission expires:
Sept 22-1907

(The above Birth Affidavit given again.)

AFFIDAVIT OF ATTENDING PHYSICIAN OR MIDWIFE

UNITED STATES OF AMERICA
INDIAN TERRITORY
Central   DISTRICT

I, S.P. Ross a Physician on oath state that I attended on Mrs. Katie Culbertson wife of Jesse W Culbertson on the 13th [sic] day of August , 190 3, that there was born to her on said date a Female child, that said child is now living, and is said to have been named Katherine Culbertson

S.P. Ross   M.D.

WITNESSETH:
Must be two witnesses who are citizens and know the child.   { B. P. Mackey
                                                               T. J. Ryan

Applications for Enrollment of Choctaw Newborn
Act of 1905 Volume VI

January   Subscribed and sworn to before me this, the   10th   day of
                        190 5

                              W.T. Culbertson   Notary Public.

　　We hereby certify that we are well acquainted with   S.P. Ross   a   Physician   and know   him   to be reputable and of good standing in the community.

$$\left\{ \begin{array}{l} \text{B. P. Mackey} \\ \text{T. J. Ryan} \end{array} \right.$$

BIRTH AFFIDAVIT.

DEPARTMENT OF THE INTERIOR.
COMMISSION TO THE FIVE CIVILIZED TRIBES.

IN RE APPLICATION FOR ENROLLMENT, as a citizen of the   Choctaw   Nation, of Katherine Culbertson   , born on the   15   day of   Aug , 1903

Name of Father: Jesse W Culbertson   a citizen of the   Choctaw   Nation.
Name of Mother: Katie Culbertson   a citizen of the   Choctaw   Nation.

Postoffice   Savanna

AFFIDAVIT OF MOTHER.

UNITED STATES OF AMERICA, Indian Territory,
　　Central   DISTRICT.

　　I,   Katie Culbertson   , on oath state that I am   31 years of age and a citizen by blood   , of the   Choctaw   Nation; that I am the lawful wife of   Jesse W Culbertson   , who is a citizen, by   Inter M   of the   Choctaw   Nation; that a Female   child was born to me on   15th   day of   August   , 1903, that said child has been named   Katherine   , and is now living.

                              Katie Culbertson

Witnesses To Mark:
$\left\{ \begin{array}{l} \text{Effie D Gorman} \\ \text{Mrs E Poe Harriss} \end{array} \right.$

　　Subscribed and sworn to before me this   13 day of   March   , 1905.

                              W.T. Culbertson
                              Notary Public.

Applications for Enrollment of Choctaw Newborn
Act of 1905   Volume VI

AFFIDAVIT OF ATTENDING PHYSICIAN OR MID-WIFE.

UNITED STATES OF AMERICA, Indian Territory, }
Central   DISTRICT.

I, SP Ross , a Physician , on oath state that I attended on Mrs. Kate[sic] Culbertson , wife of Jesse W Culbertson on the 15th day of Aug, 1903; that there was born to her on said date a Female child; that said child is now living and is said to have been named Katherine

S.P. Ross M.D.

Witnesses To Mark:
{ Effie D Gorman
{ Mrs E Poe Harriss

Subscribed and sworn to before me this 13th day of March , 1905.

W.T. Culbertson
Notary Public.

7-4711

Muskogee, Indian Territory, March 16, 1905.

Jesse W. Culberson[sic],
   Savanna, Indian Territory.

Dear Sir:

Receipt is hereby acknowledged of the affidavits of Katie Culberson[sic] and S. P. Ross to the birth of Katherine Culberson[sic], infant daughter of Jesse W. and Katie Culberson, August 15, 1903, and the same have been filed with our records as an application for the enrollment of said child.

Respectfully,

Chairman.

Applications for Enrollment of Choctaw Newborn
Act of 1905   Volume VI

Choc New Born 354
    Burnett Meadows
    (Born Jan. 15, 1905.)

BIRTH AFFIDAVIT.

DEPARTMENT OF THE INTERIOR.
COMMISSION TO THE FIVE CIVILIZED TRIBES.

IN RE APPLICATION FOR ENROLLMENT, as a citizen of the Choctaw Nation, of Burnett Meadows, born on the 15th day of January, 1905

Name of Father: Andy Meadows   Choctaw freedman ~~a citizen of the~~ ~~Nation~~.
Name of Mother: Laura Meadows   a citizen of the Choctaw Nation.

Postoffice South McAlester, I.T.

AFFIDAVIT OF MOTHER.

UNITED STATES OF AMERICA, Indian Territory, }
    Central   DISTRICT. }

I, Laura Meadows, on oath state that I am 29 years of age and a citizen by blood, of the Choctaw Nation; that I am the lawful wife of Andy Meadows, who is a ~~citizen, by~~ Choctaw ~~of the~~ freedman ~~Nation~~; that a female child was born to me on 15th day of January, 1905; that said child has been named Burnett Meadows, and was living March 4, 1905.

                                Laura Meadows

Witnesses To Mark:
{

Subscribed and sworn to before me this 17th day of March, 1905

                              Wirt Franklin
                                Notary Public.

Applications for Enrollment of Choctaw Newborn
Act of 1905   Volume VI

AFFIDAVIT OF ATTENDING PHYSICIAN OR MID-WIFE.

UNITED STATES OF AMERICA, Indian Territory, }
Central   DISTRICT.

I, E. W. South, a physician, on oath state that I attended on Mrs. Laura Meadows, wife of Andy Meadows on the 15th day of January, 1905; that there was born to her on said date a female child; that said child was living March 4, 1905, and is said to have been named Burnett Meadows

Dr. E. W. South

Witnesses To Mark:
{

Subscribed and sworn to before me this 17th day of March, 1905

Wirt Franklin
Notary Public.

7-13024
BIRTH AFFIDAVIT.

DEPARTMENT OF THE INTERIOR.
COMMISSION TO THE FIVE CIVILIZED TRIBES.

IN RE APPLICATION FOR ENROLLMENT, as a citizen of the Choctaw Nation, of Burnett Meadows, born on the 15 day of January, 1905

Name of Father: Andy Meadows   a citizen of the Choc Nation.
Name of Mother: Laura Meadows   a citizen of the Choc Nation.

Postoffice   South McAlester, I.T.

AFFIDAVIT OF MOTHER.

UNITED STATES OF AMERICA, Indian Territory, }
Central   DISTRICT.

I, Laura Meadows, on oath state that I am 30 years of age and a citizen by blood, of the Choctaw Nation; that I am the lawful wife of Andy Meadows, who is a ~~citizen, by~~ Freedman of the Choctaw Nation; that a female child was born to me on 15 day of January, 1905; that said child has been named Burnett Meadows, and was living March 4, 1905.

Laura Meadows

Applications for Enrollment of Choctaw Newborn
Act of 1905   Volume VI

Witnesses To Mark:
{

    Subscribed and sworn to before me this 26 day of   April   , 1905

                                      OL Johnson
                                        Notary Public.

AFFIDAVIT OF ATTENDING PHYSICIAN OR MID-WIFE.

UNITED STATES OF AMERICA, Indian Territory,
    Central   DISTRICT.

    I, E. W. South , a physician , on oath state that I attended on Mrs. Laura Meadows , wife of Andy Meadows on the 15 day of January , 1905; that there was born to her on said date a   female   child; that said child was living March 4, 1905, and is said to have been named Burnett Meadows

                                  Dr. E. W. South

Witnesses To Mark:
{

    Subscribed and sworn to before me this 26 day of   April   , 1905

                                      OL Johnson
                                        Notary Public.

Choc New Born 355
    Ola May Williams
    (Born July 17, 1904)

BIRTH AFFIDAVIT.
DEPARTMENT OF THE INTERIOR.
COMMISSION TO THE FIVE CIVILIZED TRIBES.

    IN RE APPLICATION FOR ENROLLMENT, as a citizen of the   Choctaw   Nation, of Ola May Williams , born on the 17th day of July , 1904

Name of Father: David Williams   a citizen of the United States Nation.
Name of Mother: Abbie Lena Williams   a citizen of the   Choctaw   Nation.

Applications for Enrollment of Choctaw Newborn
Act of 1905   Volume VI

Postoffice   McAlester, I.T.

AFFIDAVIT OF MOTHER.

UNITED STATES OF AMERICA, Indian Territory,　}
　Central　　　　　DISTRICT.

　　I,　Abbie Lena Williams　　, on oath state that I am　18　years of age and a citizen by　blood　, of the　Choctaw　Nation; that I am the lawful wife of David Williams　　, who is a citizen, ~~by~~ .... of the   United States Nation; that a　female　child was born to me on　17th day of　July　, 1904; that said child has been named   Ola May Williams　　, and was living March 4, 1905.

　　　　　　　　　　　　　　Abbie Lena Williams
Witnesses To Mark:
{

　　Subscribed and sworn to before me this　17th day of　March　　, 1905

　　　　　　　　　　　　　　Wirt Franklin
　　　　　　　　　　　　　　　　Notary Public.

AFFIDAVIT OF ATTENDING PHYSICIAN OR MID-WIFE.

UNITED STATES OF AMERICA, Indian Territory,　}
　Central　　　　　DISTRICT.

　　I,　J.O. Grubbs　　, a　physician　　, on oath state that I attended on Mrs.　Abbie Lena Williams　　, wife of　David Williams　　on the 17th day of　July　, 1904; that there was born to her on said date a　female　child; that said child was living March 4, 1905, and is said to have been named   Ola May Williams

　　　　　　　　　　　　　　J.O. Grubbs MD
Witnesses To Mark:
{

　　Subscribed and sworn to before me this　17th　day of　March　　, 1905

　　　　　　　　　　　　　　Wirt Franklin
　　　　　　　　　　　　　　　　Notary Public.

Mother of this child states that she is finally enrolled as Abbie Bevell. Her father's name is Joe Bevell and her mother's name is Alice E. Bevell. WF

Applications for Enrollment of Choctaw Newborn
Act of 1905   Volume VI

Choc New Born 356
    Nona Carney
    (Born March 16, 1903)

NEW BORN AFFIDAVIT

No ....

CHOCTAW ENROLLING COMMISSION

IN THE MATTER OF THE APPLICATION FOR ENROLLMENT as a citizen of the Choctaw Nation, of Nona Carney born on the 16th day of March 190 3

Name of father Aaron Carney   a citizen of   Choctaw   Nation, final enrollment No. ....
Name of mother Nellie Carney   a citizen of   Choctaw   Nation, final enrollment No. 13079

                           Alderson Ind. Ter.   Postoffice.

AFFIDAVIT OF MOTHER

UNITED STATES OF AMERICA
    INDIAN TERRITORY
DISTRICT   Central

    I   Nellie Carney   , on oath state that I am 30   years of age and a citizen by   blood   of the   Choctaw   Nation, and as such have been placed upon the final roll of the   Choctaw   Nation, by the Honorable Secretary of the Interior my final enrollment number being 13079   ; that I am the lawful wife of Aaron Carney , who is a citizen of the   Choctaw   Nation, and as such has been placed upon the final roll of said Nation by the Honorable Secretary of the Interior, his final enrollment number being .... and that a   Female   child was born to me on the 16th day of March 190 5[sic]; that said child has been named   Nona Carney   , and is now living.

WITNESSETH: Nellie x Carney

    Must be two witnesses { Frank Pope
    who are citizens   { Silas Nail

Applications for Enrollment of Choctaw Newborn
Act of 1905 Volume VI

Subscribed and sworn to before me this, the 15 day of March , 190 5

James Bower
Notary Public.

My Commission Expires:
Sept. 23, 1907

Affidavit of Attending Physician or Midwife

UNITED STATES OF AMERICA,
INDIAN TERRITORY,
Central   DISTRICT

I, Elizabeth James   a   Midwife
on oath state that I attended on Mrs. Nellie Carney   wife of   Aaron Carney
on the 16th day of   March , 190 3, that there was born to her on said date a Female
child, that said child is now living, and is said to have been named Nona Carney

Elizabeth x James   M. D.

Subscribed and sworn to before me this the   15   day of   March   1905

James Bower
Notary Public.

WITNESSETH:

Must be two witnesses
who are citizens and
know the child.
{ Frank Pope
  Silas Nail

We hereby certify that we are well acquainted with   Elizabeth James
a   Midwife   and know   her   to be reputable and of good standing in the community.

Must be two citizen
witnesses.
{ Silas Nail
  Frank Pope

Applications for Enrollment of Choctaw Newborn
Act of 1905   Volume VI

BIRTH AFFIDAVIT.

DEPARTMENT OF THE INTERIOR.
COMMISSION TO THE FIVE CIVILIZED TRIBES.

IN RE APPLICATION FOR ENROLLMENT, as a citizen of the Choctaw Nation, of Nona Carney, born on the 16th day of March, 1903 freedman
Name of Father: Aaron Carney   a citizen of the Chickasaw Nation.
Name of Mother: Nellie Carney   a citizen of the Choctaw Nation.

Postoffice   Alderson I.T.

AFFIDAVIT OF MOTHER.

UNITED STATES OF AMERICA, Indian Territory,
Central   DISTRICT.

I, Nellie Carney (nee Carter), on oath state that I am 30 years of age and a citizen by blood, of the Choctaw Nation; that I am the lawful wife of Aaron Carney, who is a ~~citizen, by~~ Chickasaw ~~of the~~ freedman ~~Nation~~; that a female child was born to me on 16th day of March, 1903; that said child has been named Nona Carney, and was living March 4, 1905.

　　　　　　　　　　　　　　　　　　　　her
　　　　　　　　　　　　　　　　Nellie x Carney
Witnesses To Mark:　　　　　　　　　mark
　{ Columbus Campelube
　{ Silas Nail

Subscribed and sworn to before me this 17th day of March, 1905

　　　　　　　　　　　　　　Wirt Franklin
　　　　　　　　　　　　　　　　Notary Public.

AFFIDAVIT OF ATTENDING PHYSICIAN OR MID-WIFE.

UNITED STATES OF AMERICA, Indian Territory,
Central   DISTRICT.

I, Elizabeth James, a mid-wife, on oath state that I attended on Mrs. Nellie Carney, wife of Aaron Carney on the 16th day of March, 1903; that there was born to her on said date a female child; that said child was living March 4, 1905, and is said to have been named Nona Carney

　　　　　　　　　　　　　　　　　　　her
　　　　　　　　　　　　　　Elizabeth x James
　　　　　　　　　　　　　　　　mark

Applications for Enrollment of Choctaw Newborn
Act of 1905   Volume VI

Witnesses To Mark:
- Columbus Campelube
- Silas Nail

Subscribed and sworn to before me this 17th day of March, 1905

Wirt Franklin
Notary Public.

BIRTH AFFIDAVIT.

DEPARTMENT OF THE INTERIOR.
COMMISSION TO THE FIVE CIVILIZED TRIBES.

IN RE APPLICATION FOR ENROLLMENT, as a citizen of the Choctaw Nation, of Nona Carney, born on the 16th day of March, 1903
freedman
Name of Father: Aaron Carney   a citizen of the Chickasaw Nation.
Name of Mother: Nellie Carney   a citizen of the Choctaw Nation.

Postoffice   Alderson Ind Ter

AFFIDAVIT OF MOTHER.

UNITED STATES OF AMERICA, Indian Territory,
Central DISTRICT.

I, Kellie[sic] Carney (Carter), on oath state that I am 30 years of age and a citizen by blood, of the Choctaw Nation; that I am the lawful wife of Aaron Carney, who is a ~~citizen, by~~ freedman of the Chickasaw Nation; that a female child was born to me on 16th day of March, 1903; that said child has been named Nona Carney, and was living March 4, 1905.

                    her
            Nellie x Carney
Witnesses To Mark: mark
- Silas Nail
- Henry Ward

Subscribed and sworn to before me this 14th day of June, 1905

W D Jolly
Notary Public.

Applications for Enrollment of Choctaw Newborn
Act of 1905   Volume VI

AFFIDAVIT OF ATTENDING PHYSICIAN OR MID-WIFE.

UNITED STATES OF AMERICA, Indian Territory, }
Central   DISTRICT.

    I, Elizabeth James, a Midwife, on oath state that I attended on Mrs. Nellie Carney, wife of Aaron Carney on the 16th day of March, 1903; that there was born to her on said date a female child; that said child was living March 4, 1905, and is said to have been named Nona Carney

                            her
                       Elizabeth x James
                          mark

Witnesses To Mark:
{ Silas Nail
{ Henry Ward

    Subscribed and sworn to before me this 14th day of June, 1905.

                      W D Jolly
                          Notary Public.

                          7-NB-365.

Sub

        Muskogee, Indian Territory, May 26, 1905.

Aaron Carney,
    Alderson, Indian Territory.

Dear Sir:

    There is enclosed you herewith for execution application for the enrollment of your infant child, Nona Carney.

    In the affidavits of March 17, 1905, heretofore filed in this office, the date of the applicant's birth is given as March 16, 1903, while in these of March 15, 1905, the mother gives the date of birth as March 16, 1905. In the enclosed application the former date, which appears to be the correct one, is inserted. You will please return this application, when properly executed, to this office.

    In having these affidavits executed care should be exercised to see that all names are written in full, as they appear in the body of the affidavit, and in the event that either of the persons signing the affidavit are unable to write, signatures by mark must be attested by two witnesses. Each affidavit must be executed before a Notary Public and the notarial seal and signature of the officer must be attached to each separate affidavit.

Applications for Enrollment of Choctaw Newborn
Act of 1905   Volume VI

WR 26-1.

Respectfully,

Chairman.

7 NB 356

Muskogee, Indian Territory, June 19, 1905.

Aaron Carney,
   Alderson, Indian Territory.

Dear Sir:

   Receipt is hereby acknowledged of the affidavits of Nellie Carney and Elizabeth James to the birth of Nona Carney, daughter of Aaron and Nellie Carney, March 16, 1903, and the same have been filed with our records in the matter of the enrollment of said child.

Respectfully,

Chairman.

Choc New Born 357
   Lindsy[sic] Cann
   (Born Oct. 9, 1902)

DEPARTMENT OF THE INTERIOR.
COMMISSION TO THE FIVE CIVILIZED TRIBES.
Choctaw Nation, twelve miles south of
South McAlester, I. T., January 13, 1905.

--oOo--

   In the matter of the application for the enrollment of Lizzie Carnes as a citizen by blood of the Choctaw Nation, 7-4736.
   In the matter of the application for the enrollment of Melissa McCann as a citizen by blood of the Choctaw Nation, 7-4737.

--oOo--

   Melina Cann, being duly sworn and examined through Alfred W. McClure, sworn interpreter, testified as follows:

Applications for Enrollment of Choctaw Newborn
Act of 1905   Volume VI

EXAMINATION BY THE COMMISSION.

Q What is your name? A Melina Cann.
Q How old are you? A She says she don't know how old she is.
Q About twenty-three? A She says she must be along there somewhere. They never kept any records or dates and don't know.
Q What is your post office address? A South McAlester, Indian Territory.
Q What is your mother's name? A Jincy Nail.
Q Is this your mother standing right here (Pointing to a woman by her side)? A Yes.
Q What was your father's name? A Wesley Anderson.
Q Is he living? A Dead.
Q Was he a full blood Choctaw Indian? A Wesley Anderson's mother was a Chickasaw, so that would make him a Chickasaw.
Q Are you married? A She ways she was married.
Q Were you married more than once? A She was only married once.
Q What was the name of your husband? A George Cann.
Q Is he living? A Dead.
Q There is on file with the Commission an affidavit stating that George Kaen died on May 18, 1903, is that the correct date of his death? A She says yes, that is the correct date.

The witness is identified as Melina Carnes on Choctaw card field number 4736.
The husband of the witness is identified on Choctaw card number 5629 as George Kaen.

Q Have you any children? A Yes.
q What are their names? A One of them is Lizzie; the other one is Lindsy.
Q Who is the father of Lizzie? A George Cann is the father of Lizzie.
Q The witness who testified in your case yesterday said that Alfred Nail was the father of Lizzie, was she mistaken as to that? A She says she has always thought it was George Cann's daughter.
Q When was Lizzie born? A On the last day of December was when she was born.
Q How many years ago was it? A About seven years ago.
Q Do you remember the time the Choctaw tribal authorities made the 1896 Census Roll? A She says she remembers about the time.
Q How long after that roll was made was Lizzie born, was it the next year? A Yes, it was the next year, about that time.
Q Then your daughter Lizzie was born December 31, 1897, is that correct? A Yes.
Q Who is the father of your daughter Lindsy? A George Cann.
Q When was Lindsy born as near as you can tell? How old is Lindsy now? A About two.
Q What month and day was Lindsy born? A October.
Q October two years ago? A Yes.
Q Do you remember the special election at the time the Choctaws and Chickasaws ratified the supplemental agreement on September 25, 1902? A No answer.

The witness refuses to answer further questions.

Applications for Enrollment of Choctaw Newborn
Act of 1905   Volume VI

Jincy Nail, being duly sworn and examined through sworn interpreter, Alfred W. McClure, testified as follows:

EXAMINATION BY THE COMMISSION.

Q What is your name? A Jincy Nail.
Q About how old are you? A She says she don't know.
Q About 40? A Yes, about that.
Q What is your post office address? A South McAlester, Indian Territory.
Q Are you a full blood Choctaw citizen? A Yes.
Q Have you a daughter by the name of Melissa McCann? A Yes, she says this is the girl (Pointing to a girl standing by her side who has the appearance of a full blood Indian and who appears to be 13 or 14 years old).
Q Who is the father of Melissa McCann? A William McCann.
Q Was William McCann a full blood Choctaw? A Yes.
Q Is he living? A He is dead.
Q About how old is Melissa McCann? A About thirteen.
Q Do you remember the time the Choctaws drew the leased district payment money in 1893? A Yes.
Q Was Melissa McCann living then? A She says she was crawling about that time.
Q Did you draw money for Melissa McCann in 1893, at the time that payment was made? A Yes.

Melissa McCann is identified upon the 1893 Choctaw Leased District Payment Roll, Tebuckey county[sic], page 102, number 865, as Millisie McCann.

Q Have you a daughter by the name of Melina Carnes or Cann? A Yes, says this is the girl (Pointing to a woman at her side).
Q About how old is Melina Cann? A About twenty-three.
Q Has Melina Cann any children? A Just these two.
Q What are their names? A Lizzie and Lindsy Cann.
Q Who is the father of these children? A George Cann.
Q You daughter Melina Cann stated in her testimony a few minutes ago that Lizzie Cann was born December 31, 1897, that would be seven years ago, is that the correct date of the birth of Lizzie Cann? A She says yes, that is true.
Q Were you present at the birth of Lizzie? A She says yes, she acted as the midwife.
Q When was Lindsy Cann born? A She was born on the 9th day of October.
Q Do you remember the time the Choctaws and Chickasaws voted on the ratification of the Choctaw and Chickasaw Supplemental Agreement on September 25, 1902? A Yes, she remembers that.
Q Was it on October 9th after the ratification of that treaty that Lindsy Cann was born? A She says the October before the treaty was ratified.
Q Are you positive as to that fact? A Yes, she is positive as to that.
Q Were you present at the birth of Lindsy? A She says she was not present. Melina was over at Holis Carney's and Louisiana Carney acted as midwife.
Q Then Lindsy Cann was three years old the 9th of last October? A She ways yes, she was three years old.

Applications for Enrollment of Choctaw Newborn
Act of 1905   Volume VI

Q Was any application ever made to the Commission in writing or otherwise for the enrollment of Lindsy Cann? A She says no.

Witness excused.

Robert E. Grunert, stenographer to the Commission to the Five Civilized Tribes, on oath states that he reported all the proceedings had in the above entitled case on the 13th day of January, 1905, and that the foregoing is a full, true and correct transcript of his stenographic notes in said case.

Robert E. Grunert

Subscribed and sworn to before me this 26th day of January, 1905.

Charles H. Sawyer
Notary Public.

BIRTH AFFIDAVIT.

DEPARTMENT OF THE INTERIOR.
COMMISSION TO THE FIVE CIVILIZED TRIBES.

IN RE APPLICATION FOR ENROLLMENT, as a citizen of the   Choctaw   Nation, of Lindsy Cann   , born on the 9th day of October , 1902

Name of Father: George Cann   a citizen of the   Choctaw   Nation.
Name of Mother: Melina Cann (or Carnes)   a citizen of the   Choctaw   Nation.

Postoffice   South McAlester, I.T.

Child present
W.F.   **AFFIDAVIT OF MOTHER.**

UNITED STATES OF AMERICA, Indian Territory, }
       Central   DISTRICT.}

I, Melina Cann (or Carnes)   , on oath state that I am about 24   years of age and a citizen by   blood , of the   Choctaw   Nation; that I ~~am~~ was the lawful wife of   George Cann, deceased , who ~~is~~ was a citizen, by blood   of the Choctaw   Nation; that a   female   child was born to me on 9th   day of October   , 1902; that said child has been named   Lindsy Cann   , and was living March 4, 1905.

her
Melina x Cann
mark

Witnesses To Mark:
 { Hagen Anderson
 { Alfred Worcester

Applications for Enrollment of Choctaw Newborn
Act of 1905   Volume VI

Subscribed and sworn to before me this   16th day of   March   , 1905

                                   Wirt Franklin
                                   Notary Public.

AFFIDAVIT OF ATTENDING PHYSICIAN OR MID-WIFE.

UNITED STATES OF AMERICA, Indian Territory, ⎱
   Central   **DISTRICT.** ⎰

    I,   Louisiana Carney   , a mid-wife , on oath state that I attended on Mrs.   Melina Cann (or Carnes)   , wife of   George Cann   on the 9th day of October , 1902; that there was born to her on said date a   female   child; that said child was living March 4, 1905, and is said to have been named Lindsy Cann

                                  her
                           Louisiana x Carney
Witnesses To Mark: mark
⎰ Victor M Locke Jr
⎱ Boyd O Graves

Subscribed and sworn to before me this   16th day of   March   , 1905

                                   Wirt Franklin
                                   Notary Public.

BIRTH AFFIDAVIT.
                        DEPARTMENT OF THE INTERIOR.
              COMMISSION TO THE FIVE CIVILIZED TRIBES.

    IN RE APPLICATION FOR ENROLLMENT, as a citizen of the   Choctaw   Nation, of Lindsey[sic] Cann   , born on the .... day of .... , 1........

Name of Father: George Cann   a citizen of the   Choctaw   Nation.
                                 Anderson)
Name of Mother: Melina Cann (nee Melina   a citizen of the   Choctaw   Nation.

                        Postoffice   South McAlester, I.T.

Applications for Enrollment of Choctaw Newborn
Act of 1905   Volume VI

AFFIDAVIT OF MOTHER.

UNITED STATES OF AMERICA, Indian Territory, }
Central   DISTRICT.

I, Melina Cann (nee Melina Anderson) , on oath state that I am   23   years of age and a citizen by   blood   , of the   Choctaw   Nation; that I am the lawful wife of   George Cann   , who is was a citizen, by blood   of the   Choctaw Nation; that a   female   child was born to me on 9   day of Oct   , 1903[sic]; that said child has been named   Lindsey Cann   , and was living March 4, 1905.

                                            her
                              Melina x Cann (nee Melina Anderson)
Witnesses To Mark: mark
{ Lee Silmon
{ Norris Carney

Subscribed and sworn to before me this 29   day of   April   , 1905

                              J. Anderson
                              Notary Public.

AFFIDAVIT OF ATTENDING PHYSICIAN OR MID-WIFE.

UNITED STATES OF AMERICA, Indian Territory, }
Central   DISTRICT.

I,   Louisana Carney   , a   midwife   , on oath state that I attended on Mrs.   Melina Cann   , wife of   George Cann   on the 9   day of Oct   , 1903[sic]; that there was born to her on said date a   female   child; that said child was living March 4, 1905, and is said to have been named Lindsy Cann

                                          her
                              Louisana x Carney
Witnesses To Mark: mark
{ Norris Carney
{ Lee Silmon

Subscribed and sworn to before me this 29 day of   April   , 1905

                              J. Anderson
                              Notary Public.

Applications for Enrollment of Choctaw Newborn
Act of 1905 Volume VI

BIRTH AFFIDAVIT.

DEPARTMENT OF THE INTERIOR.
COMMISSION TO THE FIVE CIVILIZED TRIBES.

IN RE APPLICATION FOR ENROLLMENT, as a citizen of the Choctaw Nation, of Lindsey[sic] Cann, born on the 9 day of October, 1902, 1........

Name of Father: George Cann   a citizen of the Choctaw Nation.
Name of Mother: Melina Cann   a citizen of the Choctaw Nation.

Postoffice   South McAlester, Ind.Ter.

AFFIDAVIT OF MOTHER.

UNITED STATES OF AMERICA, Indian Territory,
Central   DISTRICT.

I, Melina Cann, on oath state that I am 23 years of age and a citizen by blood, of the CHOCTAW Nation; that I am the lawful wife of George Cann, deceased, who ~~is~~ was a citizen, by blood of the CHOCTAW Nation; that a female child was born to me on 9th day of October, 1902; that said child has been named Lindsey Cann, and was living March 4, 1905.

                        her
                Melina x Cann
Witnesses To Mark: mark
  { Dan Russell
    Norris Carney

Subscribed and sworn to before me this 27th day of August, 1906

                HC Kessler
                    Notary Public.

AFFIDAVIT OF ATTENDING PHYSICIAN OR MID-WIFE.

UNITED STATES OF AMERICA, Indian Territory,
Central   DISTRICT.

I, Louisana Carney, a mid-wife, on oath state that I attended on Mrs. Melina Cann, wife of George Cann on the 9th day of October, 1902; that there was born to her on said date a female child; that said child was living March 4, 1905, and is said to have been named Lindsey Cann

                      her
              Louisana x Carney
                    mark

Applications for Enrollment of Choctaw Newborn
Act of 1905   Volume VI

Witnesses To Mark:
{ Dan Russell
{ Norris Carney

    Subscribed and sworn to before me this   27th day of   August   , 1906
My Commission expires
August 6th 1908   HC Kessler
                                        Notary Public.

BIRTH AFFIDAVIT.

DEPARTMENT OF THE INTERIOR.
COMMISSION TO THE FIVE CIVILIZED TRIBES.

    IN RE APPLICATION FOR ENROLLMENT, as a citizen of the   Choctaw   Nation, of Lindsy Cann   , born on the   9   day of   Oct , 1902

Name of Father: George Cann   a citizen of the   Choctaw   Nation.
Name of Mother: Melina Cann   a citizen of the   Choctaw   Nation.

                        Postoffice   South McAlester, I.T.

AFFIDAVIT OF MOTHER.

UNITED STATES OF AMERICA, Indian Territory, }
    Central   DISTRICT.}

                                    30

    I,   Melina Cann   , on oath state that I am   about ~~24~~   years of age and a citizen by   Blood   , of the   Choctaw   Nation; that I ~~am~~ was the lawful wife of George Cann, deceased , who ~~is~~ was a citizen, by Blood   of the   Choctaw   Nation; that a   Female   child was born to me on 9   day of October   , 1902; that said child has been named   Lindsy Cann   , and was living March 4, 190*6*.

                                her
                         Melina x Cann
Witnesses To Mark: mark
{ Jacob Homer
{ W.P. Covington

    Subscribed and sworn to before me this   16th day of   October   , 1906

                            Lacey P. Bobo
                            Notary Public.

Applications for Enrollment of Choctaw Newborn
Act of 1905   Volume VI

AFFIDAVIT OF ATTENDING PHYSICIAN OR MID-WIFE.

UNITED STATES OF AMERICA, Indian Territory, }
Central   DISTRICT.

am acquainted with I, Irine[sic] Fryhover, a n acquaintance, on oath state that I ~~attended~~ ~~on~~ Mrs. Melina Cann, wife of George Cann on the 9th day of October, 1902; that there was born to her on said date a Female child; that said child was living March 4, 1905, and is said to have been named Lindsy Cann

Irene Fryhover

Witnesses To Mark:
{

Subscribed and sworn to before me this 16th day of October, 1906

Lacey P. Bobo
Notary Public.

AFFIDAVIT OF ATTENDING PHYSICIAN OR MID-WIFE.

UNITED STATES OF AMERICA, Indian Territory, }
Central   DISTRICT.

I, Louisana Carney, a mid-wife, on oath state that I attended on Mrs. Melina Cann, wife of George Cann on the 9th day of October, 1902; that there was born to her on said date a Female child; that said child was living March 4, 1905, and is said to have been named Lindsy Cann

her
Louisana x Carney
mark

Witnesses To Mark:
{ Jacob Homer
  W.P. Covington

Subscribed and sworn to before me this 17th day of October, 1906

Lacey P. Bobo
Notary Public.

Applications for Enrollment of Choctaw Newborn
Act of 1905   Volume VI

Acquaintance
AFFIDAVIT OF ~~ATTENDING PHYSICIAN OR MID-WIFE~~.

UNITED STATES OF AMERICA, Indian Territory, }
   Central   District.   }

                                                                  am acquainted with
I,   Kissen Reed   , a n acquaintance   , on oath state that I ~~attended on~~ Melina Cann   , wife of   George Cann   on the ⸺ day of   October , 1902; that there was born to her on said date a   female   child; that said child was living March 4, 1906, and is said to have been named Lindsy Cann

                                                             Kissen Reed
WITNESSES TO MARK:

{

Subscribed and sworn to before me this   16th   day of   October   , 1906.

                                                         Lacey P Bobo
                                                           Notary Public.

DEPARTMENT OF THE INTERIOR,
COMMISSIONER TO THE FIVE CIVILIZED TRIBES.

South McAlester, Indian Territory, November 7, 1906.

--------oOo--------

    In the matter of the application for the enrollment, as a citizen by blood of the Choctaw Nation, of Lindsey[sic] Cann, 7-72 B-

    In the matter of the death of Robert Wilson, Choctaw by blood, Card #5701, Roll Number 15811.

    Testimony taken eight miles southeast of South McAlester, Indian Territory, October 16, 1906.

    MELINA CANN, being duly sworn, by Lacey P. Bobo, Notary Public in and for the Central District of Indian Territory, testified as follows:

                                      Jacob Homer, Official Interpreter.

BY THE COMMISSIONER:

Q What is your name? A Melina Cann.
Q What is your age? A 30.
Q What is your post office address? A McAlester, I. T?[sic]

Applications for Enrollment of Choctaw Newborn
Act of 1905   Volume VI

Q Are you a citizen by blood of the Choctaw Nation? A Yes sir.
Q Who was your husband? A George Cann.
Q How many children have you? A Two.
Q What are their names? A Lizzie and Lindsey[sic].
Q Have you a minor child that has not been placed upon the approved roll as a citizen by blood of the Choctaw Nation? A Lindsey has not.
Q When was Lindsey born? A October 9, 1902.
Q How old is this child? A Four years old this October.
Q Who attended you in the capacity of midwife when this child was born? A Louisana Carney.
Q Was any one else present save Louisana Carnet[sic] when this child was born? A No.
Q Is Lindsey Cann living at the present time? A Yes, sir.

Small Indian child, apparently about four years of age is produced and claimed by the mother to be Lindsey Cann for whom application has been made.

-------------- --------------- -------

Q Were you acquainted with Robert Wilson? A Yes.
Q Who was the mother of Robert Wilson? A Sophy, her Choctaw name was Wikey.
Q Is Robert Wilson's mother living or dead? A Dead.
Q Who was Robert Wilson's father? A Wallace Wilson.
Q Is Wallace Wilson living or dead? A Dead.
Q You state your husband was George Cann: is he living or dead? A Dead.
Q Was your husband kin to Robert Wilson, if so state the relationship?
A Yes, sir, they had the same mother but a different father.
Q Is Robert Wilson now living? A Dead.
Q What was his age at the time of his death?
A He was a little over 15.
Q When did this boy die?
A I do not know how long ago, but he was dead before my child's birth.
Q Do you refer to Lindsey, Indian Territory the child for whose enrolment[sic] you have made application to-day? A Yes, sir.
Q In what season of the year did Robert Wilson die?
A In the winter time.
Q With respect to the birth of your child Lindsey, Indian Territory who you have just stated was born October 9, 1902, when did Robert Wilson's death occur?
A I think it was two winters before Lindsey was born.
Q Do you mean it was two winters counting thr[sic] winter your child was born?
A Yes, sir.
Q Are you positive that Robert Wilson died the winter before the birth of your child? A Yes.
Q Where did Robert Wilson's death occur? A At Alfred Nail's.
Q With whom do you make your home at present?
A With Kisson Reed.
Q Did you attend the burial of Robert Wilson? A Yes.

Applications for Enrollment of Choctaw Newborn
Act of 1905   Volume VI

Q Were funeral services held?
A Yes, the funeral was preached at the grave.
Q What was the state of the weather at the time you attended Robert Wilson's burial?
A It was very cold.

Witness Excused.

Testimony taken seven miles south of South McAlester, Indian Territory, at home of Jas. H. Flyhover, October 16, 1906.

IRENE FLYHOVER, being duly sworn by Lacey P. Bobo, Notary Public in and for the Central District of Indian Territory, testified as follows:

BY THE COMMISSIONER:

Q What is your name? A Irene Flyhover.
Q How old are you? A I will be 47 years old the 18th of next month.
Q What is your post office address? A South McAlester, I. T.
Q Are you a citizen or non-citizen of the Choctaw Nation.[sic]
A I am a non-citizen, I am Missouri-born.
Q Did you know Robert Wilson? A I know of him, I was personally acquainted with his sister Cillen and with Louisana Carney, Nollis Carney's wife and his brother George Cann. I am intimately acquainted with his relations who live in this vicinity.
Q Are these brothers and sisters whom you mention and state you are so well acquainted with citizens by blood of the Choctaw Nation?
A Yes, but George Cann is dead now, he was killed by the train.
Q When was George Cann killed? A June 3, 1903; George used to come over and play ball with my boys ever[sic] Sunday and I have talked with him about Robert fifty times, and he always liked to talk about his brother.
Q Why is it you are so well acquainted with all the relatives of Robert Wilson and did not know him?
A Because they are right here near us now and we had not been here long when Robert died, we had only come in a short time, but his sisters live right near us and visit with us.
Q Do you know Robert Wilson to be dead?
A Yes, sir, I know he is dead; I know that at least my husband went to make his coffin and also laid him in it.
Q What age boy was he? A He was a great big boy from what I have heard.
Q When did Robert Wilson die? A He died January 3, 1902.
Q How do you fix in your mind that Robert Wilson died January 3, 1902?
A We first came in here in two miles of where we now live September 24, 1901; our baby died and we stayed there until November 27, 1901; in November and December 1901 we cut the logs for this house and January 3rd, 1902 we had a house raising and the day we had the house raising Robert Wilson died in the evening about three o(clock.[sic] They sent after my husband to come and make the coffin and he went and made the coffin and stayed there until twelve o'clock; he dressed him and fixed him for the coffin.
Q Who do you lease land from? A We lease from Bill Colbert.

Applications for Enrollment of Choctaw Newborn
Act of 1905   Volume VI

Q For what period did your lease run? A Five years, it will be out this coming January 1907.
Q And you had just moved on this land and taken possession under the five-year lease when Robert Wilson died? A Yes, sir.
Q Do you state under oath and as a positive fact that Robert Wilson died January 3, 1902? A Yes, sir.

Field Card Number 5701 is here shown witness:

Q Are you positive and do you know that Robert Wilson #3 hereon is the Choctaw whom you have just testified died January 3, 1902?
A Yes, sir, I am sure of it, for George Cann has talked so much to me about it and we lived here and my husband made the coffin and dressed him.

Witness Excused.

Testimony taken at same place and on same date as preceding.

KISSEN REED, being duly sworn, by lacey P. Bobo Notary Public in and for the Central District of Indian Territory, testifid[sic] as follows:

BY THE COMMISSIONER:

Q What is your name? Kissen Reed.
Q How old are you? A 46.
Q What is your post office address? A Savanna, I. T.
Q Are you a citizen by blood of the Choctaw Nation?
A No, sir, I am a Chickasaw.
Q Were you acquainted with Robert Wilson? A Yes.
Q Who was his father and mother?
Q[sic] Wallace Wilson was his father and Wikey or Sophy Wilson was his mother.
Q Are his father and mother Choctaws and are they now living?
A No, they are both dead.
Q Can you name other children of Wallace and Wikey Wilson?
A Cillen and Stephen and Robert are full sisters and brothers and George Cann and Louisana Carney are half brothers and sisters.
Q Do you know Robert Wilson to be dead, if so state when he died?
A He died January 1st, 2nd or 3rd, 1902.
Q How do you fix in your mind that Robert Wilson died the 1st, 2nd or 3rd of January 1902?
A He died the same day that Mr. James Flyhover had a house raising; Mr. Flyhover leased land from Bill Colbert for five years and his lease expires this next January and he is going to move on land he has leased from me. When he first moved on Bill Colbert's land he built a house and I know Robert Wilson died while he was having the house built.
Q Did you attend Robert during his illness? A Yes, sir.

Applications for Enrollment of Choctaw Newborn
Act of 1905 Volume VI

Q Were you present at the burial? A Yes, I helped shroud and bury him. While the boy was sick I carried him food but it did not do him any good. He stayed at my house about a month before he died and I carried him down to Alfred Nail's on New Year's day and he died about two or three days after that in January.
Q Would Alfred Nail know when Robert Wilson died?
A Alfred Nail would know but he would not telll[sic] as he does not like the Dawes Commission.
Q From the records of the Commission to the Five Civilized Tribes it appears that Louisana Carney, as half sister, and Nollis Carney, as acquaintance, have on two occasions executed affidavits affirming and reaffirming, before Wirt Franklin, Notary Public, in the first instance that Robert Wilson died the 28th of December 1902; and the same parties again executed affidabits[sic] before J. Anderson, Notary Public, that Robert Wilson died the 27th of November 1902; it further appears that Sillen[sic] Wilson as sister and Hogan Anderson, as acquaintance, before J. Lake Collins and A. E. Becker, Notaries Public, respectively, that Robert Wilson died on the 20th day of December 1902: Do you know these affidavits to be in error?
A Yes, I know they are all wrong.

Witness Excused.

JOHN FLYHOVER, being duly sworn, by Lacey P. Bobo Notary Public in and for the Central District of Indian Territory, testified as follows:

BY THE COMMISSIONER:

Q What is your name? A John Flyhover.
Q How old are you? A I will be 21 the 20th of February.
Q What is your post office? A South McAlester, I. T.
Q How long have you resided in the vicinity of where you at present live?
A About five years; we came over here from Missouri about two miles west of here September 23, 1901; my little 16-months-old sister died September 23, 1901 just after we moved over; we moved from there to a little log cabin about a quarter of a mile from here and went to cutting logs to build the house we now live in.
Q Do you know when you first began putting up this house you now live in? A We laid the foundation the 27th of December 1901 and on account of it being Christmas we did not put it up until the 3rd day of January 1902.
Q Were you acquainted with Robert Wilson?
A Yes, sir, I had seen him two or three times and knew him.
Q Are you intimately acquainted with his brothers and sisters?
A Yes, sir, I know Cillen Wilson and George Cann.
Q Was Robert Wilson and the brother and sister you mention members by blood of the Choctaw Tribe of Indians?
Q Yes, sir.
Q Is this Robert Wilson living at the present time?
A No, he's dead.

Applications for Enrollment of Choctaw Newborn
Act of 1905 Volume VI

Q When did he die? A He died the 3rd day of January 1902; I know he died the day we raised this house and we put up the house the 3rd day of January 1902.
Q You fix January 3, 1902 in your mind as the date of the death of Robert Wilson by the death of your little baby brother, by your coming to Indian Territory from Missouri and by your beginning to build the house you now live in?
A Yes, sir; also my father went over and helped make the coffin and laid him in it and stayed there until about the middle of the night.
Q It appears that certain Choctaws in this vicinity have made affidavits that Robert Wilson died nearly a year subsequent to the time you mention: Are you positive these parties are in error?
Q Yes, sir, I know that's wrong, I know exactly when that boy died.
Q Who else living near you would know when Robert Wilson died?
A My mother, Irene Flyhover and my father, James H. Flyhover and my brother, James J. Flyhover.

Witness Excused.

Testimony taken six miles southeast of South McAlester, Indian Territory, at home of Alfred Nail, October 16, 1906.

CILLEN WILSON, being duly sworn by Lacey P. Bobo, Notary Public in and for the Central District of Indian Territory, testified as follows:

Through Interpreter Jacob Homer.

BY THE COMMISSIONER:

Q What is your name? A Cillen Wilson.
Q How old are you? A About 20 or 21.
Q What is your post office address? A South McAlester.
Q Who is your father and mother?
A Wallace Wilson is my father, I do not know my mother's name.
Q Did you father and mother have any other children, if so name them?
A Stephen and Robert and George Cann and Louisana Carney, Louisana is the only one living.
Q When did Robert Wilson, your brother, die?
A He has been dead a long time but I do not know how many years he has been dead.
Q It appears from the records of the Commission to the Five Civilized Tribes that George Cann has a little child named Lindsey Cann who was born on October 9, 1902: Was Lindsey Cann born when Robert Wilson died?
A Lindsey was born after Robert's death.
Q How long had Robert been dead when Libdsey[sic] was born?
A I do not know, he had been dead some time when that child was born.
Q Do you and Lindsey Cann and mother all make your home at the same place at the present time? A Yes.
Q How old is Lindsey at the present time? A I do not know.

Applications for Enrollment of Choctaw Newborn
Act of 1905   Volume VI

Q Are you positive and do you know beyond the shadow of a doubt that Robert Wilson died before Lindsey Cann was born?
A Yes, sir, I do.
Q Can you read and write? A No, sir.
Q Do you speak English? A No.
Q Do you know the date that either of your brothers died?
A No, I do not.
Q Do you not know the month or year that either of them died?
A No, sir.
Q What year is this? A I don't know.
Q Do you know how many months weeks or days there are in a year?
A No, sir, I do not, I never did go to school and I do not know how many days or weeks make a year.
Q From the record of the Commission to the Five Civilized Tribes it appears that on the 12th day of April 1905, before L. Jake Collins, Notary Public, you made affidavit as brother that Robert Wilson died on the 20th of December 1902; said affidavit is attested by mark and is witnessed by A. E. Baker and the Noatry[sic] Public Public[sic] who took the acknowledgement: Do you remember signing this affidavit? A Yes.
Q Why did you sign an affidavit that your brother died on a definite date and now state you do not know ehen[sic] he died?
A I did not know it myself, Louisana Carney she is the one who told me to touch the pen and I did.
Q Who did the interpreting for the Notary Public when you made this affidavit? A Jake Collins.
Q You just made this affidavit simply because Louisana Carney your half sister told you to touch the pen? A Yes.
Q Did you ever receive anything for making affidavit in regard to Robert Wilson's death? A Yes.
Q How much? A I do not know how much they gave me, they never paid me all?[sic]
Q Can you count money? A No, sir.

Witness   Excused.

Testimony taken four miles south of South McAlester, Indian Territory, at home of Hagin[sic] Anderson, October 16, 1906.

HAGIN ANDERSON, being duly swirn[sic] by Lacey P. Bobo, Notary Public in and for the Central District of Indian Territory, testified as follows:

BY THE COMMISSIONER:

Q What is your name? A Hagin Anderson.
Q How old are you? A About 38.
Q Of what Tribe of Indians are you a duly enrolled member?
A Chickasaw.
Q What is your post office address? A South McAlester.

Applications for Enrollment of Choctaw Newborn
Act of 1905   Volume VI

Q How long have you resided in the vicinity of where you now live?
A I was raised here.
Q Were you acquainted with one Wikey Wilson? A Yes, sir.
Q Did this woman have children, if so state their names?
A Robert, Stephen and Cillen.
Q Who was the father of these children? A Wallace Wilson.
Q Did she have any other children that you know of?
A Louisana Carney and George Cann.
Q How many of these children that you have just mentioned are now living? A Two, Louisana Carney and Cillen Wilson.
Q When did Robert Wilson die? A I think he died in 1902.
Q What time of the year? A Some tine in January, but I could not say the day.
Q What relative facts or occurrences tend to fix in your mind that Robert Wilson died in January 1902?
A Well, the way I have it down I was up there at South McAlester on the jury and come home and he was sick and during the holidays before I went back he died.
Q Do you mean by the holidays Christmas week and the days succeeding Christmas week? A I mean Christmas week.
Q How many years ago has it been since you served on that jury?
A Next January it will be five years.
Q Was this a Federal Jury you served on at South McAlester?
A Yes, sir.
Q Who was the foreman? A I have forgot[sic] his name; it was the petit jury.
Q Do you remember any cases that were tried in U. S. Court while you were a member of the petit jury?
A Yes, I remember one case, the U. S. vs. Henry Herring for murder.
Q Did the jury that you were a member of convist[sic] Henry Herring?
A No, sir, they acquitted him.
Q Who did this Henry Herring murder?
A I forget his name, he was a negro too.
Q Did Robert Wilson die while you were a member of the petit jury, Federal Court at South McAlester? A Yes, sir.
Q Who was District Attorney and United States Judge at that time?
A Clayton and Wilkins.
Q The records of the Commission to the Five Civilized Tribes show that you, on the 14th of April 1905, before A. E. Becker, Notary Public, made affidavit that Robert Wilson died on or about the 20th of December 1902 (copy of said affidavit is shown witness): Are you confident this affidavit is in error?
A Yes, sir, that's a mistake, it chould[sic] be some tine in January 1902 instead of December 1902.

> This party examined the records of the United States Clerk's Office at South McAlester, Indian Territory, on October 17, 1906, and found, in Common Law Record on Page 491, that on December 10, 1902, a jury was empanelled including the name of Hagen Anderson for the December 1901 term of the Federal Court; and further that on Thursday December 12, 1901, December 1901 Term of Federal Court at South McAlester, Central

Applications for Enrollment of Choctaw Newborn
Act of 1905   Volume VI

District, Indian Territory, the jury of which Hagen Anderson was a member appeared in charge of bailiff and returned in open court a verdict of not guilty in the case of the U. S. vs. Henry Herring, charged with murder, and the defendent[sic] was discharged from custody. Said jury was finally discharged on the 18th day of January 1902, as appears on Witness and Jury Record Book, on Page 418, of the records of the Clerk of the United States Court, South McAlester, Central District of Indian Territory.

Testimony taken eight miles south of South McAlester, Indian Territory, October 17, 1906, at home of Nollis Carney.

LOUISANA CARNEY, being duly sworn, by Lacey P. Bobo, Notary Public in and for the Central District of Indian Territory, testified as follows:

Through Jacob Homer, Interpreter.

BY THE COMMISSIONER:

Q What is your name? A Louisana Carney.
Q What is your age? A I do not know how old I am.
Q Are you not about 30 years old, judging from the size of your children? A I guess so.
Q Who is your husband? A Nollis Carney.
Q Where do you get your mail? A Savanna, I. T.
Q Who was your mother? A Sophy Wilson.
Q Was she also known as Wikey Wilson? A Yes, that was her Choctaw name.
Q Did your mother have other children, if so name them?
Q[sic] There is only one living, Cillen.
Q State the name of the ones that are dead?
A Robert and Stephen Wilson and George Cann.
Q Who was the father of Robert Wilson? A Wallace Wilson.
Q Was George Cann your full brother, same mother and father?
A No, we had the same mother but a different father.
Q Who was the wife of your brother, George Cann? A Melina.
Q Did George Cann have a child or children by Melina Cann?
A Yes, he had children and one of them died.
Q Has he a child or children living?
A Yes, Lindsey is the only one living.
Q Is Lindsey a boy or girl? A Girl.
Q When was this child born? A October 9, 1902.
Q How old is this child at the present time? A About four years.
Q What is the name of your child that is nearest in age to Lindsey Cann? A Albert Carney.
Q When was your child Albert Carney born?
A It was in the month of August I have forgot the year but he was three years old this last August.

Applications for Enrollment of Choctaw Newborn
Act of 1905 Volume VI

Q Which is the older, your son Albert or your niece Lindsey Cann?
A Lindsey is older.
Q I will get you to state again when Lindsey Cann was born?
A She is four years old this October.
Q Was your brother Robert Wilson living October 9, 1902, when Lindsey Cann was born?
A Robert was dead when that child was born.
Q Are you positive that Robert was dead when Lindsey Cann was born? A Yes, sir, he was dead then.
Q What season of the year did Robert die?
A It was in the winter time.
Q Did one summer pass between the death of Robert and the birth of Lindsey? A I do not remember.
Q In what month did Robert Wilson die, if you know?
A I believe it was in January, but other parties think it was not in that month.
Q What makes you believe it was in the month of January that Robert died?
A They preached at Allen Carney's grand-mother's house and I was going over there to preaching but Robert Wilson was pretty bad sick and they sent after me and I went to see him and so I could not go to preaching, and I know it was in January that they had preaching.
Q Did Robert Wilson die when you went to see him at this time?
A Yes, sir.
Q What length of time elapses between January and October?
A I do not know, I do not know anything about books.
Q Do you know how many months there are in a year and can you name them in their order.[sic]
A I can't tell you, I do not know.
Q Do you know what month, this is? A No, sir.
Q If you can't mention the months in their order and do not know them, how is it that you know Lindsey Cann was born October 9, 1902 and that Robert Wilson died in January?
A When anything like that happens I hear somebody say the date and remember it.
Q From the records of the Commission to the Five Civilized Tribes it appears that you have heretofore executed two affidavits, affirming at one time that your brother Robert Wilson died the 25th of December 1902/ and again that your half brother Robert Wilson died on the 27th of December 1902: Did you know at the time you subscribed to these affidavits the dates they set forth as the time of your half-brother Robert Wilson's death, or that they alleged his death more than two months subsequent to the birth of Lindsey Cann?
A No, sir, they are wrong, because Lindsey was not born when Robert died.
Q What part of the winter did Robert Wilson die?
A It was not in the fall, it was in the middle of the winter.

Witness Excused.

Applications for Enrollment of Choctaw Newborn
Act of 1905   Volume VI

W. P. Covington, being duly sworn, states that the foregoing is a complete and correct transcript of his stenographic notes taken in said case on dates and at places set forth.

W.P. Covington

Subscribed and sworn to before me, this   8"   day of   Nov.   1906.

Lacey P.Bobo
Notary Public.

Aug. 28, 1906.

Commissioner to the Five Civilized Tribes,
Muskogee, I. T.

Dear Sir:

According to your direction embraced in letter of the 17th inst., I have secured another application for the enrollment of Lindsey Cann, so as to cure the defect in the application now existing, I trust that this will be satisfactory.

Respectfully,
J. S. Mullen.

Ardmore, Indian Territory, May 2, 1905.

Commission to the Five Civilized Tribes,
Muskogee, Indian Territory.

Gentlemen:

There are herewith transmitted, for proper disposition birth affidavits of the following named persons: Davidson Carney, Albert Carney, Lindsey Cann and Jesse Thompson.

Your attention is respectfully directed to the signature of the Notary Public before whom the affidavits in these cases were executed and to his seal thereto, as the signature is that of J. Anderson, while the seal bears the name of J. W. Anderson.

In this connection it is suggested that it might be well to ascertain whether or not there is such a person a J. Anderson, who is a Notary Public, for the Central District of the Indian Territory and if so whether or not the enclosed affidavits were executed before him.

Applications for Enrollment of Choctaw Newborn
Act of 1905 Volume VI

HC 110

Respectfully,
Fred T. Marr,
Chief Clerk.

7-NB-357.

Muskogee, Indian Territory, May 23, 1905.

Melina Cann
~~George Cann~~, 7/1/05
South McAlester, Indian Territory.

Dear Sir:

There is enclosed you herewith for execution application for the enrollment of your infant child, Lindsy Cann.

In the application filed in this office on March 16, 1905, the date of the applicants birth is given as October 9, 1902, while in those filed on the 19th inst., it is given as October 9, 1903. In the enclosed application the date of birth is left blank, in which you will please insert the correct date of birth and, when properly executed, return to this office.

In having these affidavits executed care should be exercised to see that all names are written in full, as they appear in the body of the affidavit, and in the event that either of the persons signing the affidavit are unable to write, signatures by mark must be attested by two witnesses. Each affidavit must be executed before a Notary Public and the notarial seal and signature of the officer must be attached to each separate affidavit.

Respectfully,

Chairman.

VR 23-1.

Applications for Enrollment of Choctaw Newborn
Act of 1905   Volume VI

$W^m O.B.$

COMMISSIONERS:
TAMS BIXBY,
THOMAS B. NEEDLES,
C.R. BRECKINBRIDGE.

DEPARTMENT OF THE INTERIOR,
COMMISSIONER TO THE FIVE CIVILIZED TRIBES.

REFER IN REPLY TO THE FOLLOWING:
7-NB-357.
7-5629.

WM. O. BEALL
Secretary

ADDRESS ONLY THE
COMMISSION TO THE FIVE CIVILIZED TRIBES.

Muskogee, Indian Territory, May 24, 1905.

George Cann,
    South McAlester, Indian Territory.

Dear Sir:

    There is enclosed you herewith for execution application for the enrollment of your infant child, Lindsy Cann.

    In the application filed in this office on March 16, 1905, the date of the applicants[sic] birth is given as October 9, 1902, while in these filed on the 19th inst., it is given as October 9, 1903. In the enclosed application the date of birth is left blank, in which you will please insert the correct date of birth and, when properly executed, return to this office.

    In having these affidavits executed care should be exercised to see that all names are written in full, as they appear in the body of the affidavit, and in the event that either of the persons signing the affidavit are unable to write, signatures by mark must be attested by two witnesses. Each affidavit must be executed before a Notary Public and the notarial seal and signature of the officer must be attached to each separate affidavit.

                                          Respectfully,
                                            Tams Bixby

VR 23-1.   Chairman.

7-NB-357

Muskogee, Indian Territory, July 29, 1905.

Melina Cann,
    South McAlester, Indian Territory.

Dear Madam:

    Your attention is called to a communication addressed to you by the Commission to the Five Civilized Tribes under date of May 23, 1905, with which there was inclosed for execution application for the enrollment of your infant child, Lindsy Cann.

Applications for Enrollment of Choctaw Newborn
Act of 1905 Volume VI

In said letter you were advised that in the application filed in this office March 16, 1905, the date of the applicant's birth was given as October 9, 1902, while in the affidavits filed May 19, 1905, the date of birth is given as October 9, 1903; you were requested to insert in the application the correct date of birth and have same properly executed and return to this office immediately. No reply to this letter has been received.

This matter should receive your immediate attention as no further action can be taken relative to the enrollment of your said child, until the application heretofore forwarded you is in due form filed in this office.

Respectfully,

Commissioner.

7-NB-357

Muskogee, Indian Territory, August 17, 1906.

J. S. Mullen,
    Ardmore, Indian Territory.

Dear Sir:-

Receipt is hereby acknowledged of your letter of July 27, 1906, asking the status of the applications for the enrollment of Davidson Carney and Lindsey Cann.

In reply you are advised that the information contained in your letter is not sufficient to enable this office to identify Davidson Carney as an applicant for enrollment under the Act of Congress approved March 3, 1905.

Referring to the application for the enrollment of Lindsey Cann you are advised that in the application filed in this office on March 16, 1905, the date of the applicant's birth is given as October 9, 1902, while in those filed on May 19, 1905, it is given as October 9, 1903. You are further advised that the given name of said child is spelled in the affidavits as "L-i-n-d-s-y" and "L-i-n-d-s-e-y." There is enclosed you herewith application for the enrollment of said child. You will note that the name and date of birth are left blank, in which you will please have inserted the correct name and date of birth and, when properly executed, return to this office.

In having these affidavits executed care should be exercised to see that all names are written in full, as they appear in the body of the affidavit, and in the event that either of the persons signing the affidavit are unable to write, signatures by mark must be attested by two witnesses. Each affidavit must be executed before a Notary Public and the notarial seal and signature of the officer must be attached to each separate affidavit.

Applications for Enrollment of Choctaw Newborn
Act of 1905 Volume VI

Respectfully,

WLM.
Encl. 17/1

Commissioner.

7-NB-357

Muskogee, Indian Territory, September 1, 1906.

J. S. Mullen,
    Ardmore, Indian Territory.

Dear Sir:

    Receipt is hereby acknowledged of your letter of August 28, 1906, inclosing affidavits of Melina Cann and Louisana Carney to the birth of Lindsey Cann, child of George and Melina Cann, October 9, 1902, and the same have been filed in the matter of the enrollment of said child.

Respectfully,

Acting Commissioner.

Choc New Born 358
    John B. Miller
    (Born Nov. 8, 1902)
    Clarence L. Miller
    (Born July 26, 1904)

BIRTH AFFIDAVIT.
DEPARTMENT OF THE INTERIOR.
COMMISSION TO THE FIVE CIVILIZED TRIBES.

    IN RE APPLICATION FOR ENROLLMENT, as a citizen of the Choctaw Nation, of John B. Miller, born on the 8th day of November, 1902

Name of Father: T. J. Miller   a citizen of the United States Nation.
Name of Mother: Serena J Miller   a citizen of the Choctaw Nation.

Postoffice   McAlester, I.T.

Applications for Enrollment of Choctaw Newborn
Act of 1905   Volume VI

AFFIDAVIT OF MOTHER.

UNITED STATES OF AMERICA, Indian Territory, }
   Central   DISTRICT. }

I,   Serena J. Miller   , on oath state that I am   27   years of age and a citizen by blood   , of the   Choctaw   Nation; that I am the lawful wife of   T. J. Miller , who is a citizen, ~~by~~ .... of the   United States   ~~Nation~~; that a   male   child was born to me on   8th   day of   November   , 1902; that said child has been named   John B. Miller   , and was living March 4, 1905.

                                        Serena J Miller

Witnesses To Mark:
{

Subscribed and sworn to before me this   17th   day of   March   , 1905

                                        Wirt Franklin
                                          Notary Public.

AFFIDAVIT OF ATTENDING PHYSICIAN OR MID-WIFE.

UNITED STATES OF AMERICA, Indian Territory, }
   Central   DISTRICT. }

I,   Lewis C. Tennent   , a   physician   , on oath state that I attended on Mrs.   Serena J Miller   , wife of   T. J. Miller   on the 8th   day of   November , 1902; that there was born to her on said date a   male   child; that said child was living March 4, 1905, and is said to have been named   John B. Miller

                                        L. C. Tennent, M.D.

Witnesses To Mark:
{

Subscribed and sworn to before me this   18th   day of   March   , 1905

                                        Wirt Franklin
                                        Notary Public.

Applications for Enrollment of Choctaw Newborn
Act of 1905   Volume VI

BIRTH AFFIDAVIT.

DEPARTMENT OF THE INTERIOR.
COMMISSION TO THE FIVE CIVILIZED TRIBES.

IN RE APPLICATION FOR ENROLLMENT, as a citizen of the   Choctaw   Nation, of Clarence L. Miller   , born on the   26th   day of   July   , 1904

Name of Father: T. J. Miller   a citizen of the United States Nation.
Name of Mother: Serena J Miller   a citizen of the   Choctaw   Nation.

Postoffice   McAlester, I.T.

AFFIDAVIT OF MOTHER.

UNITED STATES OF AMERICA, Indian Territory, }
       Central   DISTRICT.

I,   Serena J. Miller   , on oath state that I am   27   years of age and a citizen by blood , of the   Choctaw   Nation; that I am the lawful wife of   T. J. Miller , who is a citizen, ~~by~~ .... of the   United States   ~~Nation~~; that a   male   child was born to me on   26th   day of   July   , 1904; that said child has been named   Clarence L. Miller   , and was living March 4, 1905.

                                    Serena J Miller
Witnesses To Mark:

Subscribed and sworn to before me this   17th   day of   March   , 1905

                                    Wirt Franklin
                                       Notary Public.

AFFIDAVIT OF ATTENDING PHYSICIAN OR MID-WIFE.

UNITED STATES OF AMERICA, Indian Territory, }
       Central   DISTRICT.

I,   Lewis C. Tennent   , a   physician   , on oath state that I attended on Mrs.   Serena J Miller   , wife of   T. J. Miller   on the 26th day of   July , 1904; that there was born to her on said date a   male   child; that said child was living March 4, 1905, and is said to have been named   Clarence L. Miller

                                    L. C. Tennent, M.D.
Witnesses To Mark:

Applications for Enrollment of Choctaw Newborn
Act of 1905   Volume VI

Subscribed and sworn to before me this 18th day of March , 1905

Wirt Franklin
Notary Public.

Choc New Born 359
    Alfred Lee Alley
    (Born Dec. 19, 1902)

BIRTH AFFIDAVIT.

DEPARTMENT OF THE INTERIOR,
COMMISSION TO THE FIVE CIVILIZED TRIBES.

IN RE Application for Enrollment, as a citizen of the   Choctaw   Nation, of Alfred L Alley , born on the 19   day of December , 1902

Name of Father: Brick P. Alley   a citizen of the Choctaw Nation.
Name of Mother: Elsie Alley   a citizen of the Choctaw Nation.

Post-Office: Indianola I.T.

AFFIDAVIT OF MOTHER.

UNITED STATES OF AMERICA, ⎫
   INDIAN TERRITORY.   ⎬
   Western   District. ⎭

    I, Elsie Alley   , on oath state that I am 24   years of age and a citizen by Blood , of the Choctaw Nation; that I am the lawful wife of Brick P. Alley , who is a citizen, by marriage of the Choctaw Nation; that a male child was born to me on 19 day of December , 1902 , that said child has been named Alfred L Alley , and is now living.

                                   Elsie Alley
WITNESSES TO MARK:
{

    Subscribed and sworn to before me this 26 *day of* December , 1904

          My Commission Expires
            Aug. 1st. 1906   T.J. Rice
                         NOTARY PUBLIC.

Applications for Enrollment of Choctaw Newborn
Act of 1905 Volume VI

AFFIDAVIT OF ATTENDING PHYSICIAN OR MID-WIFE.

UNITED STATES OF AMERICA,
INDIAN TERRITORY.
Western District.

I, J A Eubank , a Physician , on oath state that I attended on Mrs. Elsie Alley , wife of Brick P. Alley on the 19 day of December , 1902; that there was born to her on said date a male child; that said child is now living and is said to have been named Alfred L Alley

Eubank[sic] MD

WITNESSES TO MARK:

Subscribed and sworn to before me this 26 day of December , 1904

My Commission Expires
Aug. 1st. 1906

T.J. Rice
NOTARY PUBLIC.

BIRTH AFFIDAVIT.

DEPARTMENT OF THE INTERIOR,
COMMISSION TO THE FIVE CIVILIZED TRIBES.

IN RE Application for Enrollment, as a citizen of the Choctaw Nation, of Alfred Lee Alley , born on the 19 day of December , 1902

Name of Father: Brick P. Alley   a citizen of the Choctaw Nation.
Name of Mother: Elsie Alley   a citizen of the Choctaw Nation.

Post-Office: Indianola I.T.

AFFIDAVIT OF MOTHER.

UNITED STATES OF AMERICA,
INDIAN TERRITORY.
Western District.

I, Elsie Alley , on oath state that I am 24 years of age and a citizen by Blood , of the Choctaw Nation; that I am the lawful wife of Brick P. Alley , who is a citizen, by Intermarriage of the Choctaw Nation; that a .... child was born to

Applications for Enrollment of Choctaw Newborn
Act of 1905   Volume VI

me on   19   day of   December   , 1902 , that said child has been named   Alfred Lee Alley , and is now living.

Elsie Alley

WITNESSES TO MARK:

{

Subscribed and sworn to before me this   18   day of   March   , 1905

T.J. Rice

NOTARY PUBLIC.

AFFIDAVIT OF ATTENDING PHYSICIAN OR MID-WIFE.

UNITED STATES OF AMERICA,
   INDIAN TERRITORY.
   Western   District.

I,   J. A. Eubank   , a   Physician   , on oath state that I attended on Mrs.   Elsie Alley   , wife of   Brick P. Alley   on the   19   day of December   , 1902; that there was born to her on said date a .... child; that said child is now living and is said to have been named   Alfred L Alley

JA Eubank

WITNESSES TO MARK:

{

Subscribed and sworn to before me this   18   day of   March   , 1905

T.J. Rice

NOTARY PUBLIC.

NEW-BORN AFFIDAVIT.

Number...............

...Choctaw Enrolling Commission...

IN THE MATTER OF THE APPLICATION FOR ENROLLMENT, as a citizen of the Choctaw   Nation, of   Alfred L Alley

born on the   19   day of   December   190 2

Name of father   Brick P. Alley   a citizen of   the Choctaw Nation final enrollment No.   762

Applications for Enrollment of Choctaw Newborn
Act of 1905 Volume VI

Name of mother   Elsie Alley   a citizen of   Choctaw
Nation final enrollment No.   12718

                                   Postoffice   Indianola I.T.

AFFIDAVIT OF MOTHER.

UNITED STATES OF AMERICA
INDIAN TERRITORY
    Western   DISTRICT

           I   Elsie Alley   , on oath state that I am   24   years of age and a citizen by   Blood   of the   Choctaw   Nation, and as such have been placed upon the final roll of the Choctaw   Nation, by the Honorable Secretary of the Interior my final enrollment number being   12718 ; that I am the lawful wife of   Brick P. Alley   , who is a citizen of the   Choctaw Nation, and as such has been placed upon the final roll of said Nation by the Honorable Secretary of the Interior, his final enrollment number being   762   and that a   male child child was born to me on the   19   day of   December   190 2; that said child has been named   Alfred L Alley   , and is now living.

Witnesseth.   Elsie Alley

Must be two Witnesses who are Citizens.
     Christopher C Choate
     John J. Beams

    Subscribed and sworn to before me this   28   day of   Dec   190 5

                                   T.J. Rice
                My Commission Expires   Notary Public.
My commission expires: Aug. 1st. 1906

AFFIDAVIT OF ATTENDING PHYSICIAN OR MIDWIFE

UNITED STATES OF AMERICA
INDIAN TERRITORY
    Western   DISTRICT

       I,   J. A. Eubank   a   Physician on oath state that I attended on Mrs.   Elsie Alley   wife of   Brick P. Alley on the   19   day of   December   , 190 2, that there was born to her on said date a   male child, that said child is now living, and is said to have been named   Alfred L Alley

                                  JA Eubank   M.D.

Applications for Enrollment of Choctaw Newborn
Act of 1905 Volume VI

Subscribed and sworn to before me this, the 28 day of January 190 5

WITNESSETH:
Must be two witnesses who are citizens

My Commission Expires Aug. 1st. 1906

Christopher C Choate
John J Beams

T.J. Rice Notary Public.

We hereby certify that we are well acquainted with J.A. Eubank a Physician and know him to be reputable and of good standing in the community.

Christopher C Choate   Indianola I.T.

John J Beams   Indianola I.T.

7-4594

Muskogee, Indian Territory, March 23, 1905.

Brick P. Alley,
    Indianola, Indian Territory.

Dear Sir:

    Receipt is hereby acknowledged of your letter of March 18, 1905, enclosing affidavits of Elsie Alley and J. A. Eubank to the birth of Alfred Lee Alley, infant son of Brick P. and Elsie Alley, December 19, 1903[sic], and the same have been filed with our records as an application for the enrollment of said child.

    Replying to that portion of your letter in which you ask when you can file for your child, you are advised that no selection of allotment can be made for children enrolled under the provisions of the Act of Congress of March 3, 1905, until their enrollment has been approved by the Secretary of the Interior.

Respectfully,

Chairman.

Applications for Enrollment of Choctaw Newborn
Act of 1905   Volume VI

(The letter below does not belong with the current applicant.)

9-NB-359

Muskogee, Indian Territory, August 8, 1905.

Joseph Gibson,
    Foster, Indian Territory.

Dear Sir:

    Receipt is hereby acknowledged of the joint affidavit of E. Park and Mrs. E. F. Park to the birth of Sylvia Gibson, daughter of Joseph and Emily Gibson, April 26, 1903, and the same has been filed with the records of this office in the matter of the enrollment of said child.

                  Respectfully,

                              Commissioner.

<u>Choc New Born 360</u>
    Dora Askew   b 11-17-04[sic]

                Marietta, Ind. Ty ___Apr 6___ 1905

Commissioners to The Five Tribes.
            Muskogee,
              I T

                Gentlemen

N.B. 360   I have received your letter of Apr 3 - in which you say that affidavit of Mollie Aaskew[sic] by Lee Askew should be signed by herself   Mrs Millie Askew My wife is now living   She died Jany 3 - 1905

                      Yours truly

                          Lee Askew

Applications for Enrollment of Choctaw Newborn
Act of 1905 Volume VI

N.B. 360
COPY
Muskogee, Indian Territory, April 3, 1905.

Lee Askew,
    Marietta, Indian Territory.

Dear Sir:

    There is inclosed you herewith for execution application for the enrollment of your infant child, Dora Askew, born November 17, 1904.

    The affidavit of the mother heretofore filed with the Commission is signed, "Mollie Askew by Lee Askew." This affidavit should be signed by the mother herself.

    In having these affidavits executed care should be exercised to see that all names are written in full, as they appear in the body of the affidavit, and in the event that either of the persons signing the affidavit are unable to write, signatures by mark must be attested by two witnesses. Each affidavit must be executed before a Notary Public and the notarial seal and signature of the officer must be attached to each separate affidavit.

Respectfully,
SIGNED
Tams Bixby
LM 3-2.   Chairman.

Wm O.B.

COMMISSIONERS:
TAMS BIXBY,
THOMAS B. NEEDLES,
C.R. BRECKINRIDGE.

**DEPARTMENT OF THE INTERIOR,
COMMISSIONER TO THE FIVE CIVILIZED TRIBES.**

REFER IN REPLY TO THE FOLLOWING:
N. B. 360

WM. O. BEALL
Secretary

ADDRESS ONLY THE
COMMISSION TO THE FIVE CIVILIZED TRIBES.

Muskogee, Indian Territory, April 10, 1905.

Lee Askew,
    Marietta, Indian Territory.

Dear Sir:

    In your communication of the 6th instant, you state that your wife, Mollie Askew, who is the mother of Dora Askew, an applicant for enrollment as a citizen of the Choctaw Nation, is dead. In this event it will be necessary that you secure the affidavits of two persons who have actual knowledge of the facts, that the child was born, the date of her birth, was living on March 4, 1905, and that Mollie Askew was her mother.

Applications for Enrollment of Choctaw Newborn
Act of 1905   Volume VI

Respectfully,

T.B. Needles
Commissioner in Charge.

---

7 NB 360

Muskogee, Indian Territory, April 21, 1905.

D. G. Bartlett,
Marietta, Indian Territory.

Dear Sir:

Receipt is hereby acknowledged of your letter of April 14, 1905, enclosing affidavits of S. A. Graham, D. Autrey and Mrs. Eliza Askew to the birth of Dora Askew, daughter of Lee and Mollie Askew, November 17, 1903, and the same have been filed with our records as an application for the enrollment of said child.

Respectfully,

Chairman.

7-NB-360.

Muskogee, Indian Territory, May 22, 1905.

Lee Askew,
Marietta, Indian Territory.

Dear Sir:

There is enclosed you herewith for execution application for the enrollment of your infant child, Dora Askew.

In the affidavits filed in this office on March 21, 1905, the date of the applicants[sic] birth is given as November 17, 1904. The affidavit executed by the physician gives it as November 17, 1903. You will please insert the correct date in the enclosed application, and when it is properly executed return it to this office.

In having these affidavits executed care should be exercised to see that all names are written in full, as they appear in the body of the affidavit, and in the event that either of the persons signing the affidavit are unable to write, signatures by mark must be attested by two witnesses. Each affidavit must be executed before a Notary Public and the notarial seal and signature of the officer must be attached to each separate affidavit.

Applications for Enrollment of Choctaw Newborn
Act of 1905 Volume VI

Respectfully,

Chairman.

VR 22-20.

(The letter below typed as given.)

Copy

Marietta, Ind. Ty June 1 1905.

Commission to The Five Tribes
   Muskogee I T

Gentlemen:

   I Return affidavit for correction You state in the affidavit that Mollie Askew is a Citizen by blood which is Not true Case she being a Citizen of the U S Lee Askew is a Citizen by blood of the Choctaw Nation the husband of Mollie Askew - on April 21 1905 you wrote to D. C. Barlett 7 N B 360 - in which you acknowledged the receipt of affidavit of S. A. Graham D. Autrey and Mrs. Eliza Askew to the birth of Dora Askew Daughter of Lee and Mollie Askew Nov 17 1903 and same had been filed with your records as an application for the Enrollment of said child. in the affidavit of Mar 21 1905 the affidavit of Lee Askew was Given as Nov 17 1903 and the only mistake was an Error in the Date and if the papers could be found it Could be rectified at once. any other enformation you wish Can be furnished at once

                          Yours truly,
                          (Signed) Lee Askew.

(The letter below typed as given.)

Copy

Marietta, I. T. June 1 1905.

Commission to The Five Tribes,
   Muskogee, I. T.

Gentlemen:

   I Enclose you a letter of Lee Askew it Seems that they have got the Dates Mixed there is Plenty Evidence here that the Said child Dora Askew is living and that it was born as stated in the affidavit Nov 17 1903 all these facts can be established and I am

Applications for Enrollment of Choctaw Newborn
Act of 1905   Volume VI

well acquainted lived here and there can be gotten any Neighbor who knows these facts there was an affidavit sent you to the death of Mrs. Mollie Askew

Yours truly
(Signed) D. G. Barlett.

7-NB-360.

Muskogee, Indian Territory, June 6, 1905.

Lee Askew,
    Marietta, Indian Territory.

Dear Sir:

    Receipt is hereby acknowledged of the affidavit of S. A. Graham to the birth of Dora Askew, your infant child, and the same has been filed with the records in the matter of the enrollment of said child.

    The error as to the citizenship of yourself and wife, which you call attention to in your letter of the first instant, has been corrected.

Respectfully,

Commissioner in Charge.

(The affidavit below typed as given.)

Indian Territory
    Chickasaw Nat } ss

    This say personally appeared Mrs. Eliza Askew, who upon oath says she was present and attended Mrs. Mollie Askew (Now deceased on Nov 17 1903 and there was Born to her on that Date a Female Child and was living Mch 4 1905 and said Child is named Dora Askew and is now living.

Witness my hand at Marietta I T this 14 day of Apr 1905

Witnesses
    Mrs Eliza x Askew
        her / mark
    J P Nance
    Mattie Nance

Applications for Enrollment of Choctaw Newborn
Act of 1905   Volume VI

1905
      Subscribed and sworn to at Marietta Ind Ter this 14 day of Apr

          D G Bartlett
          Notary Public.

Indian Territory
 Chickasaw Nation
 Southern District

      On this day Apr 14 1905 personally appeared D. Autrey a Physician who upon oath says he knows that a child was born to Mrs Mollie Askew Dec on Nov 17 1903 and that said child was living and still living on Mch 4 1905 and said child is named Dora Askew

Witness my hand at Marietta IT this 14 day of Apr 1905

         D Autrey M.D.

Subscribed and sworn at Marietta IT this 14 day of Apr 1905

         D G Bartlett
         Notary Public.

BIRTH AFFIDAVIT.

     DEPARTMENT OF THE INTERIOR.
   COMMISSION TO THE FIVE CIVILIZED TRIBES.

  IN RE APPLICATION FOR ENROLLMENT, as a citizen of the   Choctaw   Nation, of Dora Askew   , born on the   17   day of   November   , 1903

Name of Father: Lee Askew   a citizen of the   Choctaw   Nation.
Name of Mother: Mollie Askew   a citizen of the United States   Nation.

      Postoffice   Marietta Ind. Terr.

     AFFIDAVIT OF MOTHER.

UNITED STATES OF AMERICA, Indian Territory,
         .... DISTRICT.

  I,   Mollie Askew   , on oath state that I am   19   years of age and a citizen by ———, of the   United States   ~~Nation~~; that I am the lawful wife of   Lee Askew , who is a citizen, by Blood   of the   Choctaw   Nation; that a   female   child

274

Applications for Enrollment of Choctaw Newborn
Act of 1905   Volume VI

was born to me on   17 day of   November   , 1903; that said child has been named Dora Askew   , and was living March 4, 1905.

Witnesses To Mark:
{

Subscribed and sworn to before me this ...... day of ...., 1905.

Notary Public.

AFFIDAVIT OF ATTENDING PHYSICIAN OR MID-WIFE.

UNITED STATES OF AMERICA, Indian Territory, }
Southern   DISTRICT.

I,   Samuel A Graham   , a   Physician   , on oath state that I attended on Mrs.   Mollie Askew   , wife of   Lee Askew   on the 17 day of   November , 1903; that there was born to her on said date a   female   child; that said child was living March 4, 1905, and is said to have been named Dora Askew

S.A. Graham M.D.

Witnesses To Mark:
{

Subscribed and sworn to before me this   13 day of   April   , 1905

Henry F. Keller
Notary Public.

BIRTH AFFIDAVIT.

DEPARTMENT OF THE INTERIOR.
COMMISSION TO THE FIVE CIVILIZED TRIBES.

IN RE APPLICATION FOR ENROLLMENT, as a citizen of the   Choctaw   Nation, of Dora Askew   , born on the   17 day of Nov , 1903

Name of Father: Lee Askew   a citizen of the   Choctaw   Nation.
Name of Mother: Mollie Askew   a citizen of the   U.S.   Nation.

Postoffice   Marietta Ind. Ter.

Applications for Enrollment of Choctaw Newborn
Act of 1905   Volume VI

AFFIDAVIT OF MOTHER.

UNITED STATES OF AMERICA, Indian Territory, }
Southern   DISTRICT.

I, Mollie Askew, on oath state that I am 19 years of age and a citizen by ~~Blood, of the Choctaw Nation~~ U.S. ; that I am the lawful wife of Lee Askew by blood, who is a citizen, ~~by~~ —— of the ~~United States~~ Nation; that a Female child was born to me on 17 day of Nov, 1903; that said child has been named Dora Askew, and was living March 4, 1905.

Witnesses To Mark:
{

Subscribed and sworn to before me this ...... day of ...., 1905.

Notary Public.

AFFIDAVIT OF ATTENDING PHYSICIAN OR MID-WIFE.

UNITED STATES OF AMERICA, Indian Territory, }
Southern   DISTRICT.

I, S A Graham, a Physician, on oath state that I attended on Mrs. Mollie Askew, wife of Lee Askew on the 17 day of Nov, 1903; that there was born to her on said date a Female child; that said child was living March 4, 1905, and is said to have been named Dora Askew

S.A. Graham M.D.

Witnesses To Mark:
{

Subscribed and sworn to before me this 31 day of May, 1905

Henry F. Keller
Notary Public.

Applications for Enrollment of Choctaw Newborn
Act of 1905   Volume VI

BIRTH AFFIDAVIT.

Department of the Interior,
COMMISSION TO THE FIVE CIVILIZED TRIBES.

IN RE APPLICATION FOR ENROLLMENT, as a citizen of the Choctaw Nation, of Female , born on the 17 day of Nov , 190 4

Name of Father: Lee Askew   a citizen of the Choctaw Nation.
Name of Mother: Molly Askew   a citizen of the .... Nation.

Post-Office: Marietta I T

AFFIDAVIT OF MOTHER.

UNITED STATES OF AMERICA,
INDIAN TERRITORY,
Southern   District.

I, Mollie Askew , on oath state that I am 19 years of age and a citizen by Blood , of the Choctaw Nation; that I am the lawful wife of Lee Askew , who is a citizen, by —— of the —— Nation; that a Female child was born to me on 17 day of Nov , 190 4, that said child has been named Dora Askew , and is now living.

Mollie Askew
by Lee Askew

WITNESSES TO MARK:
{

Subscribed and sworn to before me this 8 day of Mat=r , 190 5

D G Bartlett
Notary Public.

AFFIDAVIT OF ATTENDING PHYSICIAN OR MID-WIFE.

UNITED STATES OF AMERICA,
~~INDIAN~~ TERRITORY, of *Oklahoma*
Caddo County   ~~District~~

I, Mrs. M.P. Walker , a Midwife , on oath state that I attended on Mrs. Mollie Askew , wife of Lee Askew on the 17 day of November , 190 3; that there was born to her on said date a Female child; that said child is now living and is said to have been named Dora Askew

M. P. Walker

Applications for Enrollment of Choctaw Newborn
Act of 1905   Volume VI

WITNESSES TO MARK:
{ M.D. Kennedy
  Lydia Woodhouse

Subscribed and sworn to before me this 13" day of March , 190 5

My Com. Exp Aug 6" 1906

(Name Illegible)
Notary Public.

Choc New Born 361
    Reader Melvin Wilson b. 8-23-03

N.B. 361

Muskogee, Indian Territory, April 3, 1905.

J. W. Wilson,
    Enville, Indian Territory.

Dear Sir:

    There is inclosed you herewith for execution application for the enrollment of your infant child, Reader Melvin Wilson, born August 23, 1903.

    In The affidavits heretofore filed with the Commission the name of the mother was written "Alizzie Wilson" and signed, "Mrs. Lizzie Wilson by Eliza Askew." In the inclosed application it is written <u>Lizzie</u> Wilson as it appears on the approved Choctaw roll.

    In having these affidavits executed care should be exercised to see that all names are written in full, as they appear in the body of the affidavit, and in the event that either of the persons signing the affidavit are unable to write, signatures by mark must be attested by two witnesses. Each affidavit must be executed before a Notary Public and the notarial seal and signature of the officer must be attached to each separate affidavit.

                    Respectfully,

LM 3-1   Chairman.

Applications for Enrollment of Choctaw Newborn
Act of 1905   Volume VI

7 N B 361

Muskogee, Indian Territory, April 14, 1905.

J. W. Wilson,
    Enville, Indian Territory.

Dear Sir:

    Receipt is hereby acknowledged of the affidavits of Mrs. Lizzie Wilson and D. Autrey to the birth of Reader Melvin Wilson, son of J. W. and Lizzie Wilson, August 23, 1903, and the same have been filed with our records as an application for the enrollment of said child.

                           Respectfully,

                           Commissioner in Charge.

BIRTH AFFIDAVIT.

Department of the Interior,
COMMISSION TO THE FIVE CIVILIZED TRIBES.

    IN RE APPLICATION FOR ENROLLMENT, as a citizen of the   Choctaw   Nation, of   Male   , born on the   23   day of   Aug   , 190 3

Name of Father: J W Wilson   a citizen of the   ———Nation.
Name of Mother: Elizzie Wilson   a citizen of the   Blood[sic]   Nation.

                  Post-Office: Enville Ind Ter

AFFIDAVIT OF MOTHER.

UNITED STATES OF AMERICA, ⎫
    INDIAN TERRITORY,   ⎬
    Southern   District. ⎭

    I,   Elizzie Wilson   , on oath state that I am   21   years of age and a citizen by   Blood , of the   Choctaw   Nation; that I am the lawful wife of   J W Wilson   , who is a citizen, by   U S   of the — Nation; that a   Male   child was born to me on   23   day of   August   , 190 3, that said child has been named Reader Melvin Wilson   , and is now living.

                           Mrs Lizzie Wilson
                           By Eliza Askew

Applications for Enrollment of Choctaw Newborn
Act of 1905   Volume VI

WITNESSES TO MARK:

{

Subscribed and sworn to before me this 8 day of Mar , 190 5

D G Bartlett
Notary Public.

AFFIDAVIT OF ATTENDING PHYSICIAN OR MID-WIFE.

UNITED STATES OF AMERICA,
  INDIAN TERRITORY,
Southern   District.

I,   D Autrey M.D.   , a   Physician   , on oath state that I attended on Mrs.   Lizzie Wilson   , wife of   J.W. Wilson   on the 23 day of   August   , 190 3; that there was born to her on said date a   male   child; that said child is now living and is said to have been named Reader Melvin Wilson

D. Autrey M.D.

WITNESSES TO MARK:

{

Subscribed and sworn to before me this 8 day of Mar , 190 5

D G Bartlett
Notary Public.

BIRTH AFFIDAVIT.

DEPARTMENT OF THE INTERIOR.
COMMISSION TO THE FIVE CIVILIZED TRIBES.

IN RE APPLICATION FOR ENROLLMENT, as a citizen of the   Choctaw   Nation, of Reader Melvin Wilson   , born on the 23 day of August , 1903

Name of Father: J W Wilson   a citizen of the   U.S.   Nation.
Name of Mother: Lizzie Wilson   a citizen of the   Choctaw   Nation.

Postoffice   Enville, Ind. Ter.

Applications for Enrollment of Choctaw Newborn
Act of 1905   Volume VI

AFFIDAVIT OF MOTHER.

UNITED STATES OF AMERICA, Indian Territory,
Southern   DISTRICT.

    I, Lizzie Wilson, on oath state that I am 21 years of age and a citizen by Blood, of the Choctaw Nation; that I am the lawful wife of J W Wilson, who is a citizen, ~~by~~ — of the United States Nation; that a Male child was born to me on 23 day of August, 1903; that said child has been named Reader Melvin Wilson, and was living March 4, 1905.

                                                Mrs Lizzie Wilson

Witnesses To Mark:
{

    Subscribed and sworn to before me this 7 day of Apr, 1905

                                                D G Bartlett
                                                  Notary Public.

AFFIDAVIT OF ATTENDING PHYSICIAN OR MID-WIFE.

UNITED STATES OF AMERICA, Indian Territory,
Southern   DISTRICT.

    I, D Autrey, a Physician, on oath state that I attended on Mrs. Lizzie Wilson, wife of JW Wilson on the 23 day of August, 1903; that there was born to her on said date a Male child; that said child was living March 4, 1905, and is said to have been named Reader Melvin Wilson

                                                D Autrey M.D.

Witnesses To Mark:
{

    Subscribed and sworn to before me this 7 day of Apr, 1905

                                                 D G Bartlett
                                                  Notary Public.

Applications for Enrollment of Choctaw Newborn
Act of 1905   Volume VI

Choc New Born 362
    Charles L. Cushman   b 6-23-04

BIRTH AFFIDAVIT.

DEPARTMENT OF THE INTERIOR.
COMMISSION TO THE FIVE CIVILIZED TRIBES.

IN RE APPLICATION FOR ENROLLMENT, as a citizen of the   Choctaw   Nation, of Charles L. Cushman   , born on the 23   day of June   , 1904
I.W.
Name of Father: Charles A Cushman   a citizen of the   Choctaw   Nation.
Name of Mother: Artee M Cushman   a citizen of the   Choctaw   Nation.

    Postoffice   Roff I.T.

AFFIDAVIT OF MOTHER.

UNITED STATES OF AMERICA, Indian Territory, }
   Southern   DISTRICT. }

    I,   Artee M Cushman   , on oath state that I am   28   years of age and a citizen by   blood   , of the   Choctaw   Nation; that I am the lawful wife of Charles A Cushman   , who is a citizen, by intermarriage   of the   Choctaw Nation; that a   male   child was born to me on   23   day of   June   , 1904; that said child has been named   Charles L Cushman   , and was living March 4, 1905.

                          Artee M Cushman
Witnesses To Mark:
{

    Subscribed and sworn to before me this   18   day of   March   , 1905

                          J C Little
                          Notary Public.

AFFIDAVIT OF ATTENDING PHYSICIAN OR MID-WIFE.

UNITED STATES OF AMERICA, Indian Territory, }
   Southern   DISTRICT. }

    I,   J L Jeffress   , a   Physician   , on oath state that I attended on Mrs.   Artee M Cushman   , wife of   Charles A Cushman   on the 23   day of June   , 1904; that there was born to her on said date a   male   child; that said child was living March 4, 1905, and is said to have been named   Charles L Cushman

Applications for Enrollment of Choctaw Newborn
Act of 1905 Volume VI

Witnesses To Mark:

J L Jeffress M.D.

{

Subscribed and sworn to before me this 18 day of   March   , 1905

J C Little
Notary Public.

Choc New Born 363
Vivian Mae McCullough b. 12-30-03

7-224

#990

CERTIFICATE OF
RECORD OF MARRIAGE

UNITED STATES OF AMERICA,
INDIAN TERRITORY, } sct.
SOUTHERN DISTRICT.

I, C. M. CAMPBELL, Clerk of the United States Court, in the Territory and District aforesaid DO HEREBY CERTIFY, that the License for and Certificate of Marriage of
MR   Carle McCullough   and
M   Quintella Vermillion
were filed in my office in said Territory and District the   6th   day of
August   A.D., 190 1   and duly recorded in Book E   of Marriage Record, Page   517

WITNESS my hand and Seal of said Court, at Ardmore, this   6th   day of   Aug.   A.D. 190 1

C. M. Campbell
CLERK.

Return this license to the United States Clerk at Ardmore, that it may be recorded, when it will be mailed to the proper address.

Applications for Enrollment of Choctaw Newborn
Act of 1905   Volume VI

No person is authorized to perform the Marriage Ceremony in the Indian Territory unless the proper credentials have first been recorded in the Clerk's office.

MARRIAGE LICENSE.

No. 990.

United States of America }
Indian Territory,   } ss   To Any Person Authorized by Law to
Southern District.   }   Solemnize Marriage, Greeting:

You are hereby Commanded to solemnize the Rite and publish the Banns of Matrimony between Mr.   Carle McCullough   of   Ardmore   in the Indian Territory, aged   20   years, and M   Quintella Vermillion   of   Ardmore   in the Indian Territory, aged   17   years, according to law; and do you officially sign and return this license to the parties therein named.

Witness my hand and official Seal, this   31st   day of   July   A. D. 190 1

(SEAL)   C. M. Campbell
                               Clerk of the United States Court.

By N. H. McCoy, Deputy

Certificate of Marriage.

United States of America }
Indian Territory,   } ss
Southern District.   }   I,   S. F. Murphy   a Gospel Minister

do hereby certify that on the   31   day of   July   A. D. 190 1 , I did duly and according to law, as commanded in the foregoing License, solemnize the Rite and publish the Banns of Matrimony between the parties therein named.

Witness my hand this   31   day of   July   A. D. 190 1

My credentials are recorded in the office of the Clerk of the United States Court, Indian Territory, Southern District, at Ardmore, Book   C , Page 30

S. F. Murphy
a Gospel Minister

NOTE. (a)- This License and Certificate of Marriages must be returned to the office of the Clerk of the United States Court in the Indian Territory, at Ardmore, within sixty days from the date thereof, or the party to whom the License was issued will be liable in the amount of ONE HUNDRED DOLLARS ($100).

Applications for Enrollment of Choctaw Newborn
Act of 1905   Volume VI

Indian Territory,
Southern District.

I, C. M. Campbell, Clerk of the United States Court, Southern District, Indian Territory, do hereby certify that the above and foregoing is a true and correct copy of the Marriage License and Certificate of Marriage of Carle McCullough and Quintella Vermillion as the same appears of record in my office at Ardmore in Book E, page 517 of Marriage License Records.

IN TESTIMONY WHEREOF, I have hereunto set my hand and affixed the seal of said Court at my office in Ardmore, Indian Territory this 21st day of March, A.D. 1905.

C. M. Campbell, Clerk,

By   N.H. McCoy   Chief Deputy.

BIRTH AFFIDAVIT.

DEPARTMENT OF THE INTERIOR.
COMMISSION TO THE FIVE CIVILIZED TRIBES.

IN RE APPLICATION FOR ENROLLMENT, as a citizen of the   Choctaw   Nation, of Vivian Mae McCullough   , born on the 30" day of December , 1903

Name of Father: Carle McCullough   a citizen of the   Choctaw   Nation.
Name of Mother: Quintella McCullough   a citizen of the   Choctaw   Nation.

Postoffice   Ardmore Ind T.

AFFIDAVIT OF MOTHER.

UNITED STATES OF AMERICA, Indian Territory, }
       Southern   DISTRICT.

I,   Quintella McCullough   , on oath state that I am   21   years of age and a citizen by   blood   , of the   Choctaw   Nation; that I am the lawful wife of   Carle McCullough   , who is a citizen, by .... of the   U. S.   Nation; that a female   child was born to me on   30" day of   December   , 1903; that said child has been named   Vivian Mae McCullough   , and was living March 4, 1905.

Quintella McCullough

Witnesses To Mark:
{

Applications for Enrollment of Choctaw Newborn
Act of 1905   Volume VI

Subscribed and sworn to before me this 20 day of   Mar   , 1905

Orrin M Redfield
Notary Public.

AFFIDAVIT OF ATTENDING PHYSICIAN OR MID-WIFE.

UNITED STATES OF AMERICA, Indian Territory, }
Southern   **DISTRICT.**

I,   W. Hardy   , a   physician   , on oath state that I attended on Mrs. Quintella McCullough   , wife of   Carle McCullough   on the 30th day of Dec , 1903; that there was born to her on said date a   female   child; that said child was living March 4, 1905, and is said to have been named Vivian Mae

W. Hardy M.D.

Witnesses To Mark:
{

Subscribed and sworn to before me this 20 day of   Mar   , 1905

Orrin M Redfield
Notary Public.

Indian Territory,   )
) S S
Southern District.)

I, Seldon T. Lindsey having first been duly sworn according to law deposes and say :

In the application of enrollment of Vivian Mae Mc. Cullough filed with the division of the Commission to the Five Civilized Tribes located at Ardmore, Ind. Ter.

That the mother of said Vivian Mae Mc. Cullough is my daughter and my wife Nina Lindsey who is a Choctaw by blood is her mother.

That my said daughter is enrolled on the Choctaw rolls as Quintella Lindsey, Indian Territory and that the person Queens Lindsey whose name appears on the certified copy of the marriage certificate of Queens Lindsey and Wm. P. Vermillion which is filed with the Commission is one and the same person and is identical with Quintella Lindsey whose name appears on the Choctaw Rolls

I further state that the records of the U.S. Clerks[sic] Office at Ardmore, I. T. give the name Queens Lindsey when it should have been Quintella Lindsey.

Witness my hand at Ardmore, I. T. this 29th. of March 1905.

Selden[sic] T Lindsey

Applications for Enrollment of Choctaw Newborn
Act of 1905   Volume VI

Subscribed and sworn to before me, by said affiant on the day and date first above written.

O.M. Redfield
Notary Public.

Indian Territory,)
) S S
Southern District.)

I Quintella McCullough having been duly sworn according to law depose and say: That I am a daughter of Seldon T. Lindsey and Nina Lindsey intermarriage and Choctaw by blood respectively That I am the same person whose name appears as Queen Lindsey on the certified copy of marriage certificate of Queen Lindsey and Wm P Vermillion.

That I am also identical with Quintella Vermillion in the certified marriage certificate of Carle McCullough and Mrs Quintella Vermillion *(the remainder illegible)*

Quintella McCullough

Subscribed and sworn to by said affiant on the day above written

David Redfield
Notary Public.

7-224

Muskogee, Indian Territory, April 10, 1905.

Quintella McCullough,
    Ardmore, Indian Territory.

Dear Madam:

Receipt is hereby acknowledged of your letter of April 2, 1905, enclosing your affidavit and the affidavit of your father Seldon T. Lindsey to the descrepancy[sic] in your name as it appears in the certified copy of the marriage certificate between yourself and William P. Vermillion which you offer in the matter of the enrollment of your child Vivian May[sic] McCullough and the same have been filed with the record in this case.

Respectfully,

Commissioner in Charge.

Applications for Enrollment of Choctaw Newborn
Act of 1905   Volume VI

Choctaw N.B. XX
363

Muskogee, Indian Territory, April 28, 1905.

Quintella McCullough,
    Ardmore, Indian Territory.

Dear Sir[sic]:

    Receipt is hereby acknowledged of your letter without date, asking if affidavits to the birth of Vivian Mae McCullough have been received, and in reply you are advised that the affidavits heretofore forwarded to the birth of Vivian Mae McCullough have been filed with our records as an application for the enrollment of said child.

        Respectfully,

        Chairman.

<u>Choc New Born 364</u>
    James Edward Sorrels   b. 5-15-04

7 NB 364

Muskogee, Indian Territory, June 30, 1905.

Alex Sorrells[sic],
    South McAlester, Indian Territory.

Dear Sir:

    Receipt is hereby acknowledged of your letter of June 23, 1905, asking when the enrollment of infants will be approved and if you may improve and hold land for your child.

    In reply to your letter you are advised that the name of your son James Edward Sorrells[sic] has been placed upon a schedule of citizens by blood of the Choctaw Nation which has been prepared for forwarding to the Secretary of the Interior, but his enrollment has not yet been approved. You will be notified when the enrollment of your son James Edward Sorrells is approved by the Department.

Applications for Enrollment of Choctaw Newborn
Act of 1905   Volume VI

You are further advised that no reservation of lands will be made for children enrolled under the provisions of the act of Congress approved March 3, 1905, until their enrollment is approved by the Secretary of the Interior, but it is believed that if you have placed improvements on lands in the Choctaw or Chickasaw Nation subsequent to March 4, 1905, you will be entitled to select the same in allotment for him when his enrollment is approved by the Secre- *(End of letter)*

(The letter below does not belong with the current applicant.)

7 NB 1420

Muskogee, Indian Territory, June 30, 1905.

Ida Green,
    Cabiness, Indian Territory.

Dear Madam:

Receipt is hereby acknowledged of the affidavit of Susan Brown to the birth of Betsey Green, daughter of Silas Folsom and Ida Green, October 25, 1904, and the same has been filed with our records in the matter of the enrollment of said child.

Respectfully,

Chairman.

BIRTH AFFIDAVIT.

DEPARTMENT OF THE INTERIOR.
COMMISSION TO THE FIVE CIVILIZED TRIBES.

IN RE APPLICATION FOR ENROLLMENT, as a citizen of the Choctaw Nation, of James Edward Sorrels, born on the 15th day of May, 1904

Name of Father: Alexander Sorrels Pitchlynn   a citizen of the United States ~~Nation~~.
Name of Mother: Ida ^ Sorrels   a citizen of the Choctaw Nation.

Postoffice   South McAlester, I.T.

Applications for Enrollment of Choctaw Newborn
Act of 1905   Volume VI

AFFIDAVIT OF MOTHER.

UNITED STATES OF AMERICA, Indian Territory, }
Central   DISTRICT.

Pitchlynn

I, Ida ^ Sorrels, on oath state that I am 19 years of age and a citizen by blood, of the Choctaw Nation; that I am the lawful wife of Alexander Sorrels, who is a citizen, by .... of the United States Nation; that a male child was born to me on 15th day of May, 1904; that said child has been named James Edward Sorrels, and was living March 4, 1905.

Ida Pitchlynn Sorrels

Witnesses To Mark:
{

Subscribed and sworn to before me this 18th day of March, 1905

Wirt Franklin
Notary Public.

AFFIDAVIT OF ATTENDING PHYSICIAN OR MID-WIFE.

UNITED STATES OF AMERICA, Indian Territory, }
Central   DISTRICT.

I, Hannah Bell, a mid-wife, on oath state that I attended on Mrs. Ida Pitchlynn Sorrels, wife of Alexander Sorrels on the 15th day of May, 1904; that there was born to her on said date a male child; that said child was living March 4, 1905, and is said to have been named James Edward Sorrels

Hannah Bell

Witnesses To Mark:
{

Subscribed and sworn to before me this 18th day of March, 1905

Wirt Franklin
Notary Public.

Applications for Enrollment of Choctaw Newborn
Act of 1905   Volume VI

Choc New Born 365
    Andy A. Pitchlynn b. 2-8-04

BIRTH AFFIDAVIT.

DEPARTMENT OF THE INTERIOR.
COMMISSION TO THE FIVE CIVILIZED TRIBES.

IN RE APPLICATION FOR ENROLLMENT, as a citizen of the Choctaw Nation, of Andy A. Pitchlynn, born on the 8th day of February, 1904

Name of Father: William B. Pitchlynn   a citizen of the Choctaw Nation.
Name of Mother: Minnie E. Pitchlynn   a citizen of the United States Nation.

    Postoffice   South McAlester, I.T.

AFFIDAVIT OF MOTHER.

UNITED STATES OF AMERICA, Indian Territory,
Central   DISTRICT.

I, Minnie E. Pitchlynn, on oath state that I am 19 years of age and a citizen by ...., of the United States ~~Nation~~; that I am the lawful wife of William B. Pitchlynn, who is a citizen, by blood of the Choctaw Nation; that a male child was born to me on 8th day of February, 1904; that said child has been named Andy A. Pitchlynn, and was living March 4, 1905.

    Minnie E. Pitchlynn

Witnesses To Mark:

Subscribed and sworn to before me this 20th day of March, 1905

    Wirt Franklin
    Notary Public.

AFFIDAVIT OF ATTENDING PHYSICIAN OR MID-WIFE.

UNITED STATES OF AMERICA, Indian Territory,
Central   DISTRICT.

I, Hannah Bell, a mid-wife, on oath state that I attended on Mrs. Minnie E. Pitchlynn, wife of William B. Pitchlynn on the 8th day of February, 1904; that there was born to her on said date a male child; that said child was living March 4, 1905, and is said to have been named Andy A Pitchlynn

Applications for Enrollment of Choctaw Newborn
Act of 1905 Volume VI

Hannah Bell

Witnesses To Mark:
{

Subscribed and sworn to before me this 20th day of March , 1905

Wirt Franklin
Notary Public.

No. 3826

Certificate of Record of Marriages.

United States of America,
The Indian Territory, } sct.
Central District.

I, E J Fannin Clerk of the United States Court, in the Indian Territory and District aforesaid, do hereby CERTIFY, that the License for and Certificate of the Marriage of

Mr. W B Pitchlynn and
Miss Minnie E Wilson was

filed in my office in said Territory and District the 31 day of Oct A.D., 190 3 , and duly recorded in Book 10 of Marriage Record, Page 617

WITNESS my hand and Seal of said Court, at So McAlester this 20 day of March A.D. 190 5

EJ Fannin
Clerk.
By WC Donnelly Deputy.

P. O. ....

Applications for Enrollment of Choctaw Newborn
Act of 1905   Volume VI

No. 3876

MARRIAGE LICENSE

United States of America,   The Indian Territory,
                             Central DISTRICT, SS.

To any Person Authorized by Law to Solemnize Marriage, Greeting:

You are hereby commanded to Solemnize the Rite and publish the Banns of Matrimony between Mr.   W. B. Pitchlynn
of   So McAlester   *in the Indian Territory, aged*   21   *years, and M* iss Minnie W Wilson   *of*   So McAlester
in the Indian Territory., aged   18   *years, according to law, and do you officially sign and return this License to the parties therein named.*

WITNESS my hand and official seal, this   19   day of   Oct   A. D. 190 3

E. J. Fannin
Clerk of the United States Court.

WC Donnelly   Deputy

Certificate of Marriage.

United States of America,
The Indian Territory, } ss.
Central   District.   I,   W.J. Pinkerton

a   Minister of the Gospel   *, do hereby certify, that on the*   25th   day *of*   Oct.   *A. D. 190* 3   *, I did, duly and according to law, as commanded in the foregoing License, solemnize the Rite and publish the Banns of Matrimony between the parties therein named.*

Witness my hand, this   25th   day of   Oct   A. D. 190 5

My credentials are recorded in the office of the Clerk of }   W.J. Pinkerton
the United States Court in the Indian Territory,
Central District, Book   B   , Page   30   *a*   Minister of the Gospel

Note—This License and Certificate of Marriage must be returned to the Office of the Clerk of the United States Court of the Indian Territory, from whence it was issued, within sixty days from the date thereof, or the party to whom the License was issued will be liable in the amount of the One Hundred Dollars ($100.00)

Applications for Enrollment of Choctaw Newborn
Act of 1905 Volume VI

Choc New Born 366
George M. Bond   b. 9-10-03

7-4598

Muskogee, Indian Territory, April 8, 1905.

Edmund M. Bond,
McAlester, Indian Territory.

Dear Sir:

Receipt is hereby acknowledged of your letter of April 3, 1905, in which you state that you have executed affidavits of the birth of your child George M. Bond and you ask when you will be able to file for him.

In reply to your letter you are informed that the affidavits heretofore forwarded to the birth of your child George M. Bond have been filed with our records as an application for the enrollment of said child.

No selection of allotment can be permitted for children for whom application was made under the act of Congress of March 3, 1905, until their enrollment has been approved by the Secretary of the Interior.

Respectfully,

Commissioner in Charge.

BIRTH AFFIDAVIT.
DEPARTMENT OF THE INTERIOR.
COMMISSION TO THE FIVE CIVILIZED TRIBES.

IN RE APPLICATION FOR ENROLLMENT, as a citizen of the   Choctaw   Nation, of George M. Bond   , born on the 10th day of Sept. , 1903

Name of Father: Edmund M. Bond   a citizen of the   Choctaw   Nation.
Name of Mother: June H Bond   a citizen of the   Choctaw   Nation.

Postoffice   McAlester, I.T.

Applications for Enrollment of Choctaw Newborn
Act of 1905   Volume VI

AFFIDAVIT OF MOTHER.

UNITED STATES OF AMERICA, Indian Territory, }
Central   DISTRICT.

    I, June H. Bond, on oath state that I am 26 years of age and a citizen by marriage, of the Choctaw Nation; that I am the lawful wife of Edmund M. Bond, who is a citizen, by blood of the Choctaw Nation; that a male child was born to me on 10th day of September, 1903; that said child has been named George M. Bond, and was living March 4, 1905.

                                           June H Bond

Witnesses To Mark:
{

    Subscribed and sworn to before me this 17th day of March, 1905

                                           Wirt Franklin
                                           Notary Public.

AFFIDAVIT OF ATTENDING PHYSICIAN OR MID-WIFE.

UNITED STATES OF AMERICA, Indian Territory, }
Central   DISTRICT.

    I, R. J. Crabill, a physician, on oath state that I attended on Mrs. June H Bond, wife of Edmund M Bond on the 10th day of September, 1903; that there was born to her on said date a male child; that said child was living March 4, 1905, and is said to have been named George M. Bond

                                           R J Crabill M.D.

Witnesses To Mark:
{

    Subscribed and sworn to before me this 17th day of March, 1905

                                           Wirt Franklin
                                           Notary Public.

Applications for Enrollment of Choctaw Newborn
Act of 1905   Volume VI

Choc New Born 367
Rex Abbott Bond   b. 3-4-04

BIRTH AFFIDAVIT.

DEPARTMENT OF THE INTERIOR.
COMMISSION TO THE FIVE CIVILIZED TRIBES.

IN RE APPLICATION FOR ENROLLMENT, as a citizen of the   Choctaw   Nation, of Rex Abbott Bond   , born on the 4th   day of   March , 1904

Name of Father: Rex Cheadle Bond   a citizen of the   Choctaw   Nation.
Name of Mother: Ruby Abbott Bond   a citizen of the United States Nation.

Postoffice   South McAlester, I.T.

AFFIDAVIT OF MOTHER.

UNITED STATES OF AMERICA, Indian Territory,
Central   DISTRICT.

I, Ruby Abbott Bond , on oath state that I am 22   years of age and a citizen by ...., of the United States   ~~Nation~~; that I am the lawful wife of   Rex Cheadle Bond   , who is a citizen, by blood   of the   Choctaw   Nation; that a   male   child was born to me on   4th   day of   March   , 1904; that said child has been named   Rex Abbott Bond   , and was living March 4, 1905.

Ruby Abbott Bond

Witnesses To Mark:
{

Subscribed and sworn to before me this   17th   day of   March   , 1905

Wirt Franklin
Notary Public.

AFFIDAVIT OF ATTENDING PHYSICIAN OR MID-WIFE.

UNITED STATES OF AMERICA, Indian Territory,
Central   DISTRICT.

I,   A. Griffith   , a   physician   , on oath state that I attended on Mrs. Ruby Abbott Bond   , wife of   Rex Cheadle Bond   on the 4th   day of   March   , 1904; that there was born to her on said date a   male   child; that said child was living March 4, 1905, and is said to have been named Rex Abbott Bond

Applications for Enrollment of Choctaw Newborn
Act of 1905   Volume VI

A Griffith, M.D.

Witnesses To Mark:

{

Subscribed and sworn to before me this   17th day of   March   , 1905

Wirt Franklin
Notary Public.

No. 3598

Certificate of Record of Marriages.

𝕌nited States of America,
The Indian Territory, } sct.
Central   *District.*

I,   E J Fannin   Clerk
of the United States Court, in the Indian Territory
and District aforesaid, do hereby CERTIFY, that the
License for and Certificate of the Marriage of

Mr.   Rex Cheadle Bond   and

M iss Ruby May Abbott   was

filed in my office in said Territory and District the
25   day of   June
A.D., 190 3 , and duly recorded in Book   10
of Marriage Record, Page   107

WITNESS my hand and Seal of said Court, at
So McAlester
this   18   day of   March
A.D. 190 3

EJ Fannin
Clerk.
By   WC Donnelly   Deputy.

P. O. ───────────

Applications for Enrollment of Choctaw Newborn
Act of 1905   Volume VI

No. 3598

MARRIAGE LICENSE

United States of America,   The Indian Territory,
Central District, SS.

To any Person Authorized by Law to Solemnize Marriage, Greeting:

You are hereby commanded to Solemnize the Rite and publish the Banns of Matrimony between Mr.   Rex Cheadle Bond
of   South McAlester   in the Indian Territory, aged   22   years,
and M iss Ruby May Abbott   of   So. McAlester
in the Indian Territory., aged   21   years, according to law, and do you officially sign and return this License to the parties therein named.

WITNESS my hand and official seal, this   24   day of   June   A. D. 1903

E. J. Fannin
Clerk of the United States Court.

WC Donnelly   Deputy

Certificate of Marriage.

United States of America,   }
The Indian Territory,   } ss.
Central   District.   }

I,   J. C. Howell

a   Christian Minister   , do hereby certify, that on the   25th day of   June A. D. 1903 , I did, duly and according to law, as commanded in the foregoing License, solemnize the Rite and publish the Banns of Matrimony between the parties therein named.

Witness my hand, this   25   day of   June   A. D. 1903

My credentials are recorded in the office of the Clerk of   }   J. C. Howell
the United States Court in the Indian Territory,   }
Central District, Book   B   , Page   129   }   a   So. McAlester

Note—This License and Certificate of Marriage must be returned to the Office of the Clerk of the United States Court of the Indian Territory, from whence it was issued, within sixty days from the date thereof, or the party to whom the License was issued will be liable in the amount of the One Hundred Dollars ($100.00).

Applications for Enrollment of Choctaw Newborn
Act of 1905 Volume VI

Choc New Born 368
May Chunn b. 7-20-04

NEW-BORN AFFIDAVIT.

Number............

...Choctaw Enrolling Commission...

IN THE MATTER OF THE APPLICATION FOR ENROLLMENT, as a citizen of the Choctaw Nation, of May Chunn

born on the 20 day of July 190 4

Name of father W. R. Chunn   a citizen of Choctaw
Nation final enrollment No. 12733
Name of mother Lucy Chunn   a citizen of Choctaw
Nation final enrollment No. 458

Postoffice Savanna

AFFIDAVIT OF MOTHER.

UNITED STATES OF AMERICA
INDIAN TERRITORY
 Central DISTRICT

I Lucy Chunn , on oath state that I am 30 years of age and a citizen by Inter M of the Choctaw Nation, and as such have been placed upon the final roll of the Choctaw Nation, by the Honorable Secretary of the Interior my final enrollment number being 458 ; that I am the lawful wife of William R Chunn , who is a citizen of the Choctaw Nation, and as such has been placed upon the final roll of said Nation by the Honorable Secretary of the Interior, his final enrollment number being 12733 and that a Female child was born to me on the 20th day of June 190 4; that said child has been named May Chunn , and is now living.

Lucy Chunn

Witnesseth.

Must be two Witnesses who are Citizens.
Belle Mackey
Katie Culbertson

Subscribed and sworn to before me this 16 day of Jan 190 5

W. T. Culbertson
Notary Public.

My commission expires: Sept 22 - 1907

Applications for Enrollment of Choctaw Newborn
Act of 1905   Volume VI

AFFIDAVIT OF ATTENDING PHYSICIAN OR MIDWIFE

UNITED STATES OF AMERICA
INDIAN TERRITORY
Central   DISTRICT

I, S. P. Ross   a   Physician on oath state that I attended on Mrs. Lucy Chunn   wife of   William R. Chunn on the 20th day of July , 190 4 , that there was born to her on said date a   Female child, that said child is now living, and is said to have been named   May Chunn

S.P. Ross   M.D.

Subscribed and sworn to before me this, the   16th   day of January   190 5

WITNESSETH: W.T. Culbertson   Notary Public.

Must be two witnesses who are citizens { Belle Mackey
Katie Culbertson

We hereby certify that we are well acquainted with   SP Ross   a   Physician   and know .... to be reputable and of good standing in the community.

_____   Belle Mackey

_____   Katie Culbertson

BIRTH AFFIDAVIT.

DEPARTMENT OF THE INTERIOR.
COMMISSION TO THE FIVE CIVILIZED TRIBES.

IN RE APPLICATION FOR ENROLLMENT, as a citizen of the   Choctaw   Nation, of May Chunn , born on the 20th   day of July , 1904

Name of Father: William R Chunn   a citizen of the   Choctaw   Nation.
Name of Mother: Lucy Chunn   a citizen of the   Choctaw   Nation.

Postoffice   Savanna

Applications for Enrollment of Choctaw Newborn
Act of 1905 Volume VI

AFFIDAVIT OF MOTHER.

UNITED STATES OF AMERICA, Indian Territory, }
   Central   DISTRICT.

    I, Lucy Chunn, on oath state that I am 30 years of age and a citizen by Interm, of the Choctaw Nation; that I am the lawful wife of William R Chunn, who is a citizen, by blood of the Choctaw Nation; that a Female child was born to me on 20th day of July, 1904, that said child has been named May Chunn, and is now living.

                                                Lucy Chunn

Witnesses To Mark:
   { Belle Mackey
     Katie Culbertson

    Subscribed and sworn to before me this 16th day of January, 1905.

                                                W.T. Culbertson
                                                Notary Public.

AFFIDAVIT OF ATTENDING PHYSICIAN OR MID-WIFE.

UNITED STATES OF AMERICA, Indian Territory, }
   Central   DISTRICT.

    I, S.P. Ross, a Physician, on oath state that I attended on Mrs. Lucy Chunn, wife of William R Chunn on the 20th day of July, 1904; that there was born to her on said date a .... child; that said child is now living and is said to have been named May Chunn

                                                S.P. Ross

Witnesses To Mark:
   { Belle Mackey
     Katie Culbertson

    Subscribed and sworn to before me this 16th day of January, 1905.

                                                W.T. Culbertson
                                                Notary Public.

Applications for Enrollment of Choctaw Newborn
Act of 1905   Volume VI

BIRTH AFFIDAVIT.

DEPARTMENT OF THE INTERIOR.
COMMISSION TO THE FIVE CIVILIZED TRIBES.

IN RE APPLICATION FOR ENROLLMENT, as a citizen of the   Choctaw   Nation, of May Chunn   , born on the 20th day of   July   , 1904

Name of Father: William R Chunn   a citizen of the   Choctaw   Nation.
Name of Mother: Lucy Chunn   a citizen of the   Choctaw   Nation.

Postoffice   Savanna

AFFIDAVIT OF MOTHER.

UNITED STATES OF AMERICA, Indian Territory, }
Central   DISTRICT.

I,   Lucy Chunn   , on oath state that I am   30   years of age and a citizen by intermarriage , of the   Choctaw   Nation; that I am the lawful wife of   William R Chunn   , who is a citizen, by blood   of the   Choctaw   Nation; that a .... child was born to me on   20th day of   July   , 1904; that said child has been named   May Chunn   , and was living March 4, 1905.

Lucy Chunn

Witnesses To Mark:
{ Belle Mackey
{ Katie Culbertson

Subscribed and sworn to before me this   15th day of   April   , 1905

W.T. Culbertson
Notary Public.

AFFIDAVIT OF ATTENDING PHYSICIAN OR MID-WIFE.

UNITED STATES OF AMERICA, Indian Territory, }
Central   DISTRICT.

I,   S.P. Ross   , a   Physician   , on oath state that I attended on Mrs.   Lucy Chunn   , wife of   William R Chunn   on the 20th day of July , 1904; that there was born to her on said date a   female   child; that said child was living March 4, 1905, and is said to have been named   May Chunn

S.P. Ross- M.D.

Applications for Enrollment of Choctaw Newborn
Act of 1905   Volume VI

Witnesses To Mark:
   { Belle Mackey
    Katie Culbertson

    Subscribed and sworn to before me this   15th day of   April   , 1905

                                W.T. Culbertson
                                  Notary Public.

(The letter below does not belong with the current applicant.)

9-NB-368

                            Muskogee, Indian Territory, July 21, 1905.

Ben Underwood,
    Norton, Indian Territory.

Dear Sir:

    Receipt is hereby acknowledged of the affidavits of Lucy Underwood and J. H. Logan M. D., to the birth of Ada Underwood, daughter of Ben and Lucy Underwood, January 14, 1905, and the same have been filed with the record in this case.

                            Respectfully,

                                        Commissioner.

---

                                      7 NB 368

                        Muskogee, Indian Territory, April 20, 1905.

W. H[sic]. Chunn,
    Savanna, Indian Territory.

Dear Sir:

    Receipt is hereby acknowledged of your letter of April 15, 1905, enclosing affidavits of Lucy Chunn and S. P. Ross to the birth of May Chunn, daughter of William R. and Lucy Chunn, July 20, 1904, and the same have been filed with our records as an application for the enrollment of said child.

    Replying to that portion of your letter in which you ask how long it will be before you can file on land for this child you are advised that no selection of allotment can be permitted for children for whom application is made under the provisions of the act of

Applications for Enrollment of Choctaw Newborn
Act of 1905   Volume VI

Congress approved March 3, 1905, until their enrollment has been approved by the Secretary of the Interior.

                Respectfully,

                              Chairman.

N.B. 368.

COPY

Muskogee, Indian Territory, April 8, 1905.

William R. Chunn,
    Savanna, Indian Territory.

Dear Sir:

    There is enclosed you herewith for execution application for the enrollment of your infant child, May Chunn, born July 20, 1904.

    The affidavit heretofore filed with the Commission show the child was living on January 16, 1905. It is necessary, for the child to be enrolled, that she was living on March 4, 1905. You will please insert the age of the mother place left blank for that purpose.

    In having these affidavits executed care should be exercised to see that all names are written in full, as they appear in the body of the affidavit, and in the event that either of the persons signing the affidavit are unable to write, signatures by mark must be attested by two witnesses. Each affidavit must be executed before a Notary Public and the notarial seal and signature of the officer must be attached to each separate affidavit.

                Respectfully,
                SIGNED
                T. B. Needles.

LER 8-3   Commissioner in Charge.

Applications for Enrollment of Choctaw Newborn
Act of 1905   Volume VI

7-4600

Muskogee, Indian Territory, March 15, 1905.

William R. Chunn,
    Savanna, Indian Territory.

Dear Sir:

    Receipt is hereby acknowledged of the affidavits of Lucy Chunn and S. P. Ross to the birth of May Chunn, infant daughter of William R. and Lucy Chunn, July 20, 1904, and the same have been filed with our records as an application for the enrollment of said child.

                Respectfully,

                      Chairman.

Choc New Born 369
    Josie Beck   b. 12-13-02
    Elisa Beck   b. 12-27-03

No. 1 died Jan. 2, 1903

No. 1 dismissed under order of Comm to FCT
July 18, 1905

Notice of decision forwarded applicant's father
Aug 23, 1905

N. B. 369

Muskogee, Indian Territory, April 10, 1905.

Joseph G. Beck,
    Bower, Indian Territory.

Dear Sir:

    There is inclosed you herewith for execution application for the enrollment of your infant child, Josie Beck, born December 13, 1902.

Applications for Enrollment of Choctaw Newborn
Act of 1905   Volume VI

The affidavit heretofore filed with the Commission shows the child was living on November 20, 1902. It is necessary, for the child to be enrolled, that she was living on March 4, 1905. You will please insert the mother's age in space for the purpose.

The above mentioned affidavit is of the mother only. The affidavit of the attending physician or midwife is also required. If there was no one in attendance at the birth of said child, it will be necessary for you to secure the affidavits of two persons who have actual knowledge of the fact that the child was born, was living on March 4, 1905, and that Frances Beck was her mother.

I having these affidavits executed care should be exercised to see that all the names are written in full as they appear in the body of the affidavit, and in the event that either of the persons signing the affidavit are unable to write, signatures by mark must be attested by two witnesses. Each affidavit must be executed before a Notary Public and the notarial seal and signature of the officer must be attached to each separate affidavit.

Respectfully,

LM 10-51

Commissioner in Charge.

Choctaw 462?.

Muskogee, Indian Territory, April 11, 1905.

Joseph G. Beck,
   Bower, Indian Territory.

Dear Sir:

Receipt is hereby acknowledged of affidavits of Francis Beck and George W. West to the birth of Elisa Beck, December 27, 1903, and the same have been filed with our records as an application for the enrollment of said child.

Respectfully,

Commissioner in Charge.

Applications for Enrollment of Choctaw Newborn
Act of 1905 Volume VI

7-NB-369.

Muskogee, Indian Territory, May 25, 1905.

Joseph G. Beck,
    Bower, Indian Territory.

Dear Sir:

There is enclosed you herewith for execution application for the enrollment of your infant child, Josie Beck, born December 13, 1902.

Your attention is called to the Commission's letter of April 10, 1905, to which you have failed to reply. In the event that the mother of the applicant is dead or that there was no attending physician or midwife present at the time of the birth of the applicant it will be necessary that you secure the affidavits of two disinterested persons who have actual knowledge of the facts that the child was born, the date of her birth; that she was living on March 4, 1905, and that Frances Beck is her mother.

In the event that this applicant is dead you will please execute the enclosed proof of death, in order that this fact may be made a matter of record.

In having these affidavits executed care should be exercised to see that all names are written in full, as they appear in the body of the affidavit, and in the event that either of the persons signing the affidavit are unable to write, signatures by mark must be attested by two witnesses. Each affidavit must be executed before a Notary Public and the notarial seal and signature of the officer must be attached to each separate affidavit.

Respectfully,

Chairman.

VR 25-8.
Encl. D-C.

Applications for Enrollment of Choctaw Newborn
Act of 1905   Volume VI

7-NB-369.

Muskogee, Indian Territory, June 20, 1905.

Joseph G. Beck,
    Bower, Indian Territory.

Dear Sir:

    Replying to your letter of June 8, 1905, in which you ask if it is necessary for you to furnish proof of death in the matter of the enrollment of your infant child, Josie Beck, who died January 2, 1903, you are informed that this proof is necessary in order to make the records in this matter complete.

    There is enclosed herewith a blank similar to the one sent you on May 25, 1905, which you will kindly execute and return to this office.

    Respectfully,

    Chairman.

D.C.

7-NB-369

Muskogee, Indian Territory, July 21, 1905.

Joseph G. Beck,
    Bower, Indian Territory.

Dear Sir:

    Receipt is hereby acknowledged of your affidavit and the affidavit of J. W. McDonald M. D., of the death of your daughter, Josie Beck, which occured[sic] January 2, 1903, and the same have been filed with the records of this office as evidence of death of the above named person.

    Respectfully,

    Commissioner.

Applications for Enrollment of Choctaw Newborn
Act of 1905 Volume VI

BIRTH AFFIDAVIT.

Department of the Interior,
COMMISSION TO THE FIVE CIVILIZED TRIBES.

IN RE APPLICATION FOR ENROLLMENT, as a citizen of the Choctaw Nation, of Josie Beck, born on the 13 day of Jan, 190 2

Name of Father: Jos. G. beck   a citizen of the Choctaw Nation.
Name of Mother: Frances Beck   a citizen of the Choctaw Nation.

Post-Office: Bower

AFFIDAVIT OF MOTHER.

UNITED STATES OF AMERICA, ⎫
   INDIAN TERRITORY,   ⎬
Central   District. ⎭

I, Jos. G. Beck, on oath state that I am 41 years of age and a citizen by marriage, of the Choctaw Nation; that I am the lawful ~~wife~~ husband of Frances Beck, who is a citizen, by blood of the Choctaw Nation; that a female child was born to ~~me~~ us on 13 day of Dec, 190 2, that said child has been named Josie Beck, and is now living.

J. G. Beck

WITNESSES TO MARK:
{

Subscribed and sworn to before me this 20 day of Dec., 190 2

T.C. Humphrey
Notary Public.

7-NB-369

Muskogee, Indian Territory, August 23, 1905.
COPY

Joseph G. Beck,
   Bower, Indian Territory.

Dear Sir:

    You are hereby advised that is appearing from the records of this office that your child, Josie Beck, died prior to March 4, 1905, the Commissioner to the Five Civilized Tribes on August 23, 1905, dismissed the application for the enrollment of said child as a citizen by blood of the Choctaw Nation.

Applications for Enrollment of Choctaw Newborn
Act of 1905 Volume VI

Respectfully,
SIGNED

Tams Bixby
Commissioner.

It appearing from the within affidavits that Josie Beck, born December 13, 1902, for whose enrollment as a citizen by blood of the Choctaw Nation, application was made under the provisions of the Act of Congress approved March 3, 1905 (33 Stats., 1071), died January 2, 1903, it is hereby ordered that the application for the enrollment of said Josie Beck as a citizen by blood of the Choctaw Nation be dismissed.

Tams Bixby
Commissioner.

Muskogee, Indian Territory.
AUG 8 1905

DEPARTMENT OF THE INTERIOR.
COMMISSION TO THE FIVE CIVILIZED TRIBES.

In the matter of the death of Josie Beck a citizen of the Choctaw Nation, who formerly resided at or near Bower , Ind. Ter., and died on the 2 second day of Jan , 1903

AFFIDAVIT OF RELATIVE.

UNITED STATES OF AMERICA, Indian Territory,
Western DISTRICT.

I, Joseph G Beck , on oath state that I am 44 years of age and a citizen by intermarriage , of the Choctaw Nation; that my postoffice address is Bower , Ind. Ter.; that I am Father of Josie Beck who was a citizen, by Blood , of the Choctaw Nation and that said Josie Beck died on the 2 day of Jan , 1903

Joseph G Beck

Witnesses To Mark:

Subscribed and sworn to before me this 13 day of July , 1905.

Sterling P Davis
Notary Public.

Applications for Enrollment of Choctaw Newborn
Act of 1905   Volume VI

AFFIDAVIT OF ACQUAINTANCE.

UNITED STATES OF AMERICA, Indian Territory,
Western   DISTRICT.

I,   J.W. McDonald M.D.   , on oath state that I am   39   years of age, and a citizen ~~by~~ .... of the   Ind. Ter.   Choctaw   Nation; that my postoffice address is Brooken[sic]   , Ind. Ter.; that I was personally acquainted with   Joseph[sic] Beck   who was a citizen, by   Blood   , of the   Choctaw   Nation; and that said   Josie Beck   died on the   2ond   day of   January   , 1903

J.W. McDonald M.D.

Witnesses To Mark:

{

Subscribed and sworn to before me this   13   day of   July   , 1905.

Sterling P Davis
Notary Public.
My commission expires Feb 9 - 07

BIRTH AFFIDAVIT.

DEPARTMENT OF THE INTERIOR.
COMMISSION TO THE FIVE CIVILIZED TRIBES.

IN RE APPLICATION FOR ENROLLMENT, as a citizen of the   Choctaw   Nation, of   Elisa Beck   , born on the   27   day of   December   , 1903

Name of Father: Joseph G. Beck   a citizen of the   Choctaw   Nation.
Name of Mother: Francis Beck   a citizen of the   Choctaw   Nation.

Postoffice   Bower, I.T.

Child present.

AFFIDAVIT OF MOTHER.

UNITED STATES OF AMERICA, Indian Territory,
Western   DISTRICT.

I,   Francis Beck   , on oath state that I am .... years of age and a citizen by blood   , of the   Choctaw   Nation; that I am the lawful wife of   Joseph G. Beck   , who is a citizen, by   intermarriage   of the   Choctaw   Nation; that a   Female   child was born to me on   27   day of   December   , 1903; that said child has been named   Elisa Beck   , and was living March 4, 1905.

Francis Beck

Applications for Enrollment of Choctaw Newborn
Act of 1905   Volume VI

Witnesses To Mark:
{

   Subscribed and sworn to before me this 7 day of   April   , 1905

Drennan C Skaggs
Notary Public.

AFFIDAVIT OF ATTENDING PHYSICIAN OR MID-WIFE.

UNITED STATES OF AMERICA, Indian Territory, }
   Western   DISTRICT.

   I,   G. W. West   , a   physician   , on oath state that I attended on Mrs.   Francis Beck   , wife of   Joseph C[sic]. Beck   on or about the 27 day of December , 1903; that there was born to her on said date a   Female   child; that said child was living March 4, 1905, and is said to have been named Elisa Beck

Geo. W. West
Witnesses To Mark:
{

   Subscribed and sworn to before me this 7 day of   April   , 1905

Drennan C Skaggs
Notary Public.

NEW-BORN AFFIDAVIT.

   Number............

...Choctaw Enrolling Commission...

   IN THE MATTER OF THE APPLICATION FOR ENROLLMENT, as a citizen of the Choctaw   Nation, of   Eliza[sic] Beck

born on the 27 day of December   190 3

Name of father   Joseph G Beck   a citizen of   Choctaw
Nation final enrollment No. 765
Name of mother   Francis Beck   a citizen of   Choctaw
Nation final enrollment No. 12787

Postoffice   Bower I.T.

Applications for Enrollment of Choctaw Newborn
Act of 1905   Volume VI

AFFIDAVIT OF MOTHER.

UNITED STATES OF AMERICA
INDIAN TERRITORY
Western   DISTRICT

I   Francis Beck   , on oath state that I am 35 years of age and a citizen by Blood of the Choctaw Nation, and as such have been placed upon the final roll of the Choctaw Nation, by the Honorable Secretary of the Interior my final enrollment number being 12787 ; that I am the lawful wife of Joseph G Beck , who is a citizen of the Choctaw Nation, and as such has been placed upon the final roll of said Nation by the Honorable Secretary of the Interior, his final enrollment number being 765 and that a Female child was born to me on the 27 day of December 190 3; that said child has been named Eliza[sic] Beck , and is now living.

Witnesseth.   Francis Beck

Must be two Witnesses who are Citizens. } Jess Walls
James Scott

Subscribed and sworn to before me this 10 day of Jan 190 5

John M Long
Notary Public.

My commission expires: Nov 27 1907

AFFIDAVIT OF ATTENDING PHYSICIAN OR MIDWIFE

UNITED STATES OF AMERICA
INDIAN TERRITORY
Western   DISTRICT

I,   Geo. W. West   a   Physician on oath state that I attended on Mrs. Francis Beck wife of Joseph G Beck on the 27 day of December , 190 3 , that there was born to her on said date a Female child, that said child is now living, and is said to have been named Eliza Beck

Geo. W. West
Subscribed and sworn to before me this, the 19th day of January 190 5

Aug 1-1906
WITNESSETH:
Must be two witnesses who are citizens   {   Thos. F. Turner   Notary Public.

313

Applications for Enrollment of Choctaw Newborn
Act of 1905   Volume VI

We hereby certify that we are well acquainted with   Geo. W. West a **Physician** and know him to be reputable and of good standing in the community.

_____   R Seary

_____   D.M. Whitaker

Choc New Born 370
Joseph W. Arudt   b. 9-2-03

BIRTH AFFIDAVIT.

DEPARTMENT OF THE INTERIOR.
COMMISSION TO THE FIVE CIVILIZED TRIBES.

IN RE APPLICATION FOR ENROLLMENT, as a citizen of the   Choctaw   Nation, of Joseph W. Arudt   , born on the   2nd   day of   September   , 1903

Name of Father: Wm. Arudt   a citizen of the United States Nation.
Name of Mother: Mary E. Arudt   a citizen of the   Choctaw   Nation.

Postoffice   McAlester, I.T.

AFFIDAVIT OF MOTHER.

UNITED STATES OF AMERICA, Indian Territory,
   Central   **DISTRICT.**

I, Mary E. Arudt   , on oath state that I am   35   years of age and a citizen by   blood   , of the   Choctaw   Nation; that I am the lawful wife of   Wm Arudt , who is a citizen, by …………… of the   United States   ~~Nation~~; that a   male   child was born to me on   2nd   day of   September   , 1903; that said child has been named Joseph W. Arudt   , and was living March 4, 1905.

                           Mary E. Arudt
Witnesses To Mark:
{

Applications for Enrollment of Choctaw Newborn
Act of 1905   Volume VI

Subscribed and sworn to before me this 20th day of March , 1905

Wirt Franklin
Notary Public.

AFFIDAVIT OF ATTENDING PHYSICIAN OR MID-WIFE.

UNITED STATES OF AMERICA, Indian Territory,
Central   DISTRICT.

I, Sarah Moore , a mid-wife , on oath state that I attended on Mrs. Mary E Arudt , wife of Wm. Arudt on the 2nd day of September , 1903; that there was born to her on said date a male child; that said child was living March 4, 1905, and is said to have been named Joseph W. Arudt

            her
          Sarah x Moore
Witnesses To Mark: mark
 { R. B. Coleman
   Silas D. Folsom

Subscribed and sworn to before me this 20th day of March , 1905

Wirt Franklin
Notary Public.

Choc New Born 371
  May Hailey b. 6-13-03

7-4683

Muskogee, Indian Territory, March 23, 1905.

Walter P. Hailey,
  Haileyville, Indian Territory.

Dear Sir:

  Receipt is hereby acknowledged of the affidavits of Grace C. Hailey and A. L. Anderson to the birth of May Hailey, daughter of Walter P. and Grace C. Hailey, June 13, 1903, and the same have been filed with our records as an application for the enrollment of said child.

Applications for Enrollment of Choctaw Newborn
Act of 1905   Volume VI

Respectfully,

Chairman.

BIRTH AFFIDAVIT.

DEPARTMENT OF THE INTERIOR.
COMMISSION TO THE FIVE CIVILIZED TRIBES.

IN RE APPLICATION FOR ENROLLMENT, as a citizen of the   Choctaw   Nation, of May Hailey   , born on the 13   day of   June , 1903

Name of Father: Walter P. Hailey   a citizen of the   Choctaw   Nation.
Name of Mother: Grace C. Hailey   a citizen of the   Choctaw   Nation.

Postoffice   Haileyville, Ind. Ter.

AFFIDAVIT OF MOTHER.

UNITED STATES OF AMERICA, Indian Territory, }
    15   ———   DISTRICT.

I,   Grace C. Hailey   , on oath state that I am   28   years of age and a citizen by   marriage   , of the   Choctaw   Nation; that I am the lawful wife of Walter P. Hailey   , who is a citizen, by blood   of the   Choctaw   Nation; that a Female   child was born to me on   13th day of   June   , 1903; that said child has been named   May Hailey   , and was living March 4, 1905.

Grace C. Hailey

Witnesses To Mark:
{

Subscribed and sworn to before me this   20   day of   March   , 1905

EH Doyle
Notary Public.

AFFIDAVIT OF ATTENDING PHYSICIAN OR MID-WIFE.

UNITED STATES OF AMERICA, Indian Territory, }
.... DISTRICT.

I,   A.L. Anderson   , a   Physician   , on oath state that I attended on Mrs.   Grace C. Hailey   , wife of   Walter P. Hailey   on the   13   day of June ,

Applications for Enrollment of Choctaw Newborn
Act of 1905   Volume VI

1903; that there was born to her on said date a   Female   child; that said child was living March 4, 1905, and is said to have been named May Hailey

AL Anderson M.D.

Witnesses To Mark:

{

Subscribed and sworn to before me this 17 day of   Mch   , 1905

(Name Illegible)
Notary Public.

Choc New Born 372
　　Sue Hailey   b. 3-5-03

BIRTH AFFIDAVIT.

DEPARTMENT OF THE INTERIOR.
COMMISSION TO THE FIVE CIVILIZED TRIBES.

IN RE APPLICATION FOR ENROLLMENT, as a citizen of the   Choctaw   Nation, of Sue Hailey   , born on the   5th day of March   , 1903

Name of Father: William E Hailey　　　　a citizen of the Choctaw Nation.
Name of Mother: Stella Doyle Hailey　　　a citizen of the Choctaw Nation.

Postoffice   Savanna, I.T.

AFFIDAVIT OF MOTHER.

UNITED STATES OF AMERICA, Indian Territory, }
　　　Central　　　　DISTRICT.　　　　　　 }

　　I,　Stella Doyle Hailey　, on oath state that I am 23 years of age and a citizen by   marriage   , of the   Choctaw   Nation; that I am the lawful wife of William E. Hailey　　　, who is a citizen, by blood   of the   Choctaw Nation; that a female child was born to me on   5th day of   March   , 1903; that said child has been named   Sue Hailey , and was living March 4, 1905.

Stella Doyle Hailey

Witnesses To Mark:

{

Applications for Enrollment of Choctaw Newborn
Act of 1905 Volume VI

Subscribed and sworn to before me this 18th day of March , 1905

Wirt Franklin
Notary Public.

AFFIDAVIT OF ATTENDING PHYSICIAN OR MID-WIFE.

UNITED STATES OF AMERICA, Indian Territory, }
    Central   DISTRICT. }

I, T.S. Chapman , a physician , on oath state that I attended on Mrs. Stella Doyle Hailey , wife of William E. Hailey on the 5th day of March , 1903; that there was born to her on said date a female child; that said child was living March 4, 1905, and is said to have been named Sue Hailey

T.S. Chapman M.D.
Witnesses To Mark:
{

Subscribed and sworn to before me this 18 day of March , 1905

Wirt Franklin
Notary Public.

Choc New Born 373
    Ethel Fairie[sic]   b. 6-22-04

BIRTH AFFIDAVIT.

DEPARTMENT OF THE INTERIOR,
COMMISSION TO THE FIVE CIVILIZED TRIBES.

IN RE *Application for Enrollment*, as a citizen of the Choctaw Nation, of Ethel Fairlie , born on the 22 day of June , 1904

Name of Father: George W. Fairlie   a citizen of the United States Nation.
Name of Mother: Rebecca Elizabeth Fairlie   a citizen of the Choctaw Nation.

Post-Office: McAlester, I.T.

Applications for Enrollment of Choctaw Newborn
Act of 1905   Volume VI

AFFIDAVIT OF MOTHER.

UNITED STATES OF AMERICA, }
    INDIAN TERRITORY.
Central   District.

I,   Rebecca Elizabeth Fairlie   , on oath state that I am   25   years of age and a citizen by   blood   , of the   Choctaw   Nation; that I am the lawful wife of George W Fairlie , who is a citizen, by .... of the United States ~~Nation~~; that a female   child was born to me on   22nd   day of   June   , 1904 , that said child has been named   Ethel Fairlie   , and is now living.

Rebecca Elizabeth Fairlie

WITNESSES TO MARK:

{

Subscribed and sworn to before me this   16th   *day of*   March   , 1905.

Wirt Franklin
NOTARY PUBLIC.

AFFIDAVIT OF ATTENDING PHYSICIAN OR MID-WIFE.

UNITED STATES OF AMERICA, }
    INDIAN TERRITORY.
Central   District.

I,   Lula Story   , ~~a~~ _____ , on oath state that I attended on Mrs.   Rebecca Elizabeth Fairlie   , wife of   George W. Fairlie   on the   22nd   day of   June   , 1904 ; that there was born to her on said date a   female   child; that said child is now living and is said to have been named   Ethel Fairlie

Mrs. Lula Story

WITNESSES TO MARK:

{

Subscribed and sworn to before me this   16th   *day of*   March   , 1905.

Wirt Franklin
NOTARY PUBLIC.

Applications for Enrollment of Choctaw Newborn
Act of 1905   Volume VI

Choc New Born 374
    Turner Silmon   b. 11-12-02
    Adam Silmon   b. 1-7-05

BIRTH AFFIDAVIT.

DEPARTMENT OF THE INTERIOR,
COMMISSION TO THE FIVE CIVILIZED TRIBES.

IN RE Application for Enrollment, as a citizen of the   Choctaw   Nation, of   Turner Silmon   , born on the   12   day of   Nov   , 1902

Name of Father: Lee Silmon   a citizen of the   Choctaw   Nation.
Name of Mother: Millie Silmon   a citizen of the   Choctaw   Nation.

Post-Office: Carbon

AFFIDAVIT OF MOTHER.

UNITED STATES OF AMERICA, ⎫
    INDIAN TERRITORY. ⎬
    Central   District. ⎭

    I,   Lee Silmon   , on oath state that I am   35   years of age and a citizen by blood   , of the   Choctaw   Nation; that I am the lawful ~~wife~~ husband of   Millie Silmon, who is a citizen, by   blood   of the   Choctaw   Nation; that a   male   child was born to ~~me~~ us on   12   day of   Nov   , 1902 , that said child has been named   Turner Silmon   , and is now living.

                                        Lee Silmon

WITNESSES TO MARK:

    Subscribed and sworn to before me this   2?   *day of*   December   , 1902

                                        T.C. Humphrey
                                              NOTARY PUBLIC.

Applications for Enrollment of Choctaw Newborn
Act of 1905   Volume VI

BIRTH AFFIDAVIT.

DEPARTMENT OF THE INTERIOR.
COMMISSION TO THE FIVE CIVILIZED TRIBES.

IN RE APPLICATION FOR ENROLLMENT, as a citizen of the   Choctaw   Nation, of Adam Silmon   , born on the   7   day of   Jan   , 1905

Name of Father: Lee Silmon   a citizen of the   Choctaw   Nation.
Name of Mother: Millie Silmon   a citizen of the   Choctaw   Nation.

Postoffice   Carbon

AFFIDAVIT OF MOTHER.

UNITED STATES OF AMERICA, Indian Territory, }
  Central   DISTRICT. }

I,   Mille[sic] Silmon   , on oath state that I am   29   years of age and a citizen by   blod[sic]   , of the   Choctaw   Nation; that I am the lawful wife of Lee Silmon   , who is a citizen, by blood   of the   Choctaw   Nation; that a male   child was born to me on   7   day of   Jan   , 1905; that said child has been named   Adam Silmon   , and was living March 4, 1905.

Millie x Silmon

Witnesses To Mark:
{ Jno Poeteet
{ Minnie Oglesby

Subscribed and sworn to before me this   22   day of   March   , 1905

....
Notary Public.

AFFIDAVIT OF ATTENDING PHYSICIAN OR MID-WIFE.

UNITED STATES OF AMERICA, Indian Territory, }
  Central   DISTRICT. }

I,   G.S. Turner   , a   Physian[sic]   , on oath state that I attended on Mrs.   Millie Silmon   , wife of   Lee Silmon   on the   7 day of   Jan   , 1905; that there was born to her on said date a   male   child; that said child was living March 4, 1905, and is said to have been named Adam Silmon

GS Turner M.D.

Applications for Enrollment of Choctaw Newborn
Act of 1905   Volume VI

Witnesses To Mark:
{

   Subscribed and sworn to before me this 22   day of   Jan   , 1905

                              W.J. Oglesby
                                    Notary Public.

- D E P A R T M E N T OF THE I N T E R I O R. -
Commision[sic] to the Five Civilized Tribes.

———APPLICATION FOR ENROLLMENT, as a citizen of the   Choctaw Natoin[sic], of   Turner Silmon   , born on the   12 Day of   Nov   , 190 2 Name of Father,   Lee Silmon   a citizen of the   Choctaw   Nation. Name of Mother; Millie Silmon   a citizen of the   Choctaw   Nation.

                    POST OFFICE: Carbon I.T.

                    Affadavit[sic] of Mother
UNITED STATES OF AMERICA |
   Indian Territory, |
   Central   District. |

   I   Millie Silmon   on oath state that I am   29   years of age and a Citizen by Blood   of the   Choctaw   Nation, that I am the lawful wife of   Lee Silmon   who is a citizen by   Blood   of the   Choctaw Nation, that a   Male   child was born to me on the   12   day of   Nov   1902, that said child has been Named   Turner Silmon   and is now liveing[sic]…...
                                her
                       Millie x Silmon
                                mark

            | Gilbert Pope
Must be to[sic] |
witnesses. | John Amos

Subscribed and sworn to before me this   9   day of   Jan   1905.

                              W.J. Oglesby
                                    Notary Public.

            Affidavid[sic] of attending Physican[sic] or Midwife.
Central District.
Indian Territory.

Applications for Enrollment of Choctaw Newborn
Act of 1905 Volume VI

I Sallie Ripley a Midwife on oath state that I attended on Mrs. Millie Silmon wife of Lee Silmon on the 12 day of Nove 1902 that there was born to her on said date a Male child; that said child is now living and is said to have been named Turner Silmon

her
Sallie x Ripley
mark

| Gilbert Pope

| John Amos

Subscribed and sworn to before me this 9 day of Jan 1905.

W.J. Oglesby   Notary Public.

BIRTH AFFIDAVIT.

DEPARTMENT OF THE INTERIOR.
COMMISSION TO THE FIVE CIVILIZED TRIBES.

IN RE APPLICATION FOR ENROLLMENT, as a citizen of the Choctaw Nation, of Turner Silmon , born on the 12 day of Nov , 1902

Name of Father: Lee Silmon   a citizen of the Choctaw Nation.
Name of Mother: Millie Silmon   a citizen of the Choctaw Nation.

Postoffice   Carbon   Indian Territory.

AFFIDAVIT OF MOTHER.

UNITED STATES OF AMERICA, Indian Territory,
Central   DISTRICT.

I, Millie Silmon , on oath state that I am 29 years of age and a citizen by Blood , of the Choctaw Nation; that I am the lawful wife of Lee Silmon , who is a citizen, by Blood of the Choctaw Nation; that a Male child was born to me on the 12 day of Nov , 1902; that said child has been named Turner Silmon , and was living March 4, 1905.

Millie x Silmon

Witnesses To Mark:
{ Jno Pueteet
{ Minnie Oglesby

Applications for Enrollment of Choctaw Newborn
Act of 1905 Volume VI

Subscribed and sworn to before me this 22 day of March , 1905

          W.J. Oglesby
          Notary Public.

AFFIDAVIT OF ATTENDING PHYSICIAN OR MID-WIFE.

UNITED STATES OF AMERICA, Indian Territory, }
  Central   DISTRICT. }

I, Sallie Riply[sic] , a Mid Wife , on oath state that I attended on Mrs. Millie Silmon , wife of Lee Silmon on the 12 day of Nov , 1902; that there was born to her on said date a male child; that said child was living March 4, 1905, and is said to have been named Turner Silmon

          Sallie x Riply

Witnesses To Mark:
  { Jno Pueteet
    Minnie Oglesby

Subscribed and sworn to before me this 22 day of March , 1905

          W.J. Oglesby
          Notary Public.

N. B. 374

Muskogee, Indian Territory, April 10, 1905.

Lee Silmon,
  Carbon, Indian Territory.

Dear Sir:

    There is inclosed you herewith for execution application for the enrollment of your infant child, Adam Silmon, born January 7, 1905.

    The affidavits heretofore filed with the Commission show the child was living on January 22, 1905. It is necessary, for the child to be enrolled, that he was living on March 4, 1905.

    In having these affidavits executed care should be exercised to see that all names are written in full, as they appear in the body of the affidavit, and in the event that either of the persons signing the affidavit are unable to write, signatures by mark must be

Applications for Enrollment of Choctaw Newborn
Act of 1905 Volume VI

attested by two witnesses. Each affidavit must be executed before a Notary Public and the notarial seal and signature of the officer must be attached to each separate affidavit.

Respectfully,

LM 11-46   Commissioner in Charge.

BIRTH AFFIDAVIT.

DEPARTMENT OF THE INTERIOR.
COMMISSION TO THE FIVE CIVILIZED TRIBES.

IN RE APPLICATION FOR ENROLLMENT, as a citizen of the Choctaw Nation, of Adam Silmon, born on the 7 day of Jan, 1905

Name of Father: Lee Silmon   a citizen of the Choctaw Nation.
Name of Mother: Millie Silmon   a citizen of the Choctaw Nation.

Postoffice   Carbon I.T.

AFFIDAVIT OF MOTHER.

UNITED STATES OF AMERICA, Indian Territory,
.... DISTRICT.

I, Millie Silmon, on oath state that I am 29 years of age and a citizen by blood, of the Choctaw Nation; that I am the lawful wife of Lee Silmon, who is a citizen, by blood of the Choctaw Nation; that a male child was born to me on the 7 day of January, 1905; that said child has been named Adam Silmon, and was living March 4, 1905.

                                  her
                        Millie x Silmon
Witnesses To Mark: mark
  { C J Hokey
    John Russell

Subscribed and sworn to before me this 8 day of July, 1905

                            M^{c}. H. Ross
                            Notary Public.

Applications for Enrollment of Choctaw Newborn
Act of 1905   Volume VI

AFFIDAVIT OF ATTENDING PHYSICIAN OR MID-WIFE.

UNITED STATES OF AMERICA, Indian Territory, }
....DISTRICT. }

I, ..., a ...., on oath state that I attended on Mrs. Millie Silmon, wife of Lee Silmon on the 7 day of January, 1905; that there was born to her on said date a .... child; that said child was living March 4, 1905, and is said to have been named Adam Silmon

GS Turner M.D.
Witnesses To Mark:
{

Subscribed and sworn to before me this 8 day of July, 1905

M^c. H. Ross
Notary Public.

- D E P A R T M E N T OF THE I N T E R I O R. -
Commision[sic] to the Five Civilized Tribes.

————APPLICATION FOR ENROLLMENT, as a citizen of the Choctaw Natoin[sic], of Adam Silmon, born on the 7 Day of Jan, 190 5 Name of Father, Lee Silmon a citizen of the Choctaw Nation. Name of Mother; Millie Silmon a citizen of the Choctaw Nation.

POST OFFICE: Carbon I.T.

Affadavit[sic] of Mother

UNITED STATES OF AMERICA |
   Indian Territory, |
   Central   District. |

I Millie Silmon on oath state that I am 29 years of age and a Citizen by Blood of the Choctaw Nation, that I am the lawful wife of Lee Silmon who is a citizen by Blood of the Choctaw Nation, that a Male child was born to me on the 7 day of Jan 1905, that said child has been Named Adam Silmon and is now liveing[sic]……

Millie x Silmon

| Gilbert Pope
Must be to[sic] |
witnesses. | John Amos

Applications for Enrollment of Choctaw Newborn
Act of 1905   Volume VI

Subscribed and sworn to before me this 9 day of Jan 1905.

                                                    W.J. Oglesby
                                                            Notary Public.

                Affidavid[sic] of attending Phycian[sic] or Midwife.

Central District.
Indian Territory.

       I G. S. Turner a Physician on oath state that I attended on Mrs. Millie Silmon   wife of   Lee Silmon   on the   7   day of   Jan   1905 that there was born to her on said date a   Male   child; that said child is now living and is said to have been named   Adam Silmon

                                                      GS Turner M.D.

Subscribed and sworn to before me this 9 day of Jan 1905.

                                       W.J. Oglesby   Notary Public.

                                                                      7-4637

                                 Muskogee, Indian Territory, January 19, 1905.

Lee Silmon,
       Carbon, Indian Territory.

Dear Sir:

       Receipt is hereby acknowledged of the affidavits of Millie Silmon and Sallie Ripley relative to the birth of Turner Silmon, infant son of Lee and Millie Silmon November 12, 1902, also the affidavits of Millie Silmon and G. S. Turner to the birth of Adam Silmon, son of Lee and Millie Silmon January 7, 1905, which it is presumed have been forwarded as an application for enrollment of the above named children.

       You are advised that under the provisions of the act of Congress approved July 1, 1902, no children born to recognized and enrolled citizens of the Choctaw and Chickasaw Nations subsequent to September 25, 1902, the date of the ratification of said act, are entitled to enrollment and allotment in the Choctaw and Chickasaw Nations.

                                    Respectfully,
                                                      Chairman.

Applications for Enrollment of Choctaw Newborn
Act of 1905   Volume VI

7-4637

Muskogee, Indian Territory, March 25, 1905.

Lee Silmon,
    Carbon, Indian Territory.

Dear Sir:

    Receipt is hereby acknowledged of the affidavits of Millie Silmon and Sallie Ripley to the birth of Turner Silmon, child of Lee and Millie Silmon, November 12, 1902; also affidavits of Millie Silmon and G. S. Turner to the birth of Adam Silmon, son of Lee and Millie Silmon, January 7, 1905, and the same have been filed with our records as an application for the enrollment of said children.

                Respectfully,

                              Chairman.

7-NB-374

Muskogee, Indian Territory, July 12, 1905.

Lee Silmon,
    Krebs, Indian Territory.

Dear Sir:

    Receipt is hereby acknowledged of your letter of July 8, 1905, transmitting affidavits of Millie Silmon and G. S. Turner to the birth of Adam Silmon, son of Lee and Millie Silmon, January 7, 1905, and the same have been filed with the records of this office in the matter of the enrollment of said child.

                Respectfully,

                              Commissioner.

Index

AASKEW
  Mollie 269
ABBOTT
  Dr W E 199
  Ruby May 297,298
  W E 198
  W E, MD 198,199
ACKER
  May 162
ADAMS
  Arthur 74
AINSWORTH
  N B 197,198
ALLEY
  Alfred L 264,265,266,267
  Alfred Lee 264,265,266,268
  Brick P 264,265,266,267,268
  Elsie 264,265,266,267,268
AMOS
  John 322,323
ANDERSON
  George 243
  Hagen 241,254,255
  Hagin 253
  Hogan 251
  J 243,251,257
  J W 257
  A L 315,316
  A L, MD 317
  Lindsey 243
  Melina 242,243
  Wesley 239
ANGELL
  W H 39,40,61,62,77,78,79,80,85,
  86,87,110,112,115,146
ANSLEY
  Dolly May 195,196
  Gilbert 195,196
  Nina Pearl 195,196
ARMSTRONG
  Annie 75,76,77,78,79,80,81,82
  Lewis 76,77
  Murrow 75,76,77,78,79,80,81,82
  Noel 77
  Wilis 76
  Willis 75,76,77,78,79,80,81,82
ARUDT

Em 315
Joseph W 314,315
Mary 314
Mary E 315
Wm 314
ASKEW
  Dora 269,270,271,272,273,274,
  275,276,277
  Eliza 271,272,273,278,279
  Lee 269,270,271,272,273,274,
  275,276,277
  Millie 269
  Mollie 270,271,272,273,274,275,
  276,277
  Molly 277
AUSTEN
  Hannah 67
AUTREY
  D 271,272,274,279,281
  D, MD 274,280,281
BAKER
  A E 253
BALDWIN
  Lee P 42,43,44,46,47
BANKS
  A 42,43,44
BARGER
  G S 157
  G S, MD 157
  H S, MD 158
BARLETT
  D C 272
  D G 273
BARTLETT
  D G 271,274,277,280,281
BATTIEST
  L G 61,62
BEAMS
  John J 267,268
BECK
  Elisa 305,306,311,312
  Eliza 313
  Frances 306,307,309
  Francis 306,311,312,313
  George W 306
  J G 309

Index

Jos G 309
Joseph 311
Joseph C 312
Joseph G 305,306,307,308,309,310,
311,312,313
Josie 305,307,308,309,310,311
BECKER
   A E 251,254
BELL
   Hannah 290,291,292
BENTLEY
   J M 206
   J M, MD 206
   J N 210
   John M 207,212
BETTS
   Autie May 37,38,39,40
   Bettie 37,38,39,40
   C A 31,32,38,39
   Charley A 16,17
   Charlie A 18,19
   Mr C A 15,16
   Ora L 17
   Ora Lee 16,17,18,19
   R D 32
   Ruby Mary 15
   Ruby May 16,17,18,19
   William W 37,38,39,40
BEVELL
   Abbie 232
   Alice E 232
   Joe 232
BIXBY
   Tams 155,164,187,259,270,310
BOATWRIGHT
   Ruth L 193,194
BOBO
   Lacey P 245,246,247,249,250,
252,255,257
BOLLING
   Geo F 148,149
   W C 197,198
BOLLINGER
   A 216
BOND
   Edmund M 294,295
   George M 294,295

June H 294,295
Rex Abbott 296
Rex Cheadle 296,297,298
Ruby Abbott 296
BOWER
   James 91,92,93,141,142,198,234
BOWMAN
   Milton M 132
BOZARTH
   C G 10,12,13,14
BREEDLOVE
   Maud 83
BRINSON
   Mollie 91
BRISTOW
   James H 41
BROCK
   Ina B 136
   Ina M 135,136
   Minnie L 135,136
   Wesley E 135,136
BROWN
   Dwight 204,205,207,208,209
   J J 149
   S F 196,200
   Susan 289
   Wm C 2
BUNN
   Wm C 160
BURNS
   Jackson 48,49
BYINGTON
   Cyrus 182
   Henry 63,64,65,66
   Lorena 63,64,65,66
   Lycid 66
   Lydia 63,64,65
   R H 63,64

CAMPBELL
   C M 283,284,285
CAMPELUBE
   Columbus 150,235,236
CANN
   George 239,240,241,242,243,
244,245,246,247,248,249,250,251,252,
255,259,261

Linbdsey 252
Lindsey 242,244,247,248,252,253,
255,256,257,260,261
Lindsy 238,239,240,241,242,243,
245,246,247,258,259,260
Lizzie 239,240,248
Malina 245
Melina 238,239,240,241,242,243,
244,245,246,247,255,258,259,261
CARL
   Frank A 178
CARNES
   Amanda 83
   Melina 239,240,241,242
CARNET
   Louisana 248
CARNEY
   Aaron 233,234,235,236,237,238
   Albert 255,257
   Allen 256
   Davidson 257,260
   Holis 240
   Kellie 236
   Louisana 243,244,246,248,249,251,
252,253,254,255,261
   Louisiana 240,242
   Mrs N A 173,174
   N A 177
   Nancy A 175,176,178
   Nellie 233,234,235,236,237,238
   Nollis 249,251,255
   Nona 233,234,235,236,237,238
   Norris 243,244,245
CARPER
   Mary 193
CARRIGER
   S E 165,166
CARTER
   J Q 74
   Kellie 236
   Mary 194
   Nellie 235
CASS
   J L 209,212
   J L, MD 208,209
   J S 210
CATLIN
   Claude M 10,11,12,13,14
   J D 15,16
   James D 13,14
   James Darrah 10,11,12
   James Darrah, Jr 9,10,11,12,13,14
CAVES
   T T 7,9
CHAPMAN
   T S 318
   T S, MD 318
CHILDS
   Dr J S 152
   J H 155
   J S 153,154,155
   J S, MD 152,153,154
CHOATE
   Amanda 88
   C C 88
   Christopher C 267,268
   G W 143
CHUNN
   Lucy 299,300,301,302,303,305
   May 299,300,301,302,303,304,305
   W H 303
   W R 299
   William R 300,301,302,303,304,305
CLABRON
   Sallie 41
CLAYTON 254
CLIFTON
   W F 182,183,184
   W F, MD 182,183
CLOWER
   Fleming P 19,20,21
   Sallie M 19,20,21
   W F 24,25
   Walter F 19,20,21
COKER
   Nannie 7
COLBERT
   Bill 249,250
   Dee 204,205,214
   R P 203,214
COLE
   John 104,105
COLEMAN
   R B 315

COLLIER
 Martha 53
COLLINS
 J Lake 251
 L Jake 253
COON
 F C 153
COOPER
 O C 220
COVINGTON
 W P 245,246,257
CRABILL
 R J 295
 R J, MD 295
CROSS
 John H 161,162,163
 M O 163
 Maggie 162
CROUCH
 N A 49,51
CULBERSON
 Jesse W 228
 Katherine 228
 Katie 228
CULBERTSON
 J W 128
 Jesse W 225,226,227,228
 Kate 98,99,170,171,228
 Katherine 225,226,227,228
 Katie 172,225,226,227,299,300, 301,302,303
 W T 98,99,100,106,126,127, 170,171,172,226,227,228,299,300,301, 302,303
CUNNINGHAM
 Alfred H 117,118,119,120,121, 122,123
 Clara Bell 123
 Clara Belle 116,117,118,119,120, 121,122
 H W 77,78
 Martha J 117,118,119,120,121, 122,123
CUSHMAN
 Artee M 282
 Charles A 282
 Charles L 282

DAVIS
 Sterling P 310,311
DAWSON
 Effie 169,171
 F E 226
 L E 98,99,170,171
 Lela E 191
DEAN
 T R 149
DELANA
 Missouri 84,85
DICKERSON
 Ada 144,145,146,147
 Joda L 146,147
 Jody 147
 Jody L 144,145
 Rhoda E 147
 Rosa 145
 Rosa E 144,145,146,147
DONNELLY
 W C 101,200,201,292,293,297,298
DOYLE
 E H 316
DUNN
 Annie Jane 148,149,150
 Josephine 148,149,150
 William B 148,149,150

EAGAN
 Isaac W 137,138
EDWARDS
 Belle 6,7,8,9
 David Jonathan 6,8,9
 Eli 203,204,205,206,207,208, 209,210,211,212,213,214
 Ely 205
 Everett 203,210,213
 Everette 205,206,207,210,211,212, 213,214
 James Robert 6,7,8,9
 Lottie Loudella 6,7,9
 Routh 203,204
 Ruth 203,207,208,209,210,211, 212,213,214
 Salle 205
 Sallie 203,204,205,206,207,208,

209,210,212,214
ELKINS
   A L 167
ETHEREDGE
   A G 32,34,35
ETHRIDGE
   S J 163
EUBANK
   J A 265,266,267,268
EUBANK, MD 265

FAIRIE
   Ethel 318
FAIRLIE
   Ethel 318,319
   George W 318,319
   Rebecca Elizabeth 318,319
FANNIN
   E J 15,16,22,23,101,102,200,
   201,292,293,297,298
FARMER
   W S 11
FERRANTE
   Isabinda 126,127
   Sante...................................126,127,128
FIZER
   James 53,54
FLORENCE
   Mary Estella 132,135
   Stella... 132
FLYHOVER
   Irene..249,252
   James H 252
   James J... 252
   Jas H 249
   John 251
   Mr... 250
FOLSOM
   A E 17,24,25,38,60,64,76,
   108,113,216
   Isaac..60,61
   Molcy 59,62
   Saul... 59
   Silas 289
   Silas D 315
FORRESTER
   J T.. 74

FRANKLIN
   Wirt 7,8,89,95,96,104,105,124,
   125,136,150,191,199,202,203,217,218,
   229,230,232,235,236,242,251,262,
   263,264,290,291,292,295,296,297,315,
   318,319
FRAZIER
   Lyman 162
FRONTERHOUSE
   Wm...31,32
FROST
   S W...167
FRYHOVER
   Irene 246
   Irine..246
FULTON
   Dr J S..18,39
   J S................. 12,13,14,17,19,32,33,35,
   36,38,40
   J S, MD 11,17,32,38
FULTON, ...11

GARDNER
   J J 3
GARY
   J L..16
GATES
   R L 218,219
GEORGE
   M J 166,167
   Mary 167,169
   Mrs M J 166
GIBSON
   Emily...269
   Joseph...269
   Sylvia 269
GLENN
   Ida B 73,74,75
   Marguerite 73,74,75
   William T 73,74,75
GORMAN
   Effie..171,172
   Effie D 170,227,228
   Effie Dawson............. 169,170,171,172
   Ira T..170
   Mike 169,170,171,172
   Ora T 169,171,172

Index

Ora Tranque 171
Ora Tranquie 170
GRAHAM
  E L 188,189
  R C 138
  S A 271,272,273,276
  S A, MD 275,276
  Samuel A 275
GRAVES
  B F 55
  Boyd O 242
  William 21
  William, DO 20
  Wm 20
GREEN
  Betsey 289
  Ida 289
GREGORY
  Edwin S 174,175
GRIFFITH
  A 296
  A, MD 297
GRUBBS
  Addie 99
  Addie M 100
  Dr J O 196
  Eli 101,102,103,104,105,106,107
  Eliza C 105
  J O 232
  J O, MD 196,232
  John D 117,118
  Liza 103,104
  Roxy Y 103,104,106
  Roy C 100,102,103,104,105,106,107
  Susie 102,103
  Susie Jane 104,105,106,107
GRUNERT
  Robert E 241

HAILEY
  Grace C 315,316
  May 315,316,317
  Stella Doyle 317
  Sue 317
  Walter P 315,316
  William E 317
HAMBY
  Mike 70
HAMLIN
  Bettie 54
HANNA
  Ollie 165,166
HARDY
  W 286
  W, MD 286
HARKREADER
  Lucy Ann 131,132,135
  Lucy M 133
  S B 131,133
  Samuel B 131,132,133,134,135
  Zoola May 131,133,134
  Zula Mary 133
  Zula May 131,132,135
HARLOW
  Sarah A 141,142
HARPER
  I W 170,226
HARRIS
  Elias 161
  Mrs E Poe 171,228
HARRISON
  Wm 69,70
HARRISS
  Mrs E Poe 172,227
HASKINS
  Levi 84
HATFIELD
  Susanah 44,48
  Susanna 51
  W R 51
HAWKINS
  Dr L R 119
  L R 117,119
  L R, MD 119
HAZEL
  Lotta 137,138,139,140
  Lottie 138,139
  Nora 137,138,139
  Norah 138,139
  Seth T 137,138,139,140
HENDERSON
  Lula 156,157,158
  Roy 156,157,158,159
  Sam Randolph 156,157,158,159

Index

HERRING
- Henry 254,255

HIGH
- P E 157

HILL
- Chas 24,25
- Rev P H 204
- Reverand 205

HOAWBBI
- David 67
- Davie 67
- James 67

HOAWBBY
- Emma 71
- Jancie 71

HOBBS
- Alice 8

HODGE
- A 59

HOKEY
- C J 325

HOLLEMAN
- Clittie Elizabeth 188,189
- Gillie A 188,189
- W J 189
- William G 188,189,190
- William J 189

HOLLIMAN
- W J 189

HOLLOWAY
- Alice 125,127,128,129,130
- Allice 125,126,127
- Frank 125,126,127,128,129,130
- Ruby 125,126,127,128,129,130

HOMER
- A H 76,77
- Jacob 245,246,247,255
- Sol J 20

HORTON
- L D 179,180
- W A 179
- W A, MD 179

HOWELL
- J C 298

HUMPHREY
- L C 1,2
- T C 309,320

HUMPHREYS
- J M 58,71

IRVINE
- A L 77,78,87

JACKSON
- Rebecca 3

JAMES
- Elizabeth 234,235,237,238

JEFFRESS
- J L 282
- J L, MD 283

JENKINS
- Mrs 123
- Sarah P 120,122

JESTICE
- Elizabeth 47
- Lizzie 45,50,52

JOBS
- B F 149

JOHNSON
- O L 231

JOHNSTON
- Dr P S 143
- P S 142,144,145,146,147
- P S, MD 142,143,145,146

JOLLY
- W D 236,237

JONES
- Henry 159,160,161,162,163,164
- Louisa 159,160,161,162,163,164
- Mary 164
- Noel 76,78,81,164
- Peter 84
- Sam 84
- T W 159,160,161,162,163,164

JUSTICE
- Lizzie 50

JUSTIS
- Elizziebeth 41

KAEN
- George 239

KARL
- Esta V 173,174,175,176,177,178
- A Frank 174,175

Index

Frank A 173,174,176,177
Viola 173,174,175,176,177,178
KELLER
   Henry F 275,276
KELLEY
   A S 192,193,194
   W F 41
KEMP
   R C 123
   Richard E 119,120,121
KENNEDY
   M D 278
KESSLER
   H C 244,245
KING
   Emma 118,119
   Mitchell 118,119,120,121

LAMB
   Addie 99,100
   Addie M 98,100
   Addie M Grubbs 97,98
   Dave 99,100
   David 97,98
   Lillie M 97,98,99,100
   Lillie May 97,98
LAWRENCE
   O S 120,121
LEFLORE
   J A 46,47
   James A 48,49
LENTZ
   John M 54,55
LESTER
   J M 136
   Joseph 90,92,97
   Josephes 90
   Josephus 91,92,93,94,95,96
   Julia Ann 90,91,95,96
   Lucy 90,91,92,93,94,95,96,97
   Ralph 90,92,93,94,95,96
   W F 173,175,176,177
   W R 174
LINDSEY
   Nina 286,287
   Queen 287
   Queens 286

Quintella 286
Selden T 286
Seldon T 286,287
LINEBAUGH
   D N 114,160
   Jno H 78
LINKER
   N L 162,163,164
   N L, MD 162
LITTLE
   J C 282,283
LIVELY
   Dr R A 3
   R A, MD 4
   Robert A 6
   Robt A, MD 3,4
LOCKE
   Victor M, Jr 242
LOGAN
   J H, MD 303
LONG
   Dr Thomas.....................................109
   John M 53,313
   T J 78,79
   T J, MD 64,79,82,109
   Thomas 109
   Thomas J 64
   Thos J 81
LOOKINGBILL
   Mary 106,107
LOOMIS
   O H 151,152
LOTT
   J H 101
LOUGHRIDGE
   Alice 200,201
LOVE
   B H 192
LUPE
   Dee 193
   Roy Ruth 193
   Ruth L 193
LUPER
   D R 191,192,194,195
   Dee 193,194
   Ray R 195
   Ray Ruth.......................................195

Roy Ruth 191,192,193,194
Ruth L 191,192,193,194
MCAFEE
   Malsey 60,61
   Molsey 60,62
MCCANN
   Melissa 238,240
   Millisie 240
   William 240
MCCARTER
   A L 162
MCCLAIN
   Mary I 174,175
MCCLURE
   Alfred W 148,238
MCCOY
   N H 284,285
MCCULLOUGH
   Carle 283,284,285,286
   Quintella 285,286,287,288
   Vivian Mae 283,285,286,288
   Vivian May 287
MCDONALD
   J W, MD 308,311
MCKENNON & DEAN 224
MACKEY
   B P 226,227
   Belle 299,300,301,302,303
MCPHERREN
   Chas 65,66
   Chas E 26,27,28,29,203,205
MCVEY
   H A 99,100
   W J 100
MANSFIELD, MCMURRAY &
   CORNISH 187
MAPLES
   J B 192,194
   J B, MD 192
MARR
   Fred T 258
MARTIN
   Lewis T 61,62
   W H 79
MASSEY
   Alice Victoria 40,41,42,43,44,45,
46,47,48,49,50,51,52
   Alis Victoria 42
   Sillin Walker 40,43,44,47,48,50,51
   Tams Bixby 40,41,42,45,46,47,
49,50,52
   William W 42,43,44,45,46,47,48,49,
50,51,52
   William Wilson 40,41
MAY
   Robt 138,139
MAYTUBBY
   Peter, Jr 217,218
   Rebecca 1
MEADOWS
   Andy 229,230,231
   Burnett 229,230,231
   Laura 229,230,231
MELTON
   J W 26
   J W, MD 25
   W J 25,27,29,30
MILLER
   Clarence L 261,263
   Geo W 153,154
   John B 261,262
   Serena J 261,262,263
   T J 261,262,263
MITCHELL
   S E 52,55,56,57
   S E, MD 52,55
MOORE
   Sarah 315
MORGAN
   Dick 182
MOSLEY
   Benjamin F 152
MOZELY
   Benjamin F 155
   Laura E 155
   Laura Lucille 155
MOZLEY
   B F 156
   Benjamin F 151,152,153,154,155
   Laura E 151,152,153,154,155
   Laura Lucile 151,152,156
   Laura Lucille 151,152,153,154,155
   Lucile 156

MULLEN
  J S 257,260,261
MURPHY
  S F 284
MURROW
  J S 83
NAIL
  Alfred 239,251,252
  Jincy 239,240
  Silas 233,234,235,236,237
NANCE
  J P 273
  Mattie 273
NEEDLES
  T B 5,9,14,72,80,96,122,123,
  130,134,140,164,168,178,222,271,304
NELSON
  Joseph E 180,181,186
  Phillip 103,104
  Philly 103
NEWMAN
  E A 59,67,68
NICHOLAS
  Emily 65,66
NICHOLSON
  O R 64
NOABBI
  David 66
NOABBY
  James 70
  James L 73
NOAWBBI
  David 68,71
  Emma 68
  Hannah 67,68,71
  James 67,68
  Jancie 68
NOWABBI
  David 69,71,72,73
  Hanna 72
  Hannah 69,72
  James 69,71,72,73
  Mary 69,72

OGLESBY
  Minnie 321,323,324

W J 322,323,324,327
OTT
  Minnie 215,216
PARK
  E269
  Mrs E F 269
PATE
  Lavinia 29
  Lavinia W 24,25,26,27,28,29
  Louvinia 22
  Lovinia 23
PATTERSON
  Albert Roy 200,202
  Alice May 202
  Robert 200,201
  Robert E Lee 202
PAYTE
  J G 163
PERKINS
  L H 143
PEYTON
  Mandy 74,75
PHILLIPS
  Charles A 180,181,182,183
PINKERTON
  W J 293
PITCHLYNN
  Andy A 291
  Minnie E 291
  W B 292,293
  William B 291
POETEET
  Jno 321
POPE
  Frank 233,234
  Gilbert 322,323,326
PUETEET
  Jno 323,324
PYBAR
  B 151,152
RAINEY
  R M 78
RALLS
  Joseph G 11
RAY

338

L D 162
REDFIELD
  David 287
  O M 287
  Orrin M 286
REED
  Kissen 247,250
  Kisson 248
RICE
  T J 88,94,143,145,147,264,265, 266,267,268
RICHARD
  Edward 198
  Mrs E T 198
RICHARDS
  Edwards 197
  Edwin T 199
  Inez Irene 197,198
  Irena 197
  Irena A 197
  Irene A 199
  Irene Inez 197,199
RICHEY
  Henry 70
RIPLEY
  Sallie 323,327,328
RIPLY
  Sallie 324
ROBINSON
  J C 124,125,202
  Jesse 182
ROSE
  C C 108,109,113,114
  Vester W 16
ROSS
  Dr S P 99,171
  Mc H 325,326
  S P 98,100,170,172,226,227, 228,300,301,302,303,305
  S P, MD 98,100,106,170,172,226, 228,300,302
ROUNDS
  Louise E 83
ROUTH
  J M 184
ROZEL
  Josephus 97

Lucy 90,92,93,94,97
Ralph 97
RUSSELL
  Dan 244,245
  John 325
RUTHERFORD
  Albert 28
  Albert B 22,23,24,25,26,27,28,29,30
  Albertine L 24,25
  A B 30
  Lavinia Albertine 21,25,26,27,28, 29,30
  Lavinia W 24,25,26,27,29,30
  Lavinia W Pate 24
RUTNER
  R R 131
RYAN
  Annie L 190,191
  Clide Bushnell 190,191
  T J 226,227
  Theron J 190,191
SAWYER
  Charles H 241
SCOTT
  James 313
  Piney 129
  Pinie 126,127,128
  Pinna 130
  Pinnia 129
SEARY
  R 314
SEE
  Geo 139
SEXTON
  Jonas 104,105
SHANAFELT
  Richard 79
SHARP
  J F 194
SHELOR
  D 112
SHONEY
  W A 3
SIEMANS
  W C 55
SILMON

Index

Adam 320,321,324,325,326,327,328
Lee 243,320,321,322,323,324, 325,326,327,328
Mille 321
Millie 320,321,322,323,324,325, 326,327,328
Turner 320,322,323,324,327,328

SKAGGS
  Drennan C 312

SLATEN
  J W 15,16

SLINKER
  J I 2,3
  James 1,4,5,6
  Lizzie 1,3,4,5,6
  Lizzy 1
  William R 1,4,5,6
  William Raymon 2,3

SMALLFIELD
  Ellen 215,216,217,221,224,225

SMISER
  Norma E 11

SORRELLS
  Alex 288
  James Edward 288

SORRELS
  Alexander 289,290
  Ida Pitchlynn 289,290
  James Edward 288,289,290

SOUTH
  Dr E W 230,231
  E W 230,231

SOUTHERLAND
  Annie 93,94,96

SPARKS
  G W 151,152

STANTON
  W H 150

STEGALL
  E L 216,218,219,220
  Edgar L 216,218,219,220,221

STEPHENS
  S D 165,166

STONE
  W B 22

STORY
  Lula 319

STUMP
  Susie 101,102

SUMTER
  Emma 108,109,110,111,112,113, 114,115,116
  Joseph 108,109,111,112,113,114
  Joseph M 109,110,114,115
  Lena Maria 109
  Lena Marie 107,108,109,110
  Magdale 110,115,116
  Magdaline 111
  Maggie 114
  Milton Leon 107,111,112,113,114, 115,116
  Mrs R E 114
  R O 38,39,108,109,113,114

SWISHER
  O P 42,43,44,46,47,48,49,50,51
  Sue 50

TALFORD
  Robt E 23

TANEHILL
  Joseph D 124
  Mintie 124
  Theodore 124,125

TAUBNER
  F R 12

TAYLOR
  Ada 141,142,143,144
  Benjamin Lawson 87,88,89
  Green 217,218
  Hugh Sylvester ... 140,141,142,143,144
  J T 87,88,89
  John W 141,142,143,144
  Talithia 87,88,89

TENNENT
  L C, MD 262,263
  Lewis C 262,263

THOMPSON
  Elias 17,18,32,58,59,60,61,62
  Jesse 257
  Listie 58,59,60,62
  Listy 58,61,62
  Lucy 58,59,60,61,62
  W S 138
  Wallace 60,61

THORNTON
  T T, MD 131
TINER
  Dora 165,166,167,169
  Leroy 165,166,167,168,169
  N T 165,166,167
  Newton 166,167,168,169
TOMLINSON
  Harriet 2
TRAUT
  Annie 215,218,219,220,221,222,
  223,224,225
  Henry 218,219,220,221,222,
  223,224,225
  Minnie .. 218,219,220,221,222,223,224
TRAUTH 222
  Annie 217
  Henry 216,217
  Minnie 215,217
TROUT
  Annie 215,216
  Henry 215,216
  Minney 215
  Minnie 215,216
TURNER
  Andrew J 128,129,188,189
  G S 321,327,328
  G S, MD 321,326,327
  H A 52
  Leona 10
  M E 180
  Robert S 88
  Thos F 313

UNDERWOOD
  Ada 303
  Ben 303
  Lucy 303

VAIL
  Arthur Floid 178,179,184,185
  Arthur Floyd 180,181,186,187
  Gilbert 178,181,182,183,184
  Jno F 183
  John 181,182,185
  John F 179,183,184,186,187
  Sophia... 179,180,181,182,183,184,186

VAILS
  Arthur Floid 179
  Arthur Floyd 179
  John F 179
  Sophia 179
VERMILLION
  Quintella 283,284,285,287
  William P 287
  Wm P 286,287

WAGONER
  Sophia 205
WALKER
  Ada 141,142
  M P 277
  Mrs M P 277
WALLS
  Catherine 52,53,54,55,56,57
  Green M 52,53,54,55,56,57
  Jess 54,313
  Thomas J 52,53,56
  Thomas J, Sr 53,54,55,56,57
  Thos J, Sr 54
WALTER
  James T 167
WARD
  Henry 236,237
WEIMER
  W G 103
WEST
  G W 312
  Geo W 312,313,314
WHITAKER
  D M 314
WILHELM
  P E 167
WILKINS 254
  L B 4,5
WILLIAMS
  Abbie Lena 231,232
  Beulah F 31,33,34,35,36
  Bulah F 31,32
  David 231,232
  H E 149,150
  H E, MD 149
  J E 132
  Ola May 231,232

T H 141,142
T R 31,32,33,34,35,36
Warneta F 17,18,31,32,33,34,35,36
WILSON
  Alizzie 278
  Cillen 250,251,252,254,255
  Elizzie 279
  J W 278,279,280,281
  Lizzie 278,279,280,281
  Minnie E 292
  Minnie W 293
  R M 160
  Reader Melvin 278,279,280,281
  Robert 247,248,249,250,251,252,
  253,254,255,256
  S W 137,139
  S W, MD 138
  Sophy 248,250,255
  Stephen 250,254,255
  Wallace 248,250,254
  Wikey 248,250,254,255
WOOD
  Annie 82,85,86
  Harrison 85,86
  Maud 85,86
WOODHOUSE
  Lydia 278
WOODS
  Annie 83,84
  Ellen 82
  Harrison 82,83,84
  Maud 83,84
WORCESTER
  Alfred 241

YORK
  Ora Lee 15,16

www.ingramcontent.com/pod-product-compliance
Lightning Source LLC
Chambersburg PA
CBHW020241030426
42336CB00010B/565